SUPERSTITION IN ALL AGES

By Jean Meslier

1732

A ROMAN CATHOLIC PRIEST, WHO, AFTER A PASTORAL SERVICE OF THIRTY YEARS AT ETREPIGNY IN CHAMPAGNE, FRANCE, WHOLLY ABJURED RELIGIOUS DOGMAS, AND LEFT AS HIS LAST WILL AND TESTAMENT TO HIS PARISHIONERS, AND TO THE WORLD, TO BE PUBLISHED AFTER HIS DEATH, THE FOLLOWING PAGES, ENTITLED: COMMON SENSE.

Translated from the French original

by

Miss Anna Knoop

LIFE OF JEAN MESLIER BY VOLTAIRE.

Jean Meslier, born 1678, in the village of Mazerny, dependency of the duchy of Rethel, was the son of a serge weaver; brought up in the country, he nevertheless pursued his studies and succeeded to the priesthood. At the seminary, where he lived with much regularity, he devoted himself to the system of Descartes.

Becoming curate of Etrepigny in Champagne and vicar of a little annexed parish named Bue, he was remarkable for the austerity of his habits. Devoted in all his duties, every year he gave hat remained of his salary to the poor of his parishes; enthusiastic, and of rigid virtue, he was very temperate, as much in regard to his appetite as in relation to women.

MM. Voiri and Delavaux, the one curate of Varq, the other curate of Boulzicourt, were his confessors, and the only ones with whom he associated.

The curate Meslier was a rigid partisan of justice, and sometimes carried his zeal a little too far. The lord of his village, M. de Touilly, having ill-treated some peasants, he refused to pray for him in his service. M. de Mailly, Archbishop of Rheims, before whom the case was brought, condemned him. But the Sunday which followed this decision, the abbot Meslier stood in his pulpit and complained of the sentence of the cardinal. "This is," said he, "the general fate of the poor country priest; the archbishops, who are great lords, scorn them and do not listen to them. Therefore, let us pray for the lord of this place. We will pray for Antoine de Touilly, that he may be converted and granted the grace that he may not wrong the poor and despoil the orphans." His lordship, who was present at this mortifying supplication, brought new complaints before the same archbishop, who ordered the curate Meslier to come to Donchery, where he ill-treated him with abusive language.

There have been scarcely any other events in his life, nor other benefice, than that of Etrepigny. He died in the odor of sanctity in the year 1733, fifty-five years old. It is believed that, disgusted with life, he expressly refused necessary food, because during his sickness he was not willing to take anything, not even a glass of wine.

At his death he gave all he possessed, which was inconsiderable, to his parishioners, and desired to be buried in his garden.

They were greatly surprised to find in his house three manuscripts, each containing three hundred and sixty-six pages, all written by his hand, signed and entitled by him, "My Testament." This work, which the author addressed to his parishioners and to M. Leroux, advocate and procurator for the parliament of Meziers, is a simple refutation of all the religious dogmas, without excepting one. The grand vicar of Rheims retained one of the three copies; another was sent to Monsieur Chauvelin, guardian of the State's seal; the third remained at the clerk's office of the justiciary of St. Minehould. The Count de Caylus had one of those three copies in his possession for some time, and soon afterward more than one hundred were at Paris, sold at ten Louis-d'or apiece. A dying priest accusing himself of having professed and taught the Christian religion, made a deeper impression upon the mind than the "Thoughts of Pascal."

The curate Meslier had written upon a gray paper which enveloped the copy destined for his parishioners these remarkable words: "I have seen and recognized the errors, the abuses, the follies, and the wickedness of men. I have hated and despised them. I did not dare say it during my life, but I will say it at least in dying, and after my death; and it is that it may be known, that I write this present memorial in order that it may serve as a witness of truth to all those who may see and read it if they choose."

At the beginning of this work is found this document (a kind of honorable amend, which in his letter to the Count of d'Argental of May 31, 1762, Voltaire qualifies as a preface), addressed to his parishioners.

"You know," said he, "my brethren, my disinterestedness; I do not sacrifice my belief to any vile interest. If I embraced a profession so directly opposed to my sentiments, it was not through cupidity. I obeyed my parents. I would have preferred to enlighten you sooner if I could have done it safely. You are witnesses to what I assert. I have not disgraced my ministry by exacting the requitals, which are a part of it.

"I call heaven to witness that I also thoroughly despised those who laughed at the simplicity of the blind people, those who furnished piously considerable sums of money to buy prayers. How horrible this monopoly! I do not blame the disdain which those who grow rich by your sweat and your pains, show for their mysteries and their superstitions; but I detest their insatiable cupidity and the signal pleasure such fellows take in railing at the ignorance of those whom they carefully keep in this state of blindness. Let them content themselves with laughing at their own ease, but at least let them not multiply their errors by abusing the blind piety of those who, by their simplicity, procured them such an easy life. You render unto me, my brethren, the justice that is due me. The sympathy which I manifested for your troubles saves me from the least suspicion. How often have I performed gratuitously the functions of my ministry. How often also has my heart been grieved at not being able to assist you as often and as abundantly as I could have wished! Have I not always proved to you that I took more pleasure in giving than in receiving? I carefully avoided exhorting you to bigotry, and I spoke to you as rarely as possible of our unfortunate dogmas. It was necessary that I should acquit myself as a priest of my ministry, but how often have I not suffered within myself when I was forced to preach to you those pious lies which I despised in my heart. What a disdain I had for my ministry, and particularly for that superstitious Mass, and those ridiculous administrations of sacraments, especially if I was compelled to perform them with the solemnity which awakened all your piety and all your good faith. What remorse I had for exciting your credulity! A thousand times upon the point of bursting forth publicly, I was going to open your eyes, but a fear superior to my strength restrained me and forced me to silence until my death."

The abbot Meslier had written two letters to the curates of his neighborhood to inform them of his Testament; he told them that he had consigned to the chancery of St. Minnehould a copy of his manuscript in 366 leaves in octavo; but he feared it would be suppressed, according to the bad custom established to prevent the poor from being instructed and knowing the truth.

The curate Meslier, the most singular phenomenon ever seen among all the meteors fatal to the Christian religion, worked his whole life secretly in order to attack the opinions he believed false. To compose his manuscript against God, against all religion, against the Bible and the

Church, he had no other assistance than the Bible itself, Moreri Montaigne, and a few fathers.

While the abbot Meslier naively acknowledged that he did not wish to be burned till after his death, Thomas Woolston, a doctor of Cambridge, published and sold publicly at London, in his own house, sixty thousand copies of his "Discourses" against the miracles of Jesus Christ.

It was a very astonishing thing that two priests should at the same time write against the Christian religion. The curate Meslier has gone further yet than Woolston; he dares to treat the transport of our Saviour by the devil upon the mountain, the wedding of Cana, the bread and the fishes, as absurd fables, injurious to divinity, which were ignored during three hundred years by the whole Roman Empire, and finally passed from the lower class to the palace of the emperors, when policy obliged them to adopt the follies of the people in order the more easily to subjugate them. The denunciations of the English priest do not approach those of the Champagne priest. Woolston is sometimes indulgent, Meslier never. He was a man profoundly embittered by the crimes he witnessed, for which he holds the Christian religion responsible. There is no miracle which to him is not an object of contempt and horror; no prophecy that he does not compare to those of Nostredamus. He wrote thus against Jesus Christ when in the arms of death, at a time when the most dissimulating dare not lie, and when the most intrepid tremble. Struck with the difficulties which he found in Scripture, he inveighed against it more bitterly than the Acosta and all the Jews, more than the famous Porphyre, Celse, Iamblique, Julian, Libanius, and all the partisans of human reason.

There were found among the books of the curate Meslier a printed manuscript of the Treatise of Fenelon, Archbishop of Cambray, upon the existence of God and His attributes, and the reflections of the Jesuit Tournemine upon Atheism, to which treatise he added marginal notes signed by his hand.

DECREE

of the NATIONAL CONVENTION upon the proposition to erect a statue to the curate Jean Meslier, the 27 Brumaire, in the year II. (November 17, 1793). The National Convention sends to the Committee of Public Instruction the proposition made by one of its members to erect a statue to Jean Meslier, curate at Etrepigny, in Champagne, the first priest who had the courage and the honesty to abjure religious errors.

PRESIDENT AND SECRETARIES.

SIGNED—P. A. Laloy, President; Bazire, Charles Duval, Philippeaux, Frecine, and Merlin (de Thionville), Secretaries.

Certified according to the original.

MEMBERS OF THE COMMITTEE OF DECREES AND PROCESS-VERBAL.

SIGNED—Batellier, Echasseriaux, Monnel, Becker, Vernetey, Pérard, Vinet, Bouillerot, Auger, Cordier, Delecloy, and Cosnard.

PREFACE OF THE AUTHOR.

When we wish to examine in a cool, calm way the opinions of men, we are very much surprised to find that in those which we consider the most essential, nothing is more rare than to find them using common sense; that is to say, the portion of judgment sufficient to know the most simple truths, to reject the most striking absurdities, and to be shocked by palpable contradictions. We have an example of this in Theology, a science revered in all times, in all countries, by the greatest number of mortals; an object considered the most important, the most useful, and the most indispensable to the happiness of society. If they would but take the trouble to sound the principles upon which this pretended science rests itself, they would be compelled to admit that the principles which were considered incontestable, are but hazardous suppositions, conceived in ignorance, propagated by enthusiasm or bad intention, adopted by timid credulity, preserved by habit, which never reasons, and revered solely because it is not comprehended. Some, says Montaigne, make the world believe that which they do not themselves believe; a greater number of others make themselves believe, not comprehending what it is to believe. In a word, whoever will consult common sense upon religious opinions, and will carry into this examination the attention given to objects of ordinary interest, will easily perceive that these opinions have no solid foundation; that all religion is but a castle in the air; that Theology is but ignorance of natural causes reduced to a system; that it is but a long tissue of chimeras and contradictions; that it presents to all the different nations of the earth only romances devoid of probability, of which the hero himself is made up of qualities impossible to reconcile, his name having the power to excite in all hearts respect and fear, is found to be but a vague word, which men continually utter, being able to attach to it only such ideas or qualities as are belied by the facts, or which evidently contradict each other. The notion of this imaginary being, or rather the word by which we designate him, would be of no consequence did it not cause ravages without number upon the earth. Born into the opinion that this phantom is for them a very interesting reality, men, instead of wisely concluding from its incomprehensibility that they are exempt from thinking of it, on the contrary, conclude that they can not occupy themselves enough about it, that they must meditate upon it without ceasing, reason without end, and never lose sight of it. The invincible ignorance in which they are kept in this respect, far from discouraging them, does but excite their curiosity; instead of putting them on guard against their imagination, this ignorance makes them positive, dogmatic, imperious, and causes them to quarrel with all those who oppose doubts to the reveries which their brains have brought forth. What perplexity, when we attempt to solve an unsolvable problem! Anxious meditations upon an object impossible to grasp, and which, however, is supposed to be very important to him, can but put a man into bad humor, and produce in his brain dangerous transports. When interest, vanity, and ambition are joined to such a morose disposition, society necessarily becomes troubled. This is why so many nations have often become the theaters of extravagances caused by nonsensical visionists, who, publishing their shallow speculations for the eternal truth, have kindled the enthusiasm of princes and of people, and have prepared them for opinions which they represented as essential to the glory of divinity and to the happiness of empires. We have seen, a thousand times, in all parts of our globe, infuriated fanatics slaughtering each other, lighting the funeral piles, committing without scruple, as a matter of duty, the greatest crimes. Why? To maintain or to propagate the impertinent conjectures of enthusiasts, or to sanction the knaveries of impostors on account of a being who exists only in their imagination, and who is known only by the ravages, the disputes, and the follies which he has caused upon the earth.

Originally, savage nations, ferocious, perpetually at war, adored, under various names, some God conformed to their ideas; that is to say, cruel, carnivorous, selfish, greedy of blood. We find in all the religions of the earth a God of armies, a jealous God, an avenging God, an exterminating God, a God who enjoys carnage and whose worshipers make it a duty to serve him to his taste. Lambs, bulls, children, men, heretics, infidels, kings, whole nations, are sacrificed to him. The zealous servants of this barbarous God go so far as to believe that they are obliged to offer themselves as a sacrifice to him. Everywhere we see zealots who, after having sadly meditated upon their terrible God, imagine that, in order to please him, they must do themselves all the harm possible, and inflict upon themselves, in his honor, all imaginable torments. In a word, everywhere the baneful ideas of Divinity, far from consoling men for misfortunes incident to their existence, have filled the heart with trouble, and given birth to follies destructive to them. How could the human mind, filled with frightful phantoms and guided by men interested in perpetuating its ignorance and its fear, make progress? Man was compelled to vegetate in his primitive stupidity; he was preserved only by invisible powers, upon whom his fate was supposed to depend. Solely occupied with his alarms and his unintelligible reveries, he was always at the mercy of his priests, who reserved for themselves the right of thinking for him and of regulating his conduct.

Thus man was, and always remained, a child without experience, a slave without courage, a loggerhead who feared to reason, and who could never escape from the labyrinth into which his ancestors had misled him; he felt compelled to groan under the yoke of his Gods, of whom he knew nothing except the fabulous accounts of their ministers. These, after having fettered him by the ties of opinion, have remained his masters or delivered him up defenseless to the absolute power of tyrants, no less terrible than the Gods, of whom they were the representatives upon the earth. Oppressed by the double yoke of spiritual and temporal power, it was impossible for the people to instruct themselves and to work for their own welfare. Thus, religion, politics, and morals became sanctuaries, into which the profane were not permitted to enter. Men had no other morality than that which their legislators and their priests claimed as descended from unknown empyrean regions. The human mind, perplexed by these theological opinions, misunderstood itself, doubted its own powers, mistrusted experience, feared truth, disdained its reason, and left it to blindly follow authority. Man was a pure machine in the hands of his tyrants and his priests, who alone had the right to regulate his movements. Always treated as a slave, he had at all times and in all places the vices and dispositions of a slave.

These are the true sources of the corruption of habits, to which religion never opposes anything but ideal and ineffectual obstacles; ignorance and servitude have a tendency to make men wicked and unhappy. Science, reason, liberty, alone can reform them and render them more happy; but everything conspires to blind them and to confirm them in their blindness. The priests deceive them, tyrants corrupt them in order to subjugate them more easily. Tyranny has been, and will always be, the chief source of the depraved morals and habitual calamities of the people. These, almost always fascinated by their religious notions or by metaphysical fictions, instead of looking upon the natural and visible causes of their miseries, attribute their vices to the imperfections of their nature, and their misfortunes to the anger of their Gods; they offer to Heaven vows, sacrifices, and presents, in order to put an end to their misfortunes, which are really due only to the negligence, the ignorance, and to the perversity of their guides, to the folly of their institutions, to their foolish customs, to their false opinions, to their unreasonable laws, and especially to their want of enlightenment. Let the mind be filled early with true ideas; let man's reason be cultivated; let justice govern him; and there will be no need of opposing to his passions the powerless barrier of the fear of Gods. Men will be good when they are well taught, well governed, chastised or censured for the evil, and justly rewarded for the good which they have done to their fellow-citizens. It is idle to pretend to cure mortals of their vices if we do not begin by curing them of their prejudices. It is only by showing them the truth that they can know their best interests and the real motives which will lead them to happiness. Long enough have the instructors of the people fixed their eyes on heaven; let them at last bring them back to the earth. Tired of an incomprehensible theology, of ridiculous fables, of impenetrable mysteries, of puerile ceremonies, let the human mind occupy itself with natural things, intelligible objects, sensible truths, and useful knowledge. Let the vain chimeras which beset the people be dissipated, and very soon rational opinions will fill the minds of those who were believed fated to be always in error. To annihilate religious prejudices, it would be sufficient to show that what is inconceivable to man can not be of any use to him. Does it need, then, anything but simple common sense to perceive that a being most clearly irreconcilable with the notions of mankind, that a cause continually opposed to the effects attributed to him; that a being of whom not a word can be said without falling into contradictions; that a being who, far from explaining the mysteries of the universe, only renders them more inexplicable; that a being to whom for so many centuries men addressed themselves so vainly to obtain their happiness and deliverance from their sufferings; does it need, I say, more than simple common sense to understand that the idea of such a being is an idea without model, and that he is himself evidently not a reasonable being? Does it require more than common sense to feel that there is at least delirium and frenzy in hating and tormenting each other for unintelligible opinions of a being of this kind? Finally, does it not all prove that morality and virtue are totally incompatible with the idea of a God, whose ministers and interpreters have painted him in all countries as the most fantastic, the most unjust, and the most cruel of tyrants, whose pretended wishes are to serve as rules and laws for the inhabitants of the earth? To discover the true principles of morality, men have no need of theology, of revelation, or of Gods; they need but common sense; they have only to look within themselves, to reflect upon their own nature, to consult their obvious interests, to consider the object of society and of each of the members who compose it, and they will easily understand that virtue is an advantage, and that vice is an injury to beings of their species. Let us teach men to be just, benevolent, moderate, and sociable, not because their Gods exact it, but to please men; let us tell them to abstain from vice and from crime, not because they will be punished in another world, but because they will suffer in the present world. There are, says Montesquieu, means to prevent crime, they are sufferings; to change the manners, these are good examples. Truth is simple, error is complicated, uncertain in its gait, full of by-ways; the voice of nature is intelligible, that of falsehood is ambiguous, enigmatical, and mysterious; the road of truth is straight, that of imposture is oblique and dark; this truth, always necessary to man, is felt by all just minds; the lessons of reason are followed by all honest souls; men are unhappy only because they are ignorant; they are ignorant only because everything conspires to prevent them from being enlightened, and they are wicked only because their reason is not sufficiently developed.

COMMON SENSE.

Detexit quo dolose Vaticinandi furore sacerdotes mysteria, illis spe ignota, audactur publicant.—PETRON. SATYR.

I.

APOLOGUE.

There is a vast empire governed by a monarch, whose conduct does but confound the minds of his subjects. He desires to be known, loved, respected, and obeyed, but he never shows himself; everything tends to make uncertain the notions which we are able to form about him. The people subjected to his power have only such ideas of the character and the laws of their invisible sovereign as his ministers give them; these suit, however, because they themselves have no idea of their master, for his ways are impenetrable, and his views and his qualities are totally incomprehensible; moreover, his ministers disagree among themselves in regard to the orders which they pretend emanated from the sovereign whose organs they claim to be; they announce them diversely in each province of the empire; they discredit and treat each other as impostors and liars; the decrees and ordinances which they promulgate are obscure; they are enigmas, made not to be understood or divined by the subjects for whose instruction they were intended. The laws of the invisible monarch need interpreters, but those who explain them are always quarreling among themselves about the true way of understanding them; more than this, they do not agree among themselves; all which they relate of their hidden prince is but a tissue of contradictions, scarcely a single word that is not contradicted at once. He is called supremely good, nevertheless not a person but complains of his decrees. He is supposed to be infinitely wise, and in his administration everything seems contrary to reason and good sense. They boast of his justice, and the best of his subjects are generally the least favored. We are assured that he sees everything, yet his presence remedies nothing. It is said that he is the friend of order, and everything in his universe is in a state of confusion and disorder; all is created by him, yet events rarely happen according to his projects. He foresees everything, but his foresight prevents nothing. He is impatient if any offend him; at the same time he puts every one in the way of offending him. His knowledge is admired in the perfection of his works, but his works are full of imperfections, and of little permanence. He is continually occupied in creating and destroying, then repairing what he has done, never appearing to be satisfied with his work. In all his enterprises he seeks but his own glory, but he does not succeed in being glorified. He works but for the good of his subjects, and most of them lack the necessities of life. Those whom he seems to favor, are generally those who are the least satisfied with their fate; we see them all continually revolting against a master whose greatness they admire, whose wisdom they extol, whose goodness they worship, and whose justice they fear, revering orders which they never follow. This empire is the world; its monarch is God; His ministers are the priests; their subjects are men.

II.

WHAT IS THEOLOGY?

There is a science which has for its object only incomprehensible things. Unlike all others, it occupies itself but with things unseen. Hobbes calls it "the kingdom of darkness." In this land all obey laws opposed to those which men acknowledge in the world they inhabit. In this marvelous region light is but darkness, evidence becomes doubtful or false, the impossible becomes credible, reason is an unfaithful guide, and common sense changed into delirium. This science is named Theology, and this Theology is a continual insult to human reason.

III.

By frequent repetition of if, but, and perhaps, we succeed in forming an imperfect and broken system which perplexes men's minds to the extent of making them forget the clearest notions, and to render uncertain the most palpable truths. By the aid of this systematic nonsense, all nature has become an inexplicable enigma for man; the visible world has disappeared to give place to invisible regions; reason is obliged to give place to imagination, which can lead us only to the land of chimeras which she herself has invented.

IV.

MAN BORN NEITHER RELIGIOUS NOR DEISTICAL.

All religious principles are founded upon the idea of a God, but it is impossible for men to have true ideas of a being who does not act upon any one of their senses. All our ideas are but pictures of objects which strike us. What can the idea of God represent to us when it is evidently an idea without an object? Is not such an idea as impossible as an effect without a cause? An idea without a prototype, is it anything but a chimera? Some theologians, however, assure us that the idea of God is innate, or that men have this idea from the time of their birth. Every principle is a judgment; all judgment is the effect of experience; experience is not acquired but by the exercise of the senses: from which it follows that religious principles are drawn from nothing, and are not innate.

V.

IT IS NOT NECESSARY TO BELIEVE IN A GOD, AND THE MOST REASONABLE THING IS NOT TO THINK OF HIM.

No religious system can be founded otherwise than upon the nature of God and of men, and upon the relations they bear to each other. But, in order to judge of the reality of these relations, we must have some idea of the Divine nature. But everybody tells us that the essence of God is incomprehensible to man; at the same time they do not hesitate to assign attributes to this incomprehensible God, and assure us that man can not dispense with a knowledge of this God so impossible to conceive of. The most important thing for men is that which is the most impossible for them to comprehend. If God is incomprehensible to man, it would seem rational never to think of Him at all; but religion concludes that man is criminal if he ceases for a moment to revere Him.

VI.

RELIGION IS FOUNDED UPON CREDULITY.

We are told that Divine qualities are not of a nature to be grasped by limited minds. The natural consequence of this principle ought to be that the Divine qualities are not made to employ limited minds; but religion assures us that limited minds should never lose sight of this inconceivable being, whose qualities can not be grasped by them: from which we see that religion is the art of occupying limited minds with that which is impossible for them to comprehend.

VII.

EVERY RELIGION IS AN ABSURDITY.

Religion unites man with God or puts them in communication; but do you say that God is infinite? If God is infinite, no finite being can have communication or any relation with Him. Where there are no relations, there can be no union, no correspondence, no duties. If there are no duties between man and his God, there exists no religion for man. Thus by saying that God is infinite, you annihilate, from that moment, all religion for man, who is a finite being. The idea of infinity is for us in idea without model, without prototype, without object.

VIII.

THE NOTION OF GOD IS IMPOSSIBLE.

If God is an infinite being, there can be neither in the actual world or in another any proportion between man and his God; thus the idea of God will never enter the human mind. In the supposition of a life where men will be more enlightened than in this one, the infinity of God will always place such a distance between his idea and the limited mind of man, that he will not be able to conceive of God any more in a future life than in the present. Hence, it evidently follows that the idea of God will not be better suited to man in the other life than in the present. God is not made for man; it follows also that intelligences superior to man—such as angels, archangels, seraphims, and saints—can have no more complete notions of God than has man, who does not understand anything about Him here below.

IX.

ORIGIN OF SUPERSTITION.

How is it that we have succeeded in persuading reasonable beings that the thing most impossible to understand was the most essential for them. It is because they were greatly frightened; it is because when men are kept in fear they cease to reason; it is because they have been expressly enjoined to distrust their reason. When the brain is troubled, we believe everything and examine nothing.

X.

ORIGIN OF ALL RELIGION.

Ignorance and fear are the two pivots of all religion. The uncertainty attending man's relation to his God is precisely the motive which attaches him to his religion. Man is afraid when in darkness—physical or moral. His fear is habitual to him and becomes a necessity; he would believe that he lacked something if he had nothing to fear.

XI.

IN THE NAME OF RELIGION CHARLATANS TAKE ADVANTAGE OF THE WEAKNESS OF MEN.

He who from his childhood has had a habit of trembling every time he heard certain words, needs these words, and needs to tremble. In this way he is more disposed to listen to the one who encourages his fears than to the one who would dispel his fears. The superstitious man wants to be afraid; his imagination demands it. It seems that he fears nothing more than having no object to fear. Men are imaginary patients, whom interested charlatans take care to encourage in their weakness, in order to have a market for their remedies. Physicians who order a great number of remedies are more listened to than those who recommend a good regimen, and who leave nature to act.

XII.

RELIGION ENTICES IGNORANCE BY THE AID OF THE MARVELOUS.

If religion was clear, it would have fewer attractions for the ignorant. They need obscurity, mysteries, fables, miracles, incredible things, which keep their brains perpetually at work. Romances, idle stories, tales of ghosts and witches, have more charms for the vulgar than true narrations.

XIII.

CONTINUATION.

In the matter of religion, men are but overgrown children. The more absurd a religion is, and the fuller of marvels, the more power it exerts; the devotee thinks himself obliged to place no limits to his credulity; the more inconceivable things are, the more divine they appear to him; the more incredible they are, the more merit he gives himself for believing them.

XIV.

THERE WOULD NEVER HAVE BEEN ANY RELIGION IF THERE HAD NEVER BEEN ANY DARK AND BARBAROUS AGES.

The origin of religious opinions dates, as a general thing, from the time when savage nations were yet in a state of infancy. It was to coarse, ignorant, and stupid men that the founders of religion addressed themselves in all ages, in order to present them with Gods, ceremonies, histories of fabulous Divinities, marvelous and terrible fables. These chimeras, adopted without examination by the fathers, have been transmitted with more or less changes to their polished children, who often do not reason more than their fathers.

XV.

ALL RELIGION WAS BORN OF THE DESIRE TO DOMINATE.

The first legislators of nations had for their object to dominate, The easiest means of succeeding was to frighten the people and to prevent them from reasoning; they led them by tortuous paths in order that they should not perceive the designs of their guides; they compelled them to look into the air, for fear they should look to their feet; they amused them upon the road by stories; in a word, they treated them in the way of nurses, who employ songs and menaces to put the children to sleep, or to force them to be quiet.

XVI.

THAT WHICH SERVES AS A BASIS FOR ALL RELIGION IS VERY UNCERTAIN.

The existence of a God is the basis of all religion. Few people seem to doubt this existence, but this fundamental principle is precisely the one which prevents every mind from reasoning. The first question of every catechism was, and will always be, the most difficult one to answer.

XVII.

IT IS IMPOSSIBLE TO BE CONVINCED OF THE EXISTENCE OF GOD.

Can one honestly say that he is convinced of the existence of a being whose nature is not known, who remains inaccessible to all our senses, and of whose qualities we are constantly assured that they are incomprehensible to us? In order to persuade me that a being exists, or can exist, he must begin by telling me what this being is; in order to make me believe the existence or the possibility of such a being, he must tell me things about him which are not contradictory, and which do not destroy one another; finally, in order to convince me fully of the existence of this being, he must tell me things about him which I can comprehend, and prove to me that it is impossible that the being to whom he attributes these qualities does not exist.

XVIII.

CONTINUATION.

A thing is impossible when it is composed of two ideas so antagonistic, that we can not think of them at the same time. Evidence can be relied on only when confirmed by the constant testimony of our senses, which alone give birth to ideas, and enable us to judge of their conformity or of their incompatibility. That which exists necessarily, is that of which the non-existence would imply contradiction. These principles, universally recognized, are at fault when the question of the existence of God is considered; what has been said of Him is either unintelligible or perfectly contradictory; and for this reason must appear impossible to every man of common sense.

XIX.

THE EXISTENCE OF GOD IS NOT PROVED.

All human intelligences are more or less enlightened and cultivated. By what fatality is it that the science of God has never been explained? The most civilized nations and the most profound thinkers are of the same opinion in regard to the matter as the most barbarous nations and the most ignorant and rustic people. As we examine the subject more closely, we will find that the science of divinity by means of reveries and subtleties has but obscured it more and more. Thus far, all religion has been founded on what is called in logic, a "begging of the question;" it supposes freely, and then proves, finally, by the suppositions it has made.

XX.

TO SAY THAT GOD IS A SPIRIT, IS TO SPEAK WITHOUT SAYING ANYTHING AT ALL.

By metaphysics, God is made a pure spirit, but has modern theology advanced one step further than the theology of the barbarians? They recognized a grand spirit as master of the world. The barbarians, like all ignorant men, attribute to spirits all the effects of which their inexperience prevents them from discovering the true causes. Ask a barbarian what causes your watch to move, he will answer, "a spirit!" Ask our philosophers what moves the universe, they will tell you "it is a spirit."

XXI.

SPIRITUALITY IS A CHIMERA.

The barbarian, when he speaks of a spirit, attaches at least some sense to this word; he understands by it an agent similar to the wind, to the agitated air, to the breath, which produces, invisibly, effects that we perceive. By subtilizing, the modern theologian becomes as little intelligible to himself as to others. Ask him what he means by a spirit? He will answer, that it is an unknown substance, which is perfectly simple, which has nothing tangible, nothing in common with matter. In good faith, is there any mortal who can form the least idea of such a substance? A spirit in the language of modern theology is then but an absence of ideas. The idea of spirituality is another idea without a model.

XXII.

ALL WHICH EXISTS SPRINGS FROM THE BOSOM OF MATTER.

Is it not more natural and more intelligible to deduce all which exists, from the bosom of matter, whose existence is demonstrated by all our senses, whose effects we feel at every moment, which we see act, move, communicate, motion, and constantly bring living beings into existence, than to attribute the formation of things to an unknown force, to a spiritual being, who can not draw from his ground that which he has not himself, and who, by the spiritual essence claimed for him, is incapable of making anything, and of putting anything in motion? Nothing is plainer than that they would have us believe that an intangible spirit can act upon matter.

XXIII.

WHAT IS THE METAPHYSICAL GOD OF MODERN THEOLOGY?

The material Jupiter of the ancients could move, build up, destroy, and propagate beings similar to himself; but the God of modern theology is a sterile being. According to his supposed nature he can neither occupy any place, nor move matter, nor produce a visible world, nor propagate either men or Gods. The metaphysical God is a workman without hands; he is able but to produce clouds, suspicions, reveries, follies, and quarrels.

XXIV.

IT WOULD BE MORE RATIONAL TO WORSHIP THE SUN THAN A SPIRITUAL GOD.

Since it was necessary for men to have a God, why did they not have the sun, the visible God, adored by so many nations? What being had more right to the homage of mortals than the star of the day, which gives light and heat; which invigorates all beings; whose presence reanimates and rejuvenates nature; whose absence seems to plunge her into sadness and languor? If some being bestowed upon men power, activity, benevolence, strength, it was no doubt the sun, which should be recognized as the father of nature, as the soul of the world, as Divinity. At least one could not without folly dispute his existence, or refuse to recognize his influence and his benefits.

XXV.

A SPIRITUAL GOD IS INCAPABLE OF WILLING AND OF ACTING.

The theologian tells us that God does not need hands or arms to act, and that He acts by His will alone. But what is this God who has a will? And what can be the subject of this divine will? Is it more ridiculous or more difficult to believe in fairies, in sylphs, in ghosts, in witches, in werewolfs, than to believe in the magical or impossible action of the spirit upon the body? As soon as we admit of such a God, there are no longer fables or visions which can not be believed. The theologians treat men like children, who never cavil about the possibilities of the tales which they listen to.

XXVI.

WHAT IS GOD?

To unsettle the existence of a God, it is only necessary to ask a theologian to speak of Him; as soon as he utters one word about Him, the least reflection makes us discover at once that what he says is incompatible with the essence which he attributes to his God. Therefore, what is God? It is an abstract word, coined to designate the hidden forces of nature; or, it is a mathematical point, which has neither length, breadth, nor thickness. A philosopher [David Hume] has very ingeniously said in speaking of theologians, that they have found the solution to the famous problem of Archimedes; a point in the heavens from which they move the world.

XXVII.

REMARKABLE CONTRADICTIONS OF THEOLOGY.

Religion puts men on their knees before a being without extension, and who, notwithstanding, is infinite, and fills all space with his immensity; before an almighty being, who never executes that which he desires; before a being supremely good, and who causes but displeasure; before a being, the friend of order, and in whose government everything is in disorder. After all this, let us conjecture what this God of theology is.

XXVIII.

TO ADORE GOD IS TO ADORE A FICTION.

In order to avoid all embarrassment, they tell us that it is not necessary to know what God is; that we must adore without knowing; that it is not permitted us to turn an eye of temerity upon His attributes. But if we must adore a God without knowing Him, should we not be assured that He exists? Moreover, how be assured that He exists without having examined whether it is possible that the diverse qualities claimed for Him, meet in Him? In truth, to adore God is to adore nothing but fictions of one's own brain, or rather, it is to adore nothing.

XXIX.

THE INFINITY OF GOD AND THE IMPOSSIBILITY OF KNOWING THE DIVINE ESSENCE, OCCASIONS AND JUSTIFIES ATHEISM.

Without doubt the more to perplex matters, theologians have chosen to say nothing about what their God is; they tell us what He is not. By negations and abstractions they imagine themselves composing a real and perfect being, while there can result from it but a being of human reason. A spirit has no body; an infinite being is a being which is not finite; a perfect being is a being which is not imperfect. Can any one form any real notions of such a multitude of deficiencies or absence of ideas? That which excludes all idea, can it be anything but nothingness? To pretend that the divine attributes are beyond the understanding of the human mind is to render God unfit for men. If we are assured that God is infinite, we admit that there can be nothing in common between Him and His creatures. To say that God is infinite, is to destroy Him for men, or at least render Him useless to them.

God, we are told, created men intelligent, but He did not create them omniscient: that is to say, capable of knowing all things. We conclude that He was not able to endow him with intelligence sufficient to understand the divine essence. In this case it is demonstrated that God has neither the power nor the wish to be known by men. By what right could this God become angry with beings whose own essence makes it impossible to have any idea of the divine essence? God would evidently be the most unjust and the most unaccountable of tyrants if He should punish an atheist for not knowing that which his nature made it impossible for him to know.

XXX.

IT IS NEITHER LESS NOR MORE CRIMINAL TO BELIEVE IN GOD THAN NOT TO BELIEVE IN HIM.

For the generality of men nothing renders an argument more convincing than fear. In consequence of this fact, theologians tell us that the safest side must be taken; that nothing is more criminal than incredulity; that God will punish without mercy all those who have the temerity to doubt His existence; that His severity is just; since it is only madness or perversity which questions the existence of an angry monarch who revenges himself cruelly upon atheists. If we examine these menaces calmly, we shall find that they assume always the thing in question. They must commence by proving to our satisfaction the existence of a God, before telling us that it is safer to believe, and that it is horrible to doubt or to deny it. Then they must prove that it is possible for a just God to punish men cruelly for having been in a state of madness, which prevented them from believing in the existence of a being whom their enlightened reason could not comprehend. In a word, they must prove that a God that is said to be full of equity, could punish beyond measure the invincible and necessary ignorance of man, caused by his relation to the divine essence. Is not the theologians' manner of reasoning very singular? They create phantoms, they fill them with contradictions, and finally assure us that the safest way is not to doubt the existence of those phantoms, which they have themselves invented. By following out this method, there is no absurdity which it would not be safer to believe than not to believe.

All children are atheists—they have no idea of God; are they, then, criminal on account of this ignorance? At what age do they begin to be obliged to believe in God? It is, you say, at the age of reason. At what time does this age begin? Besides, if the most profound theologians lose themselves in the divine essence, which they boast of not comprehending, what ideas can common people have?—women, mechanics, and, in short, those who compose the mass of the human race?

XXXI.

THE BELIEF IN GOD IS NOTHING BUT A MECHANICAL HABITUDE OF CHILDHOOD.

Men believe in God only upon the word of those who have no more idea of Him than they themselves. Our nurses are our first theologians; they talk to children of God as they talk to them of were-wolfs; they teach them from the most tender age to join the hands mechanically. Have the nurses clearer notions of God than the children, whom they compel to pray to Him?

XXXII.

IT IS A PREJUDICE WHICH HAS BEEN HANDED FROM FATHER TO CHILDREN.

Religion is handed down from fathers to children as the property of a family with the burdens. Very few people in the world would have a God if care had not been taken to give them one. Each one receives from his parents and his instructors the God which they themselves have received from theirs; only, according to his own temperament, each one arranges, modifies, and paints Him agreeably to his taste.

XXXIII.

ORIGIN OF PREJUDICES.

The brain of man is, especially in infancy, like a soft wax, ready to receive all the impressions we wish to make on it; education furnishes nearly all his opinions, at a period when he is incapable of judging for himself. We believe that the ideas, true or false, which at a tender age were forced into our heads, were received from nature at our birth; and this persuasion is one of the greatest sources of our errors.

XXXIV.

HOW THEY TAKE ROOT AND SPREAD.

Prejudice tends to confirm in us the opinions of those who are charged with our instruction. We believe them more skillful than we are; we suppose them thoroughly convinced themselves of the things they teach us. We have the greatest confidence in them. After the care they have taken of us when we were unable to assist ourselves, we judge them incapable of deceiving us. These are the motives which make us adopt a thousand errors without other foundation than the dangerous word of those who have educated us; even the being forbidden to reason upon what they tell us, does not diminish our confidence, but contributes often to increase our respect for their opinions.

XXXV.

MEN WOULD NEVER HAVE BELIEVED IN THE PRINCIPLES OF MODERN THEOLOGY IF THEY HAD NOT BEEN TAUGHT AT AN AGE WHEN THEY WERE INCAPABLE OF REASONING.

The instructors of the human race act very prudently in teaching men their religious principles before they are able to distinguish the true from the false, or the left hand from the right. It would be as difficult to tame the spirit of a man forty years old with the extravagant notions which are given us of Divinity, as to banish these notions from the head of a man who has imbibed them since his tenderest infancy.

XXXVI.

THE WONDERS OF NATURE DO NOT PROVE THE EXISTENCE OF GOD.

We are assured that the wonders of nature are sufficient to a belief in the existence of a God, and to convince us fully of this important truth. But how many persons are there in this world who have the leisure, the capacity, the necessary taste, to contemplate nature and to meditate upon its progress? The majority of men pay no attention to it. A peasant is not at all moved by the beauty of the sun, which he sees every day. The sailor is not surprised by the regular movements of the ocean; he will draw from them no theological inductions. The phenomena of nature do not prove the existence of a God, except to a few forewarned men, to whom has been shown in advance the finger of God in all the objects whose mechanism could embarrass them. The unprejudiced philosopher sees nothing in the wonders of nature but permanent and invariable law; nothing but the necessary effects of different combinations of diversified substance.

XXXVII.

THE WONDERS OF NATURE EXPLAIN THEMSELVES BY NATURAL CAUSES.

Is there anything more surprising than the logic of so many profound doctors, who, instead of acknowledging the little light they have upon natural agencies, seek outside of nature—that is to say, in imaginary regions—an agent less understood than this nature, of which they can at least form some idea? To say that God is the author of the phenomena that we see, is it not attributing them to an occult cause? What is God? What is a spirit? They are causes of which we have no idea. Sages! study nature and her laws; and when you can from them unravel the action of natural causes, do not go in search of supernatural causes, which, very far from enlightening your ideas, will but entangle them more and more and make it impossible for you to understand yourselves.

XXXVIII.

CONTINUATION.

Nature, you say, is totally inexplicable without a God; that is to say, in order to explain what you understand so little, you need a cause which you do not understand at all. You pretend to make clear that which is obscure, by magnifying its obscurity. You think you have untied a knot by multiplying knots. Enthusiastic philosophers, in order to prove to us the existence of a God, you copy complete treatises on botany; you enter into minute details of the parts of the human body; you ascend into the air to contemplate the revolutions of the stars; you return then to earth to admire the course of the waters; you fly into ecstasies over butterflies, insects, polyps, organized atoms, in which you think to find the greatness of your God; all these things will not prove the existence of this God; they will only prove that you have not the ideas which you should have of the immense variety of causes and effects that can produce the infinitely diversified combinations, of which the universe is the assemblage. This will prove that you ignore nature, that you have no idea of her resources when you judge her incapable of producing a multitude of forms and beings, of which your eyes, even by the aid of the microscope, see but the least part; finally, this will prove, that not being able to know the sensible and comprehensible agents, you find it easier to have recourse to a word, by which you designate an agent, of whom it will always be impossible for you to form any true idea.

XXXIX.

THE WORLD HAS NOT BEEN CREATED, AND MATTER MOVES BY ITSELF.

They tell us gravely that there is no effect without a cause; they repeat to us very often that the world did not create itself. But the universe is a cause, not an effect; it is not a work, has not been made, because it was impossible that it should be made. The world has always been, its existence is necessary. It is the cause of itself. Nature, whose essence is visibly acting and producing, in order to fulfill her functions, as we see she does, needs no invisible motor far more unknown than herself. Matter moves by its own energy, by the necessary result of its heterogeneity; the diversity of its movements or of its ways of acting, constitute only the diversity of substances; we distinguish one being from another but by the diversity of the impressions or movements which they communicate to our organs.

XL.

CONTINUATION.

You see that everything in nature is in a state of activity, and you pretend that nature of itself is dead and without energy! You believe that all this, acting of itself, has need of a motor! Well! who is this motor? It is a spirit, that is to say, an absolutely incomprehensible and contradictory being. Conclude then, I say to you, that matter acts of itself, and cease to reason about your spiritual motor, which has nothing that is necessary to put it into motion. Return from your useless excursions; come down from an imaginary into a real world; take hold of second causes; leave to theologians their "First Cause," of which nature has no need in order to produce all the effects which you see.

XLI.

OTHER PROOFS THAT MOTION IS IN THE ESSENCE OF MATTER, AND THAT IT IS NOT NECESSARY TO SUPPOSE A SPIRITUAL MOTOR.

It is but by the diversity of impressions or of effects which substances or bodies make upon us, that we feel them, that we have perceptions and ideas of them, that we distinguish them one from another, that we assign to them peculiarities. Moreover, in order to perceive or to feel an object, this object must act upon our organs; this object can not act upon us without exciting some motion in us; it can not produce any motion in us if it is not itself in motion. As soon as I see an object, my eyes must be struck by it; I can not conceive of light and of vision without a motion in the luminous, extended, and colored body which communicates itself to my eye, or which acts upon my retina. As soon as I smell a body, my olfactory nerve must be irritated or put into motion by the parts exhaled from an odorous body. As soon as I hear a sound, the tympanum of my ear must be struck by the air put in motion by a sonorous body, which could not act if it was not moved of itself. From which it follows, evidently, that without motion I can neither feel, see, distinguish, compare, nor judge the body, nor even occupy my thought with any matter whatever. It is said in the schools, that the essence of a being is that from which flow all the properties of that being. Now then, it is evident that all the properties of bodies or of substances of which we have ideas, are due to the motion which alone informs us of their existence, and gives us the first conceptions of it.

I can not be informed or assured of my own existence but by the motions which I experience within myself. I am compelled to conclude that motion is as essential to matter as its extension, and that it can not be conceived of without it. If one persists in caviling about the evidences which prove to us that motion is an essential property of matter, he must at least acknowledge that substances which seemed dead or deprived of all energy, take motion of themselves as soon as they are brought within the proper distance to act upon each other. Pyrophorus, when enclosed in a bottle or deprived of contact with the air, can not take fire by itself, but it burns as soon as exposed to the air. Flour and water cause fermentation as soon as they are mixed. Thus dead substances engender motion of themselves. Matter has then the power to move itself, and nature, in order to act, does not need a motor whose essence would hinder its activity.

XLII.

THE EXISTENCE OF MAN DOES NOT PROVE THAT OF GOD.

Whence comes man? What is his origin? Is he the result of the fortuitous meeting of atoms? Was the first man formed of the dust of the earth? I do not know! Man appears to me to be a production of nature like all others she embraces. I should be just as much embarrassed to tell you whence came the first stones, the first trees, the first elephants, the first ants, the first acorns, as to explain the origin of the human species. Recognize, we are told, the hand of God, of an infinitely intelligent and powerful workman, in a work so wonderful as the human machine. I would admit without question that the human machine appears to me surprising; but since man exists in nature, I do not believe it right to say that his formation is beyond the forces of nature. I will add, that I could conceive far less of the formation of the human machine, when to explain it to me they tell me that a pure spirit, who has neither eyes, nor feet, nor hands, nor head, nor lungs, nor mouth, nor breath, has made man by taking a little dust and blowing upon it. The savage inhabitants of Paraguay pretend to be descended from the moon, and appear to us as simpletons; the theologians of Europe pretend to be descended from a pure spirit. Is this pretension more sensible?

Man is intelligent, hence it is concluded that he must be the work of an intelligent being, and not of a nature devoid of intelligence. Although nothing is more rare than to see man use this intelligence, of which he appears so proud, I will admit that he is intelligent, that his necessities develop in him this faculty, that the society of other men contributes especially to cultivate it. But in the human machine and in the intelligence with which it is endowed, I see nothing that shows in a precise manner the infinite intelligence of the workman who has the honor of making it. I see that this admirable machine is subject to derangement; that at that time this wonderful intelligence is disordered, and sometimes totally disappears; from this I conclude that human intelligence depends upon a certain disposition of the material organs of the body, and that, because man is an intelligent being, it is not well to conclude that God must be an intelligent being, any more than because man is material, we are compelled to conclude that God is material. The intelligence of man no more proves the intelligence of God than the malice of men proves the malice of this God, of whom they pretend that man is the work. In whatever way theology is taken, God will always be a cause contradicted by its effects, or of whom it is impossible to judge by His works. We shall always see evil, imperfections, and follies resulting from a cause claimed to be full of goodness, of perfections, and of wisdom.

XLIII.

HOWEVER, NEITHER MAN NOR THE UNIVERSE IS THE EFFECT OF CHANCE.

Then you will say that intelligent man and even the universe and all it encloses, are the effects of chance. No, I answer, the universe is not an effect; it is the cause of all effects; all the beings it embraces are the necessary effects of this cause which sometimes shows to us its manner of acting, out which often hides from us its way. Men may use the word "chance" to cover their ignorance of the true causes; nevertheless, although they may ignore them, these causes act, but by certain laws. There is no effect without a cause.

Nature is a word which we make use of to designate the immense assemblage of beings, diverse substances, infinite combinations, and all the various motions which we see. All bodies, whether organized or not organized, are the necessary results of certain causes, made to produce necessarily the effects which we see. Nothing in nature can be made by chance; all follow fixed laws; these laws are but the necessary union of certain effects with their causes. An atom of matter does not meet another atom by accident or by hazard; this rencounter is due to permanent laws, which cause each being to act by necessity as it does, and can not act otherwise under the same circumstances. To speak about the accidental coming together of atoms, or to attribute any effects to chance, is to say nothing, if not to ignore the laws by which bodies act, meet, combine, or separate.

Everything is made by chance for those who do not understand nature, the properties of beings, and the effects which must necessarily result from the concurrence of certain causes. It is not chance that has placed the sun in the center of our planetary system; it is by its very essence, the substance of which it is composed, that it occupies this place, and from thence diffuses itself to invigorate the beings who live in these planets.

XLIV.

NEITHER DOES THE ORDER OF THE UNIVERSE PROVE THE EXISTENCE OF A GOD.

The worshipers of a God find, especially in the order of the universe, an invincible proof of the existence of an intelligent and wise being who rules it. But this order is only a result of motions necessarily brought on by causes or by circumstances which are sometimes favorable and sometimes injurious to ourselves; we approve the former and find fault with the latter.

Nature follows constantly the same progress; that is to say, the same causes produce the same effects, as long as their action is not interrupted by other causes which occasion the first ones to produce different effects. When the causes, whose effects we feel, are interrupted in their action by causes which, although unknown to us, are no less natural and necessary, we are stupefied, we cry out miracles: and we attribute them to a cause far less known than all those we see operating before us. The universe is always in order; there can be no disorder for it. Our organization alone is suffering if we complain about disorder. Bodies, causes, beings, which this world embraces, act necessarily in the manner in which we see them act, whether we approve or disapprove their action. Earthquakes, volcanoes, inundations, contagions, and famines are effects as necessary in the order of nature as the fall of heavy bodies, as the course of rivers, as the periodical movements of the seas, the blowing of the winds, the abundant rains, and the favorable effects for which we praise and thank Providence for its blessings.

To be astonished that a certain order reigns in the world, is to be surprised to see the same causes constantly producing the same effects. To be shocked at seeing disorder, is to forget that the causes being changed or disturbed in their action, the effects can no longer be the same. To be astonished to see order in nature, is to be astonished that anything can exist; it is to be surprised at one's own existence. What is order for one being, is disorder for another. All wicked beings find that everything is in order when they can with impunity put everything into disorder; they find, on the contrary, that everything is in disorder when they are prevented from exercising their wickedness.

XLV.

CONTINUATION.

Supposing God to be the author and the motor of nature, there could be no disorder relating to Him; all causes which He would have made would necessarily act according to their properties the essences and the impulsions that He had endowed them with. If God should change the ordinary course of things, He would not be immutable. If the order of the universe—in which we believe we see the most convincing proof of His existence, of His intelligence, His power, and His goodness—should be inconsistent, His existence might be doubted; or He might be accused at least of inconstancy, of inability, of want of foresight, and of wisdom in the first arrangement of things; we would have a right to accuse Him of blundering in His choice of agents and instruments. Finally, if the order of nature proves the power and the intelligence, disorder ought to prove the weakness, inconstancy, and irrationality of Divinity. You say that God is everywhere; that He fills all space; that nothing was made without Him; that matter could not act without Him as its motor. But in this case you admit that your God is the author of disorder; that it is He who deranges nature; that He is the Father of confusion; that He is in man; and that He moves man at the moment when he sins. If God is everywhere, He is in me; He acts with me; He is deceived when I am deceived; He questions with me the existence of God; He offends God with me. Oh, theologians! you never understand yourselves when you speak of God.

XLVI.

A PURE SPIRIT CAN NOT BE INTELLIGENT, AND TO ADORE A DIVINE INTELLIGENCE IS A CHIMERA.

To be what we call intelligent, we must have ideas, thoughts, will; to have ideas, thoughts, and will, we must have organs; to have organs, we must have a body; to act upon bodies, we must have a body; to experience trouble, we must be capable of suffering; from which it evidently follows that a pure spirit can not be intelligent, and can not be affected by that which takes place in the universe.

Divine intelligence, divine ideas, divine views, you say, have nothing in common with those of men. So much the better! But in this case, how can men judge of these views—whether good or evil—reason about these ideas, or admire this intelligence? It would be to judge, to admire, to adore that of which we can form no idea. To adore the profound views of divine wisdom, is it not to worship that of which it is impossible for us to judge? To admire these same views, is it not admiring without knowing wry? Admiration is always the daughter of ignorance. Men admire and worship only what they do not understand.

XLVII.

ALL THE QUALITIES WHICH THEOLOGY GIVES TO ITS GOD ARE CONTRARY TO THE VERY ESSENCE WHICH IT SUPPOSES HIM TO HAVE.

All these qualities which are given to God are not suited to a being who, by His own essence, is devoid of all similarity to human beings. It is true, they think to find this similarity by exaggerating the human qualities with which they have clothed Divinity; they thrust them upon the infinite, and from that moment cease to understand themselves. What is the result of this combination of man with God, or of this theanthropy? Its only result is a chimera, of which nothing can be affirmed without causing the phantom to vanish which they had taken so much trouble to conjure up.

Dante, in his poem of Paradise, relates that the Divinity appeared to him under the figure of three circles, which formed an iris, whose bright colors arose from each other; but having wished to retain its brilliant light, the poet saw only his own face. In worshiping God, man adores himself.

XLVIII.

CONTINUATION.

The slightest reflection suffices to prove to us that God can not have any of the human qualities, virtues, or perfections. Our virtues and our perfections are the results of our temperament modified. Has God a temperament like ours? Our good qualities are our habits relative to the beings in whose society we live. God, according to you, is a solitary being. God has no one like Him; He does not live in society; He has no need of any one; He enjoys a happiness which nothing can alter. Admit, then, upon your own principles, that God can not possess what we call virtues, and that man can not be virtuous in regard to Him.

XLIX.

IT IS ABSURD TO SAY THAT THE HUMAN RACE IS THE OBJECT AND THE END OF CREATION.

Man, charmed with his own merits, imagines that it is but his own kind that God proposed as the object and the end in the formation of the universe. Upon what is this so flattering opinion based? It is, we are told, upon this: that man is the only being endowed with an intelligence which enables him to know the Divine nature, and to render to it homage worthy of it. We are assured that God created the world for His own glory, and that the human race was included in His plan, in order that He might have somebody to admire and glorify Him in His works. But by these intentions has not God visibly missed His end?

1. According to you, it would always be impossible for man to know his God, and he would be kept in the most invincible ignorance of the Divine essence.

2. A being who has no equals, can not be susceptible of glory. Glory can result but from the comparison of his own excellence with that of others.

3. If God by Himself is infinitely happy and is sufficient unto Himself, why does He need the homage of His feeble creatures?

4. In spite of all His works, God is not glorified; on the contrary, all the religions of the world show Him to us as

perpetually offended; their great object is to reconcile sinful, ungrateful, and rebellious man with his wrathful God.

L.

GOD IS NOT MADE FOR MAN, NOR MAN FOR GOD.

If God is infinite, He is created still less for man, than man is for the ants. Would the ants of a garden reason pertinently with reference to the gardener, if they should attempt to occupy themselves with his intentions, his desires, and his projects? Would they reason correctly if they pretended that the park of Versailles was made but for them, and that a fastidious monarch had had as his only object to lodge them superbly? But according to theology, man in his relation to God is far beneath what the lowest insect is to man. Thus by the acknowledgment of theology itself, theology, which does but occupy itself with the attributes and views of Divinity, is the most complete of follies.

LI.

IT IS NOT TRUE THAT THE OBJECT OF THE FORMATION OF THE UNIVERSE WAS TO RENDER MEN HAPPY.

It is pretended, that in forming the universe, God had no object but to render man happy. But, in a world created expressly for him and governed by an all-mighty God, is man after all very happy? Are his enjoyments durable? Are not his pleasures mingled with sufferings? Are there many people who are contented with their fate? Is not mankind the continual victim of physical and moral evils? This human machine, which is shown to us as the masterpiece of the Creator's industry, has it not a thousand ways of deranging itself? Would we admire the skill of a mechanic, who should show us a complicated machine, liable to be out of order at any moment, and which would after a while destroy itself?

LII.

WHAT IS CALLED PROVIDENCE IS BUT A WORD VOID OF SENSE.

We call Providence the generous care which Divinity shows in providing for our needs, and in watching over the happiness of its beloved creatures. But, as soon as we look around, we find that God provides for nothing. Providence neglects the greatest part of the inhabitants of this world. Against a very small number of men, who are supposed to be happy, what a multitude of miserable ones are groaning beneath oppression, and languishing in misery! Whole nations are compelled to starve in order to indulge the extravagances of a few morose tyrants, who are no happier than the slaves whom they oppress! At the same time that our philosophers energetically parade the bounties of Providence, and exhort us to place confidence in it, do we not see them cry out at unforeseen catastrophes, by which Providence plays with the vain projects of men; do we not see that it overthrows their designs, laughs at their efforts, and that its profound wisdom pleases itself in misleading mortals? But how can we place confidence in a malicious Providence which laughs at and sports with mankind? How can I admire the unknown course of a hidden wisdom whose manner of acting is inexplicable to me? Judge it by its effects! you will say; it is by these I do judge it, and I find that these effects are sometimes useful and sometimes injurious to me.

We think to justify Providence by saying, that in this world there are more blessings than evil for each individual man. Let us suppose that the blessings which this Providence makes us enjoy are as one hundred, and that the evils are as ten per cent.; would it not always result that against these hundred degrees of goodness, Providence possesses a tenth degree of malignity?—which is incompatible with the perfection we suppose it to have.

All the books are filled with the most flattering praises of Providence, whose attentive care is extolled; it would seem to us, as if in order to live happy here below, man would have no need of exerting himself. However, without labor, man could scarcely live a day. In order to live, I see him obliged to sweat, work, hunt, fish, toil without relaxation; without these secondary causes, the First Cause (at least in the majority of countries) could provide for none of his needs. If I examine all parts of this globe, I see the uncivilized as well as the civilized man in a perpetual struggle with Providence; he is compelled to ward off the blows which it sends in the form of hurricanes, tempests, frost, hail, inundations, sterility, and the divers accidents which so often render all their labors useless. In a word, I see the human race continually occupied in protecting itself from the wicked tricks of this Providence, which is said to be busy with the care of their happiness. A devotee admired Divine Providence for having wisely made rivers to flow through all the places where men had built large cities. Is not this man's way of reasoning as sensible as that of many learned men who do not cease from telling us of Final Causes, or who pretend to perceive clearly the benevolent views of God in the formation of things?

LIII.

THIS PRETENDED PROVIDENCE IS LESS OCCUPIED IN CONSERVING THAN IN DISTURBING THE WORLD— MORE AN ENEMY THAN A FRIEND OF MAN.

Do we see, then, that Divine Providence manifests itself in a sensible manner in the conservation of its admirable works, for which we honor it? If it is Divine Providence which governs the world, we find it as much occupied in destroying as in creating; in exterminating as in producing. Does it not at every instant cause thousands of those same men to perish, to whose preservation and well-being it is supposed to give its continual attention? Every moment it loses sight of its beloved creatures; sometimes it tears down their dwellings; sometimes it destroys their harvests, inundates their fields, devastates by a drought, arms all nature against man, sets man against man, and finishes by causing him to expire in pain. Is this what you call preserving a universe? If we attempted to consider without prejudice the equivocal conduct of Providence relative to mankind and to all sentient beings, we should find that very far from resembling a tender and careful mother, it rather resembles those unnatural mothers who, forgetting the unfortunate fruits of their illicit amours, abandon their children as soon as they are born; and who, pleased to have conceived them, expose them without mercy to the caprices of fate.

The Hottentots—wiser in this particular than other nations, who treat them as barbarians—refuse, it is said, to adore God, because if He sometimes does good, He as often does harm. Is not this reasoning more just and more conformed to experience than that of so many men who persist in seeing in their God but kindness, wisdom, and foresight; and who refuse to see that the countless evils, of which the world is the theater, must come from the same Hand which they kiss with transport?

LIV.

NO! THE WORLD IS NOT GOVERNED BY AN INTELLIGENT BEING.

The logic of common sense teaches us that we should judge a cause but by its effects. A cause can not be reputed as constantly good, except when it constantly produces good, useful, and agreeable effects. A cause which produces good at one time, and evil at another, is a cause which is sometimes good and sometimes bad. But the logic of Theology destroys all this. According to it, the phenomena of nature, or the effects which we see in this world, prove to us the existence of an infinitely good Cause, and this Cause is God. Although this world is full of evils, although disorder reigns here very often, although men groan every moment under the fate which oppresses them, we ought to be convinced that these effects are due to a benevolent and immutable Cause; and many people believe it, or pretend to believe it!

Everything which takes place in the world proves to us in the clearest way that it is not governed by an intelligent being. We can judge of the intelligence of a being but by the means which he employs to accomplish his proposed design. The aim of God, it is said, is the happiness of our race; however, the same necessity regulates the fate of all sentient beings—which are born to suffer much, to enjoy little, and to die. Man's cup is full of joy and of bitterness; everywhere good is side by side with evil; order is replaced by disorder; generation is followed by destruction. If you tell me that the designs of God are mysteries, and that His views are impossible to understand, I will answer, that in this case it is impossible for me to judge whether God is intelligent.

LV.

GOD CAN NOT BE CALLED IMMUTABLE.

You pretend that God is immutable! But what is it that occasions the continual instability in this world, which you claim as His empire? Is any state subject to more frequent and cruel revolutions than that of this unknown monarch? How can we attribute to an immutable God, powerful enough to give solidity to His works, the government of a world where everything is in a continual vicissitude? If I think to see a God unchanging in all the effects advantageous to my kind, what God can I discover in the continual misfortunes by which my kind is oppressed? You tell me that it is our sins that force Him to punish us. I will answer that God, according to yourselves, is not immutable, because the sins of men compel Him to change His conduct in regard to them. Can a being who is sometimes irritated, and sometimes appeased, be constantly the same?

LVI.

EVIL AND GOOD ARE THE NECESSARY EFFECTS OF NATURAL CAUSES. WHAT IS A GOD WHO CAN CHANGE NOTHING?

The universe is but what it can be; all sentient beings enjoy and suffer here: that is to say, they are moved sometimes in an agreeable, and at other times in a disagreeable way. These effects are necessary; they result from causes that act according to their inherent tendencies., These effects necessarily please or displease me, according to my own nature. This same nature compels me to avoid, to remove, and to combat the one, and to seek, to desire, and to procure the other. In a world where everything is from necessity, a God who remedies nothing, and allows things to follow their own course, is He anything else but destiny or necessity personified? It is a deaf God who can effect no change on the general laws to which He is subjected Himself. What do I care for the infinite power of a being who can do but a very few things to please me? Where is the infinite kindness of a being who is indifferent to my happiness? What good to me is the favor of a being who, able to bestow upon me infinite good, does not even give me a finite one?

LVII.

THE VANITY OF THEOLOGICAL CONSOLATIONS IN THE TROUBLES OF THIS LIFE. THE HOPE OF A HEAVEN, OF A FUTURE LIFE, IS BUT IMAGINARY.

When we ask why, under a good God, so many are wretched, we are reminded that the present world is but a pass-way, designed to conduct man to a happier sphere; we are assured that our sojourn on the earth, where we live, is for trial; they silence us by saying that God would not impart to His creatures either the indifference to the sufferings of others, or the infinite happiness which He reserved for Himself alone. How can we be satisfied with these answers?

1. The existence of another life has no other guaranty than the imagination of men, who, in supposing it, have but manifested their desire to live again, in order to enter upon a purer and more durable state of happiness than that which they enjoy at present.

2. How can we conceive of a God who, knowing all things, must know to their depths the nature of His creatures, and yet must have so many proofs in order to assure Himself of their proclivities?

3. According to the calculations of our chronologists, the earth which we inhabit has existed for six or seven

thousand years; during this time the nations have, under different forms, experienced many vicissitudes and calamities; history shows us that the human race in all ages has been tormented and devastated by tyrants, conquerors, heroes; by wars, inundations, famines, epidemics, etc. Is this long catalogue of proofs of such a nature as to inspire us with great confidence in the hidden views of the Divinity? Do such constant evils give us an exalted idea of the future fate which His kindness is preparing for us?

4. If God is as well-disposed as they assure us He is, could He not at least, without bestowing an infinite happiness upon men, communicate to them that degree of happiness of which finite beings are susceptible? In order to be happy, do we need an Infinite or Divine happiness?

5. If God has not been able to render men happier than they are here below, what will become of the hope of a Paradise, where it is pretended that the elect or chosen few will rejoice forever in ineffable happiness? If God could not or would not remove evil from the earth (the only sojourning place we know of), what reason could we have to presume that He can or will remove it from another world, of which we know nothing? More than two thousand years ago, according to Lactance, the wise epicure said: "Either God wants to prevent evil, and can not, or He can and will not; or He neither can nor will, or He will and can. If He wants to, without the power, He is impotent; if He can, and will not, He is guilty of malice which we can not attribute to Him; if He neither can nor will, He is both impotent and wicked, and consequently can not be God; if He wishes to and can, whence then comes evil, or why does He not prevent it?" For more than two thousand years honest minds have waited for a rational solution of these difficulties; and our theologians teach us that they will not be revealed to us until the future life.

LVIII.

ANOTHER IDLE FANCY.

We are told of a pretended scale for human beings; it is supposed that God has divided His creatures into different classes, each one enjoying the degree of happiness of which he is susceptible. According to this romantic arrangement, all beings, from the oyster to the angel, enjoy the happiness which belongs to them. Experience contradicts this sublime revery. In the world where we are, we see all sentient beings living and suffering in the midst of dangers. Man can not step without wounding, tormenting, crushing a multitude of sentient beings which he finds in his path, while he himself, at every step, is exposed to a throng of evils seen or unseen, which may lead to his destruction. Is not the very thought of death sufficient to mar his greatest enjoyment? During the whole course of his life he is subject to sufferings; there is not a moment when he feels sure of preserving his existence, to which he is so strongly attached, and which he regards as the greatest gift of Divinity.

LIX.

IN VAIN DOES THEOLOGY EXERT ITSELF TO ACQUIT GOD OF MAN'S DEFECTS. EITHER THIS GOD IS NOT FREE, OR HE IS MORE WICKED THAN GOOD.

The world, it will be said, has all the perfection of which it was susceptible; by the very reason that the world was not the God who made it, it was necessary that it should have great qualities and great defects. But we will answer, that the world necessarily having great defects, it would have been better suited to the nature of a good God not to create a world which He could not render completely happy. If God, who was, according to you, supremely happy before the world was created, had continued to be supremely happy in the created world, why did He not remain in peace? Why must man suffer? Why must man exist What is his existence to God? Nothing or something. If his existence is not useful or necessary to God, why did He not leave him in nothingness? If man's existence is necessary to His glory, He then needed man, He lacked something before this man existed!

We can forgive an unskillful workman for doing imperfect work, because he must work, well or ill, or starve; this workman is excusable; but your God is not. According to you, He is self-sufficient; in this case, why does He create men? He has, according to you, all that is necessary to render man happy; why, then, does He not do it? You must conclude that your God has more malice than goodness, or you must admit that God was compelled to do what He has done, without being able to do otherwise. However, you assure us that your God is free; you say also that He is immutable, although beginning in time and ceasing in time to exercise His power, like all the inconstant beings of this world. Oh, theologians! you have made vain efforts to acquit your God of all the defects of man; there is always visible in this God so perfect, "a tip of the [human] ear."

LX.

WE CAN NOT BELIEVE IN A DIVINE PROVIDENCE, IN AN INFINITELY GOOD AND POWERFUL GOD.

Is not God the master of His favors? Has He not the right to dispense His benefits? Can He not take them back again? His creature has no right to ask the reason of His conduct; He can dispose at will of the works of His hands. Absolute sovereign of mortals, He distributes happiness or unhappiness, according to His pleasure. These are the solutions which theologians give in order to console us for the evils which God inflicts upon us. We would tell them that a God who was infinitely good, would not be the master of His favors, but would be by His own nature obliged to distribute them among His creatures; we would tell them that a truly benevolent being would not believe he had the right to abstain from doing good; we would tell them that a truly generous being does not take back what he has given, and any man who does it, forfeits gratitude, and has no right to complain of ingratitude. How can the arbitrary and whimsical conduct which theologians ascribe to God, be reconciled with the religion which supposes a compact or mutual agreement between this God and men? If God owes nothing to His creatures, they, on their part, can not owe anything to their God. All religion is founded upon the happiness which men believe they have a right to expect from the Divinity, who is supposed to tell them: "Love, adore, obey me, and I will render you happy!" Men on their side say to Him: "Make us happy, be faithful to your promises, and we will love you, we will adore you, we will obey your laws!" In neglecting the happiness of His creatures, in distributing His favors and His graces according to His caprice, and taking back His gifts, does not God violate the contract which serves as a base for all religion?

Cicero has said with reason that if God does not make Himself agreeable to man, He can not be his God. [Nisi Deus homini placuerit, Deus non erit.] Goodness constitutes Divinity; this Goodness can manifest itself to man only by the advantages he derives from it. As soon as he is unfortunate, this Goodness disappears and ceases to be Divinity. An infinite Goodness can be neither partial nor exclusive. If God is infinitely good, He owes happiness to all His creatures; one unfortunate being alone would be sufficient to annihilate an unlimited goodness. Under an infinitely good and powerful God, is it possible to conceive that a single man could suffer? An animal, a mite, which suffers, furnishes invincible arguments against Divine Providence and its infinite benefactions.

LXI.

CONTINUATION.

According to theologians, the afflictions and evils of this life are chastisements which culpable men receive from Divinity. But why are men culpable? If God is Almighty, does it cost Him any more to say, "Let everything remain in order!"—"let all my subjects be good, innocent, fortunate!"—than to say, "Let everything exist?" Was it more difficult for this God to do His work well than to do it so badly? Was it any farther from the nonexistence of beings to their wise and happy existence, than from their non-existence to their insensate and miserable existence? Religion speaks to us of a hell—that is, of a fearful place where, notwithstanding His goodness, God reserves eternal torments for the majority of men. Thus, after having rendered mortals very miserable in this world, religion teaches them that God can make them much more wretched in another. They meet our objections by saying, that otherwise the goodness of God would take the place of His justice. But goodness which takes the place of the most terrible cruelty, is not infinite kindness. Besides, a God who, after having been infinitely good, becomes infinitely wicked, can He be regarded as an immutable being? A God filled with implacable fury, is He a God in whom we can find a shadow of charity or goodness?

LXII.

THEOLOGY MAKES OF ITS GOD A MONSTER OF NONSENSE, OF INJUSTICE, OF MALICE, AND ATROCITY—A BEING ABSOLUTELY HATEFUL.

Divine justice, such as our theologians paint it, is, without doubt, a quality intended to make us love Divinity. According to the notions of modern theology, it appears evident that God has created the majority of men with the view only of punishing them eternally. Would it not have been more in conformity with kindness, with reason, with equity, to create but stones or plants, and not sentient beings, than to create men whose conduct in this world would cause them eternal chastisements in another? A God so perfidious and wicked as to create a single man and leave him exposed to the perils of damnation, can not be regarded as a perfect being, but as a monster of nonsense, injustice, malice, and atrocity. Far from forming a perfect God, the theologians have made the most imperfect of beings. According to theological ideas, God resembles a tyrant who, having deprived the majority of his slaves of their eyesight, would confine them in a cell where, in order to amuse himself he could observe incognito their conduct through a trap-door, in order to have occasion to cruelly punish all those who in walking should hurt each other; but who would reward splendidly the small number of those to whom the sight was spared, for having the skill to avoid an encounter with their comrades. Such are the ideas which the dogma of gratuitous predestination gives of Divinity!

Although men repeat to us that their God is infinitely good, it is evident that in the bottom of their hearts they can believe nothing of it. How can we love anything we do not know? How can we love a being, the idea of whom is but liable to keep us in anxiety and trouble? How can we love a being of whom all that is told conspires to render him supremely hateful?

LXIII.

ALL RELIGION INSPIRES BUT A COWARDLY AND INORDINATE FEAR OF THE DIVINITY.

Many people make a subtle distinction between true religion and superstition; they tell us that the latter is but a cowardly and inordinate fear of Divinity, that the truly religious man has confidence in his God, and loves Him sincerely; while the superstitious man sees in Him but an enemy, has no confidence in Him, and represents Him as a suspicious and cruel tyrant, avaricious of His benefactions and prodigal of His chastisements. But does not all religion in reality give us these same ideas of God? While we are told that God is infinitely good, is it not constantly repeated to us that He is very easily offended, that He bestows His favors but upon a few, that He chastises with fury those to whom He has not been pleased to grant them?

LXIV.

THERE IS IN REALITY NO DIFFERENCE BETWEEN RELIGION AND THE MOST SOMBRE AND SERVILE SUPERSTITION.

If we take our ideas of God from the nature of the things where we find a mixture of good and evil, this God, according to the good and evil which we experience, does naturally appear to us capricious, inconstant, sometimes good, sometimes wicked, and in this way, instead of exciting our love, He must produce suspicion, fear, and uncertainty in our hearts. There is no real difference between natural religion and the most sombre and servile superstition. If the Theist sees God but on the beautiful side, the superstitious man looks upon Him from the most hideous side. The folly of the one is gay of the other is lugubrious; but both are equally delirious.

LXV.

ACCORDING TO THE IDEAS WHICH THEOLOGY GIVES OF DIVINITY, TO LOVE GOD IS IMPOSSIBLE.

If I take my ideas of God from theology, God shows Himself to me in such a light as to repel love. The devotees who tell us that they love their God sincerely, are either liars or fools who see their God but in profile; it is impossible to love a being, the thought of whom tends to excite terror, and whose judgments make us tremble. How can we face without fear, a God whom we suppose sufficiently barbarous to wish to damn us forever? Let them not speak to us of a filial or respectful fear mingled with love, which men should have for their God. A son can not love his father when he knows he is cruel enough to inflict exquisite torments upon him; in short, to punish him for the least faults. No man upon earth can have the least spark of love for a God who holds in reserve eternal, hard, and violent chastisements for ninety-nine hundredths of His children.

LXVI.

BY THE INVENTION OF THE DOGMA OF THE ETERNAL TORMENTS OF HELL, THEOLOGIANS HAVE MADE OF THEIR GOD A DETESTABLE BEING, MORE WICKED THAN THE MOST WICKED OF MEN, A PERVERSE AND CRUEL TYRANT WITHOUT AIM.

The inventors of the dogma of eternal torments in hell, have made of the God whom they call so good, the most detestable of beings. Cruelty in man is the last term of corruption. There is no sensitive soul but is moved and revolts at the recital alone of the torments which the greatest criminal endures; but cruelty merits the greater indignation when we consider it gratuitous or without motive. The most sanguinary tyrants, Caligula, Nero, Domitian, had at least some motive in tormenting their victims and insulting their sufferings; these motives were, either their own safety, the fury of revenge, the design to frighten by terrible examples, or perhaps the vanity to make parade of their power, and the desire to satisfy a barbarous curiosity. Can a God have any of these motives? In tormenting the victims of His wrath, He would punish beings who could not really endanger His immovable power, nor trouble His felicity, which nothing can change. On the other hand, the sufferings of the other life would be useless to the living, who can not witness them; these torments would be useless to the damned, because in hell is no more conversion, and the hour of mercy is passed; from which it follows, that God, in the exercise of His eternal vengeance, would have no other aim than to amuse Himself and insult the weakness of His creatures. I appeal to the whole human race! Is there in nature a man so cruel as to wish in cold blood to torment, I do not say his fellow-beings, but any sentient being whatever, without fee, without profit, without curiosity, without having anything to fear? Conclude, then, O theologians! that according to your own principles, your God is infinitely more wicked than the most wicked of men. You will tell me, perhaps, that infinite offenses deserve infinite chastisements, and I will tell you that we can not offend a God whose happiness is infinite. I will tell you further, that offenses of finite beings can not be infinite; that a God who does not want to be offended, can not consent to make His creatures' offenses last for eternity; I will tell you that a God infinitely good, can not be infinitely cruel, nor grant His creatures infinite existence solely for the pleasure of tormenting them forever.

It could have been but the most cruel barbarity, the most notorious imposition, but the blindest ambition which could have created the dogma of eternal damnation. If there exists a God who could be offended or blasphemed, there would not be upon earth any greater blasphemers than those who dare to say that this God is perverse enough to take pleasure in dooming His feeble creatures to useless torments for all eternity.

LXVII.

THEOLOGY IS BUT A SERIES OF PALPABLE CONTRADICTIONS.

To pretend that God can be offended with the actions of men, is to annihilate all the ideas that are given to us of this being. To say that man can disturb the order of the universe, that he can grasp the lightning from God's hand, that he can upset His projects, is to claim that man is stronger than his God, that he is the arbiter of His will, that it depends on him to change His goodness into cruelty. Theology does nothing but destroy with one hand that which it builds with the other. If all religion is founded upon a God who becomes angry, and who is appeased, all religion is founded upon a palpable contradiction.

All religions agree in exalting the wisdom and the infinite power of the Divinity; but as soon as they expose His conduct, we discover but imprudence, want of foresight, weakness, and folly. God, it is said, created the world for Himself; and so far He has not succeeded in making Himself properly respected! God has created men in order to have in His dominion subjects who would render Him homage; and we continually see men revolt against Him!

LXVIII.

THE PRETENDED WORKS OF GOD DO NOT PROVE AT ALL WHAT WE CALL DIVINE PERFECTION.

We are continually told of the Divine perfections; and as soon as we ask the proofs of them, we are shown the works in which we are assured that these perfections are written in ineffaceable characters. All these works, however, are imperfect and perishable; man, who is regarded as the masterpiece, as the most marvelous work of Divinity, is full of imperfections which render him disagreeable in the eyes of the Almighty workman who has formed him; this surprising work becomes often so revolting and so odious to its Author, that He feels Himself compelled to cast him into the fire. But if the choicest work of Divinity is imperfect, by what are we to judge of the Divine perfections? Can a work with which the author himself is so little satisfied, cause us to admire his skill? Physical man is subject to a thousand infirmities, to countless evils, to death; the moral man is full of defects; and yet they exhaust themselves by telling us that he is the most beautiful work of the most perfect of beings.

LXIX.

THE PERFECTION OF GOD DOES NOT SHOW TO ANY MORE ADVANTAGE IN THE PRETENDED CREATION OF ANGELS AND PURE SPIRITS.

It appears that God, in creating more perfect beings than men, did not succeed any better, or give stronger proofs of His perfection. Do we not see in many religions that angels and pure spirits revolted against their Master, and even attempted to expel Him from His throne? God intended the happiness of angels and of men, and He has never succeeded in rendering happy either angels or men; pride, malice, sins, the imperfections of His creatures, have always been opposed to the wishes of the perfect Creator.

LXX.

THEOLOGY PREACHES THE OMNIPOTENCE OF ITS GOD, AND CONTINUALLY SHOWS HIM IMPOTENT.

All religion is visibly founded upon the principle that "God proposes and man disposes." All the theologies of the world show us an unequal combat between Divinity on the one side, and His creatures on the other. God never relies on His honor; in spite of His almighty power, He could not succeed in making the works of His hands as He would like them to be. To complete the absurdity, there is a religion which pretends that God Himself died to redeem the human race; and, in spite of His death, men are not in the least as this God would desire them to be!

LXXI.

ACCORDING TO ALL THE RELIGIOUS SYSTEMS OF THE EARTH, GOD WOULD BE THE MOST CAPRICIOUS AND THE MOST INSENSATE OF BEINGS.

Nothing could be more extravagant than the role which in every country theology makes Divinity play. If the thing was real, we would be obliged to see in it the most capricious and the most insane of beings; one would be obliged to believe that God made the world to be the theater of dishonoring wars with His creatures; that He created angels, men, demons, wicked spirits, but as adversaries, against whom He could exercise His power. He gives them liberty to offend Him, makes them wicked enough to upset His projects, obstinate enough to never give up: all for the pleasure of getting angry, and being appeased, of reconciling Himself, and of repairing the confusion they have made. Had Divinity formed at once His creatures such as they ought to be in order to please Him, what trouble He might have spared Himself! or, at least, how much embarrassment He might have saved to His theologians! According to all the religious systems of the earth, God seems to be occupied but in doing Himself injury; He does it as those charlatans do who wound themselves, in order to have occasion to show the public the value of their ointments. We do not see, however, that so far Divinity has been able to radically cure itself of the evil which is caused by men.

LXXII.

IT IS ABSURD TO SAY THAT EVIL DOES NOT COME FROM GOD.

God is the author of all; still we are assured that evil does not come from God. Whence, then, does it come? From men? But who has made men? It is God: then that evil comes from God. If He had not made men as they are, moral evil or sin would not exist in the world. We must blame God, then, that man is so perverse. If man has the power to do wrong or to offend God, we must conclude that God wishes to be offended; that God, who has created man, resolved that evil should be done by him: without this, man would be an effect contrary to the cause from which he derives his being.

LXXIII.

THE FORESIGHT ATTRIBUTED TO GOD, WOULD GIVE TO GUILTY MEN WHOM HE PUNISHES, THE RIGHT TO COMPLAIN OF HIS CRUELTY.

The faculty of foresight, or the ability to know in advance all which is to happen in the world, is attributed to God. But this foresight can scarcely belong to His glory, nor spare Him the reproaches which men could legitimately heap upon Him. If God had the foresight of the future, did He not foresee the fall of His creatures whom He had destined to happiness? If He resolved in His decrees to allow this fall, there is no doubt that He desired it to take place: otherwise it would not have happened. If the Divine foresight of the sin of His creatures had been necessary or forced, it might be supposed that God was compelled by His justice to punish the guilty; but God, enjoying the faculty of foresight and the power to predestinate everything, would it not depend upon Himself not to impose upon men these cruel laws? Or, at least, could He not have dispensed with creating beings whom He might be compelled to punish and to render unhappy by a subsequent decree? What does it matter whether God destined men to happiness or to misery by a previous decree, the effect of His foresight, or by a subsequent decree, the effect of His justice. Does the arrangement of these decrees change the fate of the miserable? Would they not have the right to complain of a God who, having the power of leaving them in oblivion, brought them forth, although He foresaw very well that His justice would force Him sooner or later to punish them?

LXXIV.

ABSURDITY OF THE THEOLOGICAL FABLES UPON ORIGINAL SIN AND UPON SATAN.

Man, say you, issuing from the hands of God, was pure, innocent, and good; but his nature became corrupted in consequence of sin. If man could sin, when just leaving the hands of God, his nature was then not perfect! Why did God permit him to sin, and his nature to become corrupt? Why did God allow him to be seduced, knowing well that he would be too weak to resist the tempter? Why did God create a Satan, a malicious spirit, a tempter? Why did not God, who was so desirous of doing good to mankind, why did He not annihilate, once for all, so many evil genii whose nature rendered them enemies of our happiness? Or rather, why did God create evil spirits, whose victories and terrible influences upon the human race He must have foreseen? Finally, by what fatality, in all the religions of the world, has the evil principle such a marked advantage over the good principle or over Divinity?

LXXV.

THE DEVIL, LIKE RELIGION, WAS INVENTED TO ENRICH THE PRIESTS.

We are told a story of the simple-heartedness of an Italian monk, which does him honor. This good man preaching one day felt obliged to announce to his auditory that, thanks to Heaven, he had at last discovered a sure means of rendering all men happy. "The devil," said he, "tempts men but to have them as comrades of his misery in hell. Let us address ourselves, then, to the Pope, who possesses the keys of paradise and of hell; let us ask him to beseech God, at the head of the whole Church, to reconcile Himself with the devil; to take him back into His favor; to re-establish him in His first rank. This can not fail to put an end to his sinister projects against mankind." The good monk did not see, perhaps, that the devil is at least fully as useful as God to the ministers of religion. These reap too many benefits from their differences to lend themselves willingly to a reconciliation between the two enemies ties, upon whose contests their existence and their revenues depend. If men would cease to be tempted and to sin, the ministry of priests would become useless to them. Manicheism is evidently the support of all religions; but unfortunately the devil, being invented to remove all suspicion of malice from Divinity, proves to us at every moment the powerlessness or the awkwardness of his celestial Adversary.

LXXVI.

IF GOD COULD NOT RENDER HUMAN NATURE SINLESS, HE HAS NO RIGHT TO PUNISH MAN.

Man's nature, it is said, must necessarily become corrupt. God could not endow him with sinlessness, which is an inalienable portion of Divine perfection. But if God could not render him sinless, why did He take the trouble of creating man, whose nature was to become corrupt, and which, consequently, had to offend God? On the other side, if God Himself was not able to render human nature sinless, what right had He to punish men for not being sinless? It is but by the right of might. But the right of the strongest is violence; and violence is not suited to the most Just of Beings. God would be supremely unjust if He punished men for not having a portion of the Divine perfections, or for not being able to be Gods like Himself.

Could not God have at least endowed men with that sort of perfection of which their nature is susceptible? If some men are good or render themselves agreeable to their God, why did not this God bestow the same favor or give the same dispositions to all beings of our kind? Why does the number of wicked exceed so greatly the number of good people? Why, for every friend, does God find ten thousand enemies in a world which depended upon Him alone to people with honest men? If it is true that God intends to form in heaven a court of saints, of chosen ones, or of men who have lived in this world according to His views, would He not have had a court more numerous, more brilliant, and more honorable to Him, if it were composed of all the men to whom, in creating them, He could have granted the degree of goodness necessary to obtain eternal happiness? Finally, were it not easier not to take man from nothingness than to create him full of defects, rebellious to his Creator, perpetually exposed to lose himself by a fatal abuse of his liberty? Instead of creating men, a perfect God ought to have created only docile and submissive angels. The angels, it is said, are free; a few among them have sinned; but all of them have not sinned; all have not abused their liberty by revolting against their Master. Could not God have created only angels of the good kind? If God could create angels who have not sinned, could He not create men sinless, or those who would never abuse their liberty by doing evil. If the chosen ones are incapable of sinning in heaven, could not God have made sinless men upon the earth?

LXXVII.

IT IS ABSURD TO SAY THAT GOD'S CONDUCT MUST BE A MYSTERY TO MAN, AND THAT HE HAS NO RIGHT TO EXAMINE AND JUDGE IT.

We are told that the enormous distance which separates God from men, makes God's conduct necessarily a mystery for us, and that we have no right to interrogate our Master. Is this statement satisfactory? But according to you, when my eternal happiness is involved, have I not the right to examine God's own conduct? It is but with the hope of happiness that men submit to the empire of a God. A despot to whom men are subjected but through fear, a master whom they can not interrogate, a totally inaccessible sovereign, can not merit the homage of intelligent beings. If God's conduct is a mystery to me, it is not made for me. Man can not adore, admire, respect, or imitate a conduct of which everything is impossible to conceive, or of which he can not form any but revolting ideas; unless it is pretended that he should worship all the things of which he is forced to be ignorant, and then all that he does not understand becomes admirable.

Priests! you teach us that the designs of God are impenetrable; that His ways are not our ways; that His thoughts are not our thoughts; that it is folly to complain of His administration, whose motives and secret ways are entirely unknown to us; that there is temerity in accusing Him of unjust judgments, because they are incomprehensible to us. But do you not see that by speaking in this manner, you destroy with your own hands all your profound systems which have no design but to explain the ways of Divinity that you call impenetrable? These judgments, these ways, and these designs, have you penetrated them? You dare not say so; and, although you season incessantly, you do not understand them more than we do. If by chance you know the plan of God, which you tell us to admire, while there are many people who find it so little worthy of a just, good, intelligent, and rational being; do not say that this plan is impenetrable. If you are as ignorant as we, have some indulgence for those who ingenuously confess that they comprehend nothing of it, or that they see nothing in it Divine. Cease to persecute for opinions which you do not understand yourselves; cease to slander each other for dreams and conjectures which are altogether contradictory; speak to us of intelligible and truly useful things; and no longer tell us of the impenetrable ways of a God, about which you do nothing but stammer and contradict yourselves.

In speaking to us incessantly of the immense depths of Divine wisdom, in forbidding us to fathom these depths by telling us that it is insolence to call God to the tribunal of our humble reason, in making it a crime to judge our Master, the theologians only confess the embarrassment in which they find themselves as soon as they have to render account of the conduct of a God, which they tell us is marvelous, only because it is totally impossible for them to understand it themselves.

LXXVIII.

IT IS ABSURD TO CALL HIM A GOD OF JUSTICE AND GOODNESS, WHO INFLICTS EVIL INDISCRIMINATELY ON THE GOOD AND THE WICKED, UPON THE INNOCENT AND THE GUILTY; IT IS IDLE TO DEMAND THAT THE UNFORTUNATE SHOULD CONSOLE THEMSELVES FOR THEIR MISFORTUNES, IN THE VERY ARMS OF THE ONE WHO ALONE IS THE AUTHOR OF THEM.

Physical evil commonly passes as the punishment of sin. Calamities, diseases, famines, wars, earthquakes, are the means which God employs to chastise perverse men. Therefore, they have no difficulty in attributing these evils to the severity of a just and good God. However, do we not see these plagues fall indiscriminately upon the good and the wicked, upon the impious and the pious, upon the innocent and the guilty? How can we be made to admire, in this proceeding, the justice and the goodness of a being, the idea of whom appears so consoling to the unfortunate? Doubtless the brain of these unfortunate ones has been disturbed by their misfortunes, since they forget that God is the arbiter of things, the sole dispenser of the events of this world. In this case ought they not to blame Him for the evils for which they would find consolation in His arms? Unfortunate father! you console yourself in the bosom of Providence for the loss of a cherished child or of a wife, who made your happiness! Alas! do you not see that your God has killed them? Your God has rendered you miserable; and you want Him to console you for the fearful blows He has inflicted upon you.

The fantastic and supernatural notions of theology have succeeded so thoroughly in overcoming the simplest, the clearest, the most natural ideas of the human spirit, that the pious, incapable of accusing God of malice, accustom themselves to look upon these sad afflictions as indubitable proofs of celestial goodness. Are they in affliction, they are told to believe that God loves them, that God visits them, that God wishes to try them. Thus it is that religion changes evil into good! Some one has said profanely, but with reason: "If the good God treats thus those whom He loves, I beseech Him very earnestly not to think of me." Men must have formed very sinister and very cruel ideas of their God whom they call so good, in order to persuade themselves that the most frightful calamities and the most painful afflictions are signs of His favor! Would a wicked Genii or a Devil be more ingenious in tormenting his enemies, than sometimes is this God of goodness, who is so often occupied with inflicting His chastisements upon His dearest friends?

LXXIX.

A GOD WHO PUNISHES THE FAULTS WHICH HE COULD HAVE PREVENTED, IS A FOOL, WHO ADDS INJUSTICE TO FOOLISHNESS.

What would we say or a father who, we are assured, watches without relaxation over the welfare of his feeble and unforeseeing children, and who, however, would leave them at liberty to go astray in the midst of rocks, precipices, and waters; who would prevent them but rarely from following their disordered appetites; who would permit them to handle, without precaution, deadly arms, at the risk of wounding themselves severely? What would we think of this same father, if, instead of blaming himself for the harm which would have happened to his poor children, he should punish them for their faults in the most cruel way? We would say, with reason, that this father is a fool, who joins injustice to foolishness. A God who punishes the faults which He could have prevented, is a being who lacks wisdom, goodness, and equity. A God of foresight would prevent evil, and in this way would be saved the trouble of punishing it. A good God would not punish weaknesses which He knows to be inherent in human nature. A just God, if He has made man, would not punish him for not being strong enough to resist his desires. To punish weakness, is the most unjust tyranny. Is it not calumniating a just God, to say that He punishes men for their faults, even in the present life? How would He punish beings whom He alone could correct, and who, as long as they had not received grace, can not act otherwise than they do?

According to the principles of theologians themselves, man, in his actual state of corruption, can do nothing but evil, for without Divine grace he has not the strength to do good. Moreover, if man's nature, abandoned to itself, of destitute of Divine help, inclines him necessarily to evil, or renders him incapable of doing good, what becomes of his free will? According to such principles, man can merit neither reward nor punishment; in rewarding man for the good he does, God would but recompense Himself; in punishing man for the evil he does, God punishes him for not having been given the grace, without which it was impossible for him to do better.

LXXX.

FREE WILL IS AN IDLE FANCY.

Theologians tell and repeat to us that man is free, while all their teachings conspire to destroy his liberty. Trying to justify Divinity, they accuse him really of the blackest injustice. They suppose that, without grace, man is compelled to do evil: and they maintain that God will punish him for not having been given the grace to do good! With a little reflection, we will be obliged to see that man in all things acts by compulsion, and that his free will is a chimera, even according to the theological system. Does it depend upon man whether or not he shall be born of such or such parents? Does it depend upon man to accept or not to accept the opinions of his parents and of his teachers? If I were born of idolatrous or Mohammedan parents, would it have depended upon me to become a Christian? However, grave Doctors of Divinity assure us that a just God will damn without mercy all those to whom He has not given the grace to know the religion of the Christians.

Man's birth does not depend upon his choice; he was not asked if he would or would not come into the world; nature did not consult him upon the country and the parents that she gave him; the ideas he acquired, his opinions, his true or false notions are the necessary fruits of the education which he has received, and of which he has not been the master; his passions and his desires are the necessary results of the temperament which nature has given him, and of the ideas with which he has been inspired; during the whole course of his life, his wishes and his actions are determined by his surroundings, his habits, his occupations, his pleasures, his conversations, and by the thoughts which present themselves involuntarily to him; in short, by a multitude of events and accidents which are beyond his control. Incapable of foreseeing the future, he knows neither what he will wish, nor what he will do in the time which must immediately follow the present. Man passes his life, from the moment of his birth to that of his death, without having been free one instant. Man, you say, wishes, deliberates, chooses, determines; hence you conclude that his actions are free. It is true that man intends, but he is not master of his will or of his desires. He can desire and wish only what he judges advantageous for himself; he can not love pain nor detest pleasure. Man, it will be said, sometimes prefers pain to pleasure; but then, he prefers a passing pain in the hope of procuring a greater and more durable pleasure. In this case, the idea of a greater good determines him to deprive himself of one less desirable.

It is not the lover who gives to his mistress the features by which he is enchanted; he is not then the master to love or not to love the object of his tenderness; he is not the master of the imagination or the temperament which dominates him; from which it follows, evidently, that man is not the master of the wishes and desires which rise in his soul, independently of him. But man, say you, can resist his desires; then he is free. Man resists his desires when the motives which turn him from an object are stronger than those which draw him toward it; but then, his resistance is necessary. A man who fears dishonor and punishment more than he loves money, resists necessarily the desire to take possession of another's money. Are we not free when we deliberate?—but has one the power to know or not to know, to be uncertain or to be assured? Deliberation is the necessary effect of the uncertainty in which we find ourselves with reference to the results of our actions. As soon as we believe ourselves certain of these results, we necessarily decide; and then we act necessarily according as we shall have judged right or wrong. Our judgments, true or false, are not free; they are necessarily determined by ideas which we have received, or which our mind has formed. Man is not free in his choice; he is evidently compelled to choose what he judges the most useful or the most agreeable for himself. When he suspends his choice, he is not more free; he is forced to suspend it till he knows or believes he knows the qualities of the objects presented to him, or until he has weighed the consequence of his actions. Man, you will say, decides every moment on actions which he knows will endanger him; man kills himself sometimes, then he is free. I deny it! Has man the ability to reason correctly or incorrectly? Do not his reason and his wisdom depend either upon opinions that he has formed, or upon his mental constitution? As neither the one nor the other depends upon his will, they can not in any wise prove his liberty.

If I make the wager to do or not to do a thing, am I not free? Does it not depend upon me to do or not to do it? No; I will answer you, the desire to win the wager will necessarily determine you to do or not to do the thing in question. "But if I consent to lose the wager?" Then the desire to prove to me that you are free will have become to you a stronger motive than the desire to win the wager; and this motive will necessarily have determined you to do or not to do what was understood between us. But you will say, "I feel myself free." It is an illusion which may be compared to that of the fly in the fable, which, lighting on the shaft of a heavy wagon, applauded itself as driver of the vehicle which carried it. Man who believes himself free, is a fly who believes himself the master-motor in the machine of the universe, while he himself, without his own volition, is carried on by it. The feeling which makes us believe that we are free to do or not to do a thing, is but a pure illusion. When we come to the veritable principle of our actions, we will find that they are nothing but the necessary results of our wills and of our desires, which are never within our power. You believe yourselves free because you do as you choose; but are you really free to will or not to will, to desire or not to desire? Your wills and your desires, are they not necessarily excited by objects or by qualities which do not depend upon you at all?

LXXXI.

WE SHOULD NOT CONCLUDE FROM THIS THAT SOCIETY HAS NOT THE RIGHT TO CHASTISE THE WICKED.

If the actions of men are necessary, if men are not free, what right has society to punish the wicked who infest it? Is it not very unjust to chastise beings who could not act otherwise than they did? If the wicked act from the impulse of their corrupt nature, society in punishing them acts necessarily on its side from the desire to preserve itself. Certain objects produce in us the feeling of pain; therefore our nature compels us to hate them, and incites us to remove them. A tiger pressed by hunger, attacks the man whom he wishes to devour; but the man is not the master of his fear of the tiger, and seeks necessarily the means of exterminating it.

LXXXII.

REFUTATION OF THE ARGUMENTS IN FAVOR OF FREE WILL.

If everything is necessary, if errors, opinions, and ideas of men are fated, how or why can we pretend to reform them? The errors of men are the necessary results of their ignorance; their ignorance, their obstinacy, their credulity, are the necessary results of their inexperience, of their indifference, of their lack of reflection; the same as congestion of the brain or lethargy are the natural effects of some diseases. Truth, experience, reflection, reason, are the proper remedies to cure ignorance, fanaticism, and follies; the same as bleeding is good to soothe congestion of the brain. But you will say, why does not truth produce this effect upon many of the sick heads? There are some diseases which resist all remedies; it is impossible to cure obstinate patients who refuse to take the remedies which are given them; the interest of some men and the folly of others naturally oppose them to the admission of truth. A cause produces its effect only when it is not interrupted in its action by other causes which are stronger, or which weaken the action of the first cause or render it useless. It is entirely impossible to have the best arguments accepted by men who are strongly interested in error; who are prejudiced in its favor; who refuse to reflect; but it must necessarily be that truth undeceives the honest souls who seek it in good faith. Truth is a cause; it produces necessarily its effect when its impulse is not interrupted by causes which suspend its effects.

LXXXIII.

CONTINUATION.

To take away from man his free will, is, we are told, to make of him a pure machine, an automaton without liberty; there would exist in him neither merit nor virtue What is merit in man?

It is a certain manner of acting which renders him estimable in the eyes of his fellow beings. What is virtue? It is the disposition that causes us to do good to others. What can there be contemptible in automatic machines capable of producing such desirable effects? Marcus Aurelius was a very useful spring to the vast machine of the Roman Empire. By what right will a machine despise another machine, whose springs would facilitate its own play? Good people are springs which assist society in its tendency to happiness; wicked men are badly-formed springs, which disturb the order, the progress, and harmony of society. If for its own interests society loves and rewards the good, she hates, despises, and removes the wicked, as useless or dangerous motors.

LXXXIV.

GOD HIMSELF, IF THERE WAS A GOD, WOULD NOT BE FREE; HENCE THE USELESSNESS OF ALL RELIGION.

The world is a necessary agent; all the beings which compose it are united to each other, and can not do otherwise than they do, so long as they are moved by the same causes and possessed of the same qualities. If they lose these qualities, they will act necessarily in a different way. God Himself (admitting His existence a moment) can not be regarded as a free agent; if there existed a God, His manner of acting would necessarily be determined by the qualities inherent in His nature; nothing would be able to alter or to oppose His wishes. This considered, neither our actions nor our prayers nor our sacrifices could suspend or change His invariable progress and His immutable designs, from which we are compelled to conclude that all religion would be entirely useless.

LXXXV.

EVEN ACCORDING TO THEOLOGICAL PRINCIPLES, MAN IS NOT FREE ONE INSTANT.

If theologians were not constantly contradicting each other, they would know, from their own hypotheses, that man can not be called free for an instant. Is not man supposed to be in a continual dependence upon God? Is one free, when one could not have existed or can not live without God, and when one ceases to exist at the pleasure of His supreme will? If God created man of nothing, if the preservation of man is a continual creation, if God can not lose sight of His creature for an instant, if all that happens to him is a result of the Divine will, if man is nothing of himself, if all the events which he experiences are the effects of Divine decrees, if he can not do any good without assistance from above, how can it be pretended that man enjoys liberty during one moment of his life? If God did not save him in the moment when he sins, how could man sin? If God preserves him, God, therefore, forces him to live in order to sin.

LXXXVI.

ALL EVIL, ALL DISORDER, ALL SIN, CAN BE ATTRIBUTED BUT TO GOD; AND CONSEQUENTLY, HE HAS NO RIGHT TO PUNISH OR REWARD.

Divinity is continually compared to a king, the majority of whose subjects revolt against Him and it is pretended that He has the right to reward His faithful subjects, and to punish those who revolt against Him. This comparison is not just in any of its parts. God presides over a machine, of which He has made all the springs; these springs act according to the way in which God has formed them; it is the fault of His inaptitude if these springs do not contribute to the harmony of the machine in which the workman desired to place them. God is a creating King, who created all kinds of subjects for Himself; who formed them according to His pleasure, and whose wishes can never find any resistance. If God in His empire has rebellious subjects, it is God who resolved to have rebellious subjects. If the sins of men disturb the order of the world, it is God who desired this order to be disturbed. Nobody dares to doubt Divine justice; however, under the empire of a just God, we find nothing but injustice and violence. Power decides the fate of nations. Equity seems to be banished from the earth; a small number of men enjoy with impunity the repose, the fortunes, the liberty, and the life of all the others. Everything is in disorder in a world governed by a God of whom it is said that disorder displeases Him exceedingly.

LXXXVII.

MEN'S PRAYERS TO GOD PROVE SUFFICIENTLY THAT THEY ARE NOT SATISFIED WITH THE DIVINE ECONOMY.

Although men incessantly admire the wisdom the goodness, the justice, the beautiful order of Providence, they are, in fact, never contented with it. The prayers which they continually offer to Heaven, prove to us that they are not at all satisfied with God's administration. Praying to God, asking a favor of Him, is to mistrust His vigilant care; to pray God to avert or to suppress an evil, is to endeavor to put obstacles in the way of His justice; to implore the assistance of God in our calamities, means to appeal to the very author of these calamities in order to represent to Him our welfare; that He ought to rectify in our favor His plan, which is not beneficial to our interests. The optimist, or the one who thinks that everything is good in the world, and who repeats to us incessantly that we live in the best world possible, if he were consistent, ought never to pray; still less should he expect another world where men will be happier. Can there be a better world than the best possible of all worlds? Some of the theologians have treated the optimists as impious for having claimed that God could not have made a better world than the one in which we live; according to these doctors it is limiting the Divine power and insulting it. But do not theologians see that it is less offensive for God, to pretend that He did His best in creating the world, than to say that He, having the power to produce a better one, had the malice to make a very bad one? If the optimist, by his system, does wrong to the

Divine power, the theologian, who treats him as impious, is himself a reprobate, who wounds the Divine goodness under pretext of taking interest in God.

LXXXVIII.

THE REPARATION OF THE INIQUITIES AND THE MISERIES OF THIS WORLD IN ANOTHER WORLD, IS AN IDLE CONJECTURE AND AN ABSURD SUPPOSITION.

When we complain of the evils of which this world is the theater, we are referred to another world; we are told that there God will repair all the iniquities and the miseries which He permits for a time here below. However, if leaving His eternal justice to sleep for a time, God could consent to evil during the period of the existence of our globe, what assurance have we that during the existence of another globe, Divine justice will not likewise sleep during the misfortunes of its inhabitants? They console us in our troubles by saying, that God is patient, and that His justice, although often very slow, is not the less certain. But do you not see, that patience can not be suited to a being just, immutable, and omnipotent? Can God tolerate injustice for an instant? To temporize with an evil that one knows of, evinces either uncertainty, weakness, or collusion; to tolerate evil which one has the power to prevent, is to consent that evil should be committed.

LXXXIX.

THEOLOGY JUSTIFIES THE EVIL AND INJUSTICE PERMITTED BY ITS GOD, ONLY BY CONCEDING TO THIS GOD THE RIGHT OF THE STRONGEST, THAT IS TO SAY, THE VIOLATION OF ALL RIGHTS, OR IN COMMANDING FROM MEN A STUPID DEVOTION.

I hear a multitude of theologians tell me on all sides, that God is infinitely just, but that His justice is not that of men! Of what kind, or of what nature is this Divine justice then? What idea can I form of a justice which so often resembles human injustice? Is it not confounding all our ideas of justice and of injustice, to tell us that what is equitable in God is iniquitous in His creatures? How can we take as a model a being whose Divine perfections are precisely contrary to human perfections? God, you say, is the sovereign arbiter of our destinies; His supreme power, that nothing can limit, authorizes Him to do as He pleases with His works; a worm, such as man, has not the right to murmur against Him. This arrogant tone is literally borrowed from the language which the ministers of tyrants hold, when they silence those who suffer by their violences; it can not, then, be the language of the ministers of a God of whose equity they boast. It can not impose upon a being who reasons. Ministers of a just God! I tell you then, that the greatest power is not able to confer even upon your God Himself the right to be unjust to the vilest of His creatures. A despot is not a God. A God who arrogates to Himself the right to do evil, is a tyrant; a tyrant is not a model for men. He ought to be an execrable object in their eyes. Is it not strange that, in order to justify Divinity, they made of Him the most unjust of beings? As soon as we complain of His conduct, they think to silence us by claiming that God is the Master; which signifies that God, being the strongest, He is not subjected to ordinary rules. But the right of the strongest is the violation of all rights; it can pass as a right but in the eyes of a savage conqueror, who, in the intoxication of his fury, imagines he has the right to do as he pleases with the unfortunate ones whom he has conquered; this barbarous right can appear legitimate only to slaves, who are blind enough to think that everything is allowed to tyrants, who are too strong for them to resist.

By a foolish simplicity, or rather by a plain contradiction of terms, do we not see devotees exclaim, amidst the greatest calamities, that the good Lord is the Master? Well, illogical reasoners, you believe in good faith that the good Lord sends you the pestilence; that your good Lord gives war; that the good Lord is the cause of famine; in a word, that the good Lord, without ceasing to be good, has the will and the right to do you the greatest evils you can endure! Cease to call your Lord good when He does you harm; do not say that He is just; say that He is the strongest, and that it is impossible for you to avert the blows which His caprice inflicts upon you. God, you say, punishes us for our highest good; but what real benefit can result to a nation in being exterminated by contagion, murdered by wars, corrupted by the examples of perverse masters, continually pressed by the iron scepter of merciless tyrants, subjected to the scourge of a bad government, which often for centuries causes nations to suffer its destructive effects? The eyes of faith must be strange eyes, if we see by their means any advantage in the most dreadful miseries and in the most durable evils, in the vices and follies by which our kind is so cruelly afflicted!

XC.

REDEMPTION, AND THE CONTINUAL EXTERMINATIONS ATTRIBUTED TO JEHOVAH IN THE BIBLE, ARE SO MANY ABSURD AND RIDICULOUS INVENTIONS WHICH PRESUPPOSE AN UNJUST AND BARBAROUS GOD.

What strange ideas of the Divine justice must the Christians have who believe that their God, with the view of reconciling Himself with mankind, guilty without knowledge of the fault of their parents, sacrificed His own innocent and sinless Son! What would we say of a king, whose subjects having revolted against him, in order to appease himself could find no other expedient than to put to death the heir to his crown, who had taken no part in the general rebellion? It is, the Christian will say, through kindness for His subjects, incapable of satisfying themselves of His Divine justice, that God consented to the cruel death of His Son. But the kindness of a father to strangers does not give him the right to be unjust and cruel to his son. All the qualities that theology gives to its God annul each other. The exercise of one of His perfections is always at the expense of another.

Has the Jew any more rational ideas than the Christian of Divine justice? A king, by his pride, kindles the wrath of Heaven. Jehovah sends pestilence upon His innocent people; seventy thousand subjects are exterminated to expiate the fault of a monarch that the kindness of God resolved to spare.

XCI.

HOW CAN WE DISCOVER A TENDER, GENEROUS, AND EQUITABLE FATHER IN A BEING WHO HAS CREATED HIS CHILDREN BUT TO MAKE THEM UNHAPPY?

In spite of the injustice with which all religions are pleased to blacken the Divinity, men can not consent to accuse Him of iniquity; they fear that He, like the tyrants of this world, will be offended by the truth, and redouble the weight of His malice and tyranny upon them. They listen, then, to their priests, who tell them that their God is a tender Father; that this God is an equitable Monarch, whose object in this world is to assure Himself of the love, obedience, and respect of His subjects; who gives them the liberty to act, in order to give them occasion to deserve His favors and to acquire eternal happiness, which He does not owe them in any way. In what way can we recognize the tenderness of a Father who created the majority of His children but for the purpose of dragging out a life of pain, anxiety, and bitterness upon this earth? Is there any more fatal boon than this pretended liberty which, it is said, men can abuse, and thereby expose themselves to the risk of eternal misery?

XCII.

THE LIFE OF MORTALS, ALL WHICH TAKES PLACE HERE BELOW, TESTIFIES AGAINST MAN'S LIBERTY AND AGAINST THE JUSTICE AND GOODNESS OF A PRETENDED GOD.

In calling mortals into life, what a cruel and dangerous game does the Divinity force them to play! Thrust into the world without their wish, provided with a temperament of which they are not the masters, animated by passions and desires inherent in their nature, exposed to snares which they have not the skill to avoid, led away by events which they could neither foresee nor prevent, the unfortunate beings are obliged to follow a career which conducts them to horrible tortures.

Travelers assert that in some part of Asia reigns a sultan full of phantasies, and very absolute in his will. By a strange mania this prince spends his time sitting before a table, on which are placed six dice and a dice-box. One end of the table is covered with a pile of gold, for the purpose of exciting the cupidity of the courtiers and of the people by whom the sultan is surrounded. He, knowing the weak point of his subjects, speaks to them in this way: "Slaves! I wish you well; my aim is to enrich you and render you all happy. Do you see these treasures? Well, they are for you! try to win them; let each one in turn take this box and these dice; whoever shall have the good luck to raffle six, will be master of this treasure; but I warn you that he who has not the luck to throw the required number, will be precipitated forever into an obscure cell, where my justice exacts that he shall be burned by a slow fire." Upon this threat of the monarch, they regarded each other in consternation; no one willing to take a risk so dangerous. "What!" said the angry sultan, "no one wants to play? Oh, this does not suit me! My glory demands that you play. You will raffle then; I wish it; obey without replying!" It is well to observe that the despot's dice are prepared in such a way, that upon a hundred thousand throws there is but one that wins; thus the generous monarch has the pleasure to see his prison well filled, and his treasures seldom carried away. Mortals! this Sultan is your God; His treasures are heaven; His cell is hell; and you hold the dice!

XCIII.

IT IS NOT TRUE THAT WE OWE ANY GRATITUDE TO WHAT WE CALL PROVIDENCE.

We are constantly told that we owe an infinite gratitude to Providence for the countless blessings It is pleased to lavish upon us. They boast above all that our existence is a blessing. But, alas! how many mortals are really satisfied with their mode of existence? If life has its sweets, how much of bitterness is mingled with it? Is not one bitter trouble sufficient to blight all of a sudden the most peaceful and happy life? Is there a great number of men who, if it depended upon them, would wish to begin, at the same sacrifice, the painful career into which, without their consent, destiny has thrown them? You say that existence itself is a great blessing. But is not this existence continually troubled by griefs, fears, and often cruel and undeserved maladies. This existence, menaced on so many sides, can we not be deprived of it at any moment? Who is there, after having lived for some time, who has not been deprived of a beloved wife, a beloved child, a consoling friend, whose loss fills his mind constantly? There are very few mortals who have not been compelled to drink from the cup of bitterness; there are but few who have not often wished to die. Finally, it did not depend upon us to exist or not to exist. Would the bird be under such great obligations to the bird-catcher for having caught it in his net and for having put it into his cage, in order to eat it after being amused with it?

XCIV.

TO PRETEND THAT MAN IS THE BELOVED CHILD OF PROVIDENCE, GOD'S FAVORITE, THE ONLY OBJECT OF HIS LABORS, THE KING OF NATURE, IS FOLLY.

In spite of the infirmities, the troubles, the miseries to which man is compelled to submit in this world; in spite of the danger which his alarmed imagination creates in regard to another, he is still foolish enough to believe himself to be God's favorite, the only aim of all His works. He imagines that the entire universe was made for him; he calls himself arrogantly the king of nature, and ranks himself far above other animals. Poor mortal! upon what can you establish your high pretensions? It is, you say, upon your soul, upon your reason, upon your sublime faculties, which place you in a condition to exercise an absolute authority over the beings which surround you. But weak sovereign of this world, art thou sure one instant of the duration of thy reign? The least atoms of matter which you despise, are they not sufficient to deprive you of your throne and life? Finally, does not the king of animals terminate always by becoming food for the worms?

You speak of your soul. But do you know what your soul is? Do you not see that this soul is but the assemblage of your organs, from which life results? Would you refuse a soul to other animals who live, who think, who judge, who compare, who seek pleasure, and avoid pain even as you do, and who often possess organs which are better than your own? You boast of your intellectual faculties, but these faculties which render you so proud, do they make you any happier than other creatures? Do you often make use of this reason which you glory in, and which religion commands you not to listen to? Those animals which you disdain because they are weaker or less cunning than yourself, are they subject to troubles, to mental anxieties, to a thousand frivolous passions, to a thousand imaginary needs, of which your heart is continually the prey? Are they, like you, tormented by the past, alarmed for the future?

Limited solely to the present, what you call their instinct, and what I call their intelligence, is it not sufficient to preserve and to defend them and to provide for their needs? This instinct, of which you speak with disdain, does it not often serve them much better than your wonderful faculties? Their peaceable ignorance, is it not more advantageous than these extravagant meditations and these futile investigations which render you miserable, and for which you are driven to murdering beings of your own noble kind? Finally, these animals, have they, like mortals, a troubled imagination which makes them fear not only death, but even eternal torments? Augustus, having heard that Herod, king of Judea, had murdered his sons, cried out: "It would be better to be Herod's pig than his son!" We can say as much of men; this beloved child of Providence runs much greater risks than all other animals. After having suffered a great deal in this world, do we not believe ourselves in danger of suffering for eternity in another?

XCV.

COMPARISON BETWEEN MAN AND ANIMALS.

What is the exact line of demarcation between man and the other animals which he calls brutes? In what way does he essentially differ from the beasts? It is, we are told, by his intelligence, by the faculties of his mind, by his reason, that man is superior to all the other animals, which in all they do, act but by physical impulsions, reason taking no part. But the beasts, having more limited needs than men, do very well without these intellectual faculties, which would be perfectly useless in their way of living. Their instinct is sufficient for them, while all the faculties of man are hardly sufficient to render his existence endurable, and to satisfy the needs which his imagination, his prejudices, and his institutions multiply to his torment.

The brute is not affected by the same objects as man; it has neither the same needs, nor the same desires, nor the same whims; it early reaches maturity, while nothing is more rare than to see the human being enjoying all of his faculties, exercising them freely, and making a proper use of them for his own happiness.

XCVI.

THERE ARE NO MORE DETESTABLE ANIMALS IN THIS WORLD THAN TYRANTS.

We are assured that the human soul is a simple substance; but if the soul is such a simple substance, it ought to be the same in all the individuals of the human race, who all ought to have the same intellectual faculties; however, this is not the case; men differ as much in qualities of mind as in the features of the face. There are in the human race, beings as different from one another as man is from a horse or a dog. What conformity or resemblance do we find between some men? What an infinite distance between the genius of a Locke, of a Newton, and that of a peasant, of a Hottentot, or of a Laplander!

Man differs from other animals but by the difference of his organization, which causes him to produce effects of which they are not capable. The variety which we notice in the organs of individuals of the human race, suffices to explain to us the difference which is often found between them in regard to the intellectual faculties. More or less of delicacy in these organs, of heat in the blood, of promptitude in the fluids, more or less of suppleness or of rigidity in the fibers and the nerves, must necessarily produce the infinite diversities which are noticeable in the minds of men. It is by exercise, by habitude, by education, that the human mind is developed and succeeds in rising above the beings which surround it; man, without culture and without experience, is a being as devoid of reason and of industry as the brute. A stupid individual is a man whose organs are acted upon with difficulty, whose brain is hard to move, whose blood circulates slowly; a man of mind is he whose organs are supple, who feels very quickly, whose brain moves promptly; a learned man is one whose organs and whose brain have been exercised a long while upon objects which occupy him.

The man without culture, experience, or reason, is he not more despicable and more abominable than the vilest insects, or the most ferocious beasts? Is there a more detestable being in nature than a Tiberius, a Nero, a Caligula? These destroyers of the human race, known by the name of conquerors, have they better souls than those of bears, lions, and panthers? Are there more detestable animals in this world than tyrants?

XCVII.

REFUTATION OF MAN'S EXCELLENCE.

Human extravagances soon dispel, in the eyes of reason, the superiority which man arrogantly claims over other animals. Do we not see many animals show more gentleness, more reflection and reason than the animal which calls itself reasonable par excellence? Are there amongst men, who are so often enslaved and oppressed, societies as well organized as those of ants, bees, or beavers? Do we ever see ferocious beasts of the same kind meet upon the plains to devour each other without profit? Do we see among them religious wars? The cruelty of beasts against other species is caused by hunger, the need of nourishment; the cruelty of man against man has no other motive than the vanity of his masters and the folly of his impertinent prejudices. Theorists who try to make us believe that everything in the universe was made for man, are very much embarrassed when we ask them in what way can so many mischievous animals which continually infest our life here, contribute to the welfare of men. What known advantage results for God's friend to be bitten by a viper, stung by a gnat, devoured by vermin, torn into pieces by a tiger? Would not all these animals reason as wisely as our theologians, if they should pretend that man was made for them?

XCVIII.

AN ORIENTAL LEGEND.

At a short distance from Bagdad a dervis, celebrated for his holiness, passed his days tranquilly in agreeable solitude. The surrounding inhabitants, in order to have an interest in his prayers, eagerly brought to him every day provisions and presents. The holy man thanked God incessantly for the blessings Providence heaped upon him. "O Allah," said he, "how ineffable is Thy tenderness toward Thy servants. What have I done to deserve the benefactions which Thy liberality loads me with! Oh, Monarch of the skies! oh, Father of nature! what praises could be worthy to celebrate Thy munificence and Thy paternal cares! O Allah, how great are Thy gifts to the children of men!" Filled with gratitude, our hermit made a vow to undertake for the seventh time the pilgrimage to Mecca. The war, which then existed between the Persians and the Turks, could not make him defer the execution of his pious enterprise. Full of confidence in God, he began his journey; under the inviolable safeguard of a respected garb, he passed through without obstacle the enemies' detachments; far from being molested, he receives at every step marks of veneration from the soldiers of both sides. At last, overcome by fatigue, he finds himself obliged to seek a shelter from the rays of the burning sun; he finds it beneath a fresh group of palm-trees, whose roots were watered by a limpid rivulet. In this solitary place, where the silence was broken only by the murmuring of the waters and the singing of the birds, the man of God found not only an enchanting retreat, but also a delicious repast; he had but to extend the hand to gather dates and other agreeable fruits; the rivulet can appease his thirst; very soon a green plot invites him to take sweet repose. As he awakens he performs the holy cleansing; and in a transport of ecstasy, he exclaimed: "O Allah! HOW GREAT IS THY GOODNESS TO THE CHILDREN OF MEN!" Well rested, refreshed, full of life and gayety, our holy man continues on his road; it conducts him for some time through a delightful country, which offers to his sight but blooming shores and trees filled with fruit. Softened by this spectacle, he worships incessantly the rich and liberal hand of Providence, which is everywhere seen occupied with the welfare of the human race. Going a little farther, he comes across a few mountains, which were quite hard to ascend; but having arrived at their summit, a hideous sight suddenly meets his eyes; his soul is all consternation. He discovers a vast plain entirely devastated by the sword and fire; he looks at it and finds it covered with more than a hundred thousand corpses, deplorable remains of a bloody battle which had taken place a few days previous. Eagles, vultures, ravens, and wolves were devouring the dead bodies with which the earth was covered. This sight plunges our pilgrim into a sad reverie. Heaven, by a special favor, had made him understand the language of beasts. He heard a wolf, gorged with human flesh, exclaim in his excessive joy: "O Allah! how great is Thy kindness for the children of wolves! Thy foreseeing wisdom takes care to send infatuation upon these detestable men who are so dangerous to us. Through an effect of Thy Providence which watches over Thy creatures, these, our destroyers, murder each other, and thus furnish us with sumptuous repasts. O Allah! HOW GREAT IS THY GOODNESS TO THE CHILDREN OF WOLVES!"

XCIX.

IT IS FOOLISH TO SEE IN THE UNIVERSE ONLY THE BENEFACTIONS OF HEAVEN, AND TO BELIEVE THAT THIS UNIVERSE WAS MADE BUT FOR MAN.

An exalted imagination sees in the universe but the benefactions of Heaven; a calm mind finds good and evil in it. I exist, you will say; but is this existence always a benefit? You will say, look at this sun, which shines for you; this earth, which is covered with fruits and verdure; these flowers, which bloom Tor our sight and smell; these trees, which bend beneath the weight of fruits; these pure streams, which flow but to quench your thirst; these seas, which embrace the universe to facilitate your commerce; these animals, which a foreseeing nature produces for your use! Yes, I see all these things, and I enjoy them when I can. But in some climates this beautiful sun is most always obscured from me; in others, its excessive heat torments me, produces storm, gives rise to dreadful diseases, dries up the fields; the meadows have no grass, the trees are fruitless, the harvests are scorched, the springs are dried up; I can scarcely exist, and I sigh under the cruelty of a nature which you find so benevolent. If these seas bring me spices, riches, and useless things, do they not destroy a multitude of mortals who are dupes enough to go after them?

Man's vanity persuades him that he is the sole center of the universe; he creates for himself a world and a God; he thinks himself of sufficient consequence to derange nature at his will, but he reasons as an atheist when the question of other animals is involved. Does he not imagine that the individuals different from his species are automatons unworthy of the cares of universal Providence, and that the beasts can not be the objects of its justice and kindness? Mortals consider fortunate or unfortunate events, health or sickness, life and death, abundance or famine, as rewards or punishments for the use or misuse of the liberty which they arrogate to themselves. Do they reason on this principle when animals are taken into consideration? No; although they see them under a just God enjoy and suffer, be healthy and sick, live and die, like themselves, it does not enter their mind to ask what crimes these beasts have committed in order to cause the displeasure of the Arbiter of nature. Philosophers, blinded by their theological prejudices, in order to disembarrass themselves, have gone so far as to pretend that beasts have no feelings!

Will men never renounce their foolish pretensions? Will they not recognize that nature was not made for them? Will they not see that this nature has placed on equal footing all the beings which she produced? Will they not see that all organized beings are equally made to be born and to die, to enjoy and to suffer? Finally, instead of priding themselves preposterously on their mental faculties, are they not compelled to admit that they often render them more unhappy than the beasts, in which we find neither opinions, prejudices, vanities, nor the weaknesses which decide at every moment the well-being of men?

C.

WHAT IS THE SOUL? WE KNOW NOTHING ABOUT IT. IF THIS PRETENDED SOUL WAS OF ANOTHER ESSENCE FROM THAT OF THE BODY, THEIR UNION WOULD BE IMPOSSIBLE.

The superiority which men arrogate to themselves over other animals, is principally founded upon the opinion of possessing exclusively an immortal soul. But as soon as we ask what this soul is, they begin to stammer. It is an unknown substance; it is a secret force distinguished from their bodies; it is a spirit of which they can form no idea. Ask them how this spirit, which they suppose like their God, totally deprived of a physical substance, could combine itself with their material bodies? They will tell you that they know nothing about it; that it is a mystery to them; that this combination is the effect of the Almighty power. These are the clear ideas which men form of the hidden, or, rather, imaginary substance which they consider the motor of all their actions! If the soul is a substance essentially different from the body, and which can have no affinity with it, their union would be, not a mystery, but a thing impossible. Besides, this soul, being of an essence different from that of the body, ought to act necessarily in a different way from it. However, we see that the movements of the body are felt by this pretended soul, and that these two substances, so different in essence, always act in harmony. You will tell us that this harmony is a mystery; and I will tell you that I do not see my soul, that I know and feel but my body; that it is my body which feels, which reflects, which judges, which suffers, and which enjoys, and that all of its faculties are the necessary results of its own mechanism or of its organization.

CI.

THE EXISTENCE OF A SOUL IS AN ABSURD SUPPOSITION, AND THE EXISTENCE OF AN IMMORTAL SOUL IS A STILL MORE ABSURD SUPPOSITION.

Although it is impossible for men to have the least idea of the soul, or of this pretended spirit which animates them, they persuade themselves, however, that this unknown soul is exempt from death; everything proves to them that they feel, think, acquire ideas, enjoy or suffer, but by the means of the senses or of the material organs of the body. Even admitting the existence of this soul, one can not refuse to recognize that it depends wholly on the body, and suffers conjointly with it all the vicissitudes which it experiences itself; and however it is imagined that it has by its nature nothing analogous with it; it is pretended that it can act and feel without the assistance of this body; that deprived of this body and robbed of its senses, this soul will be able to live, to enjoy, to suffer, be sensitive of enjoyment or of rigorous torments. Upon such a tissue of conjectural absurdities the wonderful opinion of the immortality of the soul is built.

If I ask what ground we have for supposing that the soul is immortal: they reply, it is because man by his nature desires to be immortal, or to live forever. But I rejoin, if you desire anything very much, is it sufficient to conclude that this desire will be fulfilled? By what strange logic do they decide that a thing can not fail to happen because they ardently desire it to happen? Man's childish desires of the imagination, are they the measure of reality? Impious people, you say, deprived of the flattering hopes of another life, desire to be annihilated. Well, have they not just as much right to conclude by this desire that they will be annihilated, as you to conclude that you will exist forever because you desire it?

CII.

IT IS EVIDENT THAT THE WHOLE OF MAN DIES.

Man dies entirely. Nothing is more evident to him who is not delirious. The human body, after death, is but a mass, incapable of producing any movements the union of which constitutes life. We no longer see circulation, respiration, digestion, speech, or reflection. It is claimed then that the soul has separated itself from the body. But to say that this soul, which is unknown, is the principle of life, is saying nothing, unless that an unknown force is the invisible principle of imperceptible movements. Nothing is more natural and more simple than to believe that the dead man lives no more, nothing more absurd than to believe that the dead man is still living.

We ridicule the simplicity of some nations whose fashion is to bury provisions with the dead—under the idea that this food might be useful and necessary to them in another life. Is it more ridiculous or more absurd to believe that men will eat after death than to imagine that they will think; that they will have agreeable or disagreeable ideas; that they will enjoy; that they will suffer; that they will be conscious of sorrow or joy when the organs which produce sensations or ideas are dissolved and reduced to dust? To claim that the souls of men will be happy or unhappy after the death of the body, is to pretend that man will be able to see without eyes, to hear without ears, to taste without a palate, to smell without a nose, and to feel without hands and without skin. Nations who believe themselves very rational, adopt, nevertheless, such ideas.

CIII.

INCONTESTABLE PROOFS AGAINST THE SPIRITUALITY OF THE SOUL.

The dogma of the immortality of the soul assumes that the soul is a simple substance, a spirit; but I will always ask, what is a spirit? It is, you say, a substance deprived of expansion, incorruptible, and which has nothing in common with matter. But if this is true, how came your soul into existence? how did it grow? how did it strengthen? how weaken itself, get out of order, and grow old with your body? In reply to all these questions, you say that they are mysteries; but if they are mysteries, you understand nothing about them. If you do not understand anything about them, how can you positively affirm anything about them? In order to believe or to affirm anything, it is necessary at least to know what that consists of which we believe and which we affirm. To believe in the existence of your immaterial soul, is to say that you are persuaded of the existence of a thing of which it is impossible for you to form any true idea; it is to believe in words without attaching any sense to them; to affirm that the thing is as you claim, is the highest folly or assumption.

CIV.

THE ABSURDITY OF SUPERNATURAL CAUSES, WHICH THEOLOGIANS CONSTANTLY CALL TO THEIR AID.

Are not theologians strange reasoners? As soon as they can not guess the natural causes of things, they invent causes, which they call supernatural; they imagine them spirits, occult causes, inexplicable agents, or rather words much more obscure than the things which they attempt to explain. Let us remain in nature when we desire to understand its phenomena; let us ignore the causes which are too delicate to be seized by our organs; and let us be assured that by seeking outside of nature we can never find the solution of nature's problems. Even upon the theological hypothesis—that is to say, supposing an Almighty motor in matter—what right have theologians to refuse their God the power to endow this matter with thought? Would it be more difficult for Him to create combinations of matter from which results thought, than spirits which think? At least, in supposing a substance endowed with thought, we could form some idea of the object of our thoughts, or of what thinks in us; while attributing thought to an immaterial being, it is impossible for us to form the least idea of it.

CV.

IT IS FALSE THAT MATERIALISM CAN BE DEBASING TO THE HUMAN RACE.

Materialism, it is objected, makes of man a mere machine, which is considered very debasing to the human race. But will the human race be more honored when it can be said that man acts by the secret impulsions of a spirit, or a certain something which animates him without his knowing how? It is easy to perceive that the superiority which is given to mind over matter, or to the soul over the body, is based upon the ignorance of the nature of this soul; while we are more familiarized with matter or the body, which we imagine we know, and of which we believe we have understood the springs; but the most simple movements of our bodies are, for every thinking man, enigmas as difficult to divine as thought.

CVI.

CONTINUATION.

The esteem which so many people have for the spiritual substance, appears to result from the impossibility they find in defining it in an intelligible way. The contempt which our metaphysicians show for matter, comes from the fact that "familiarity breeds contempt." When they tell us that the soul is more excellent and noble than the body, they tell us nothing, except that what they know nothing about must be more beautiful than that of which they have some faint ideas.

CVII.

THE DOGMA OF ANOTHER LIFE IS USEFUL BUT FOR THOSE WHO PROFIT BY IT AT THE EXPENSE OF THE CREDULOUS PUBLIC.

We are constantly told of the usefulness of the dogma of life hereafter. It is pretended that even if it should be a fiction, it is advantageous, because it imposes upon men and leads them to virtue. But is it true that this dogma renders men wiser and more virtuous? The nations where this fiction is established, are they remarkable for the morality of their conduct? Is not the visible world always preferred to the invisible world? If those who are charged to instruct and to govern men had themselves enlightenment and virtue, they would govern them far better by realities than by vain chimeras; but deceitful, ambitious, and corrupt, the legislators found it everywhere easier to put the nations to sleep by fables than to teach them truths; than to develop their reason; than to excite them to virtue by sensible and real motives; than to govern them in a reasonable way.

Theologians, no doubt, have had reasons for making the soul immaterial. They needed souls and chimeras to populate the imaginary regions which they have discovered in the other life. Material souls would have been subjected, like all bodies, to dissolution. Moreover, if men believe that everything is to perish with the body, the geographers of the other world would evidently lose the chance of guiding their souls to this unknown abode. They would draw no profits from the hopes with which they feast them, and from the terrors with which they take care to overwhelm them. If the future is of no real utility to the human race, it is at least of the greatest advantage to those who take upon themselves the responsibility of conducting mankind thither.

CVIII.

IT IS FALSE THAT THE DOGMA OF ANOTHER LIFE CAN BE CONSOLING; AND IF IT WERE, IT WOULD BE NO PROOF THAT THIS ASSERTION IS TRUE.

But, it will be said, is not the dogma of the immortality of the soul consoling for beings who often find themselves very unhappy here below? If this should be an illusion, is it not a sweet and agreeable one? Is it not a benefit for man to believe that he can live again and enjoy, sometime, the happiness which is refused to him on earth? Thus, poor mortals! you make your wishes the measure of the truth! Because you desire to live forever, and to be happier, you conclude from thence that you will live forever, and that you will be more fortunate in an unknown world than in the known world, in which you so often suffer! Consent, then, to leave without regret this world, which causes more trouble than pleasure to the majority of you. Resign yourselves to the order of destiny, which decrees that you, like all other beings, should not endure forever. But what will become of me? you ask! What you were several millions of years ago. You were then, I do not know what; resign yourselves, then, to become again in an instant, I do not know what; what you were then; return peaceably to the universal home from which you came without your knowledge into your material form, and pass by without murmuring, like all the beings which surround you!

We are repeatedly told that religious ideas offer infinite consolation to the unfortunate; it is pretended that the idea of the immortality of the soul and of a happier life has a tendency to lift up the heart of man and to sustain him in the midst of the adversities with which he is assailed in this life. Materialism, on the contrary, is, we are told, an afflicting system, tending to degrade man, which ranks him among brutes; which destroys his courage, whose only hope is complete annihilation, tending to lead him to despair, and inducing him to commit suicide as soon as he suffers in this world. The grand policy of theologians is to blow hot and to blow cold, to afflict and to console, to frighten and to reassure.

According to the fictions of theology, the regions of the other life are happy and unhappy. Nothing more difficult than to render one worthy of the abode of felicity; nothing easier than to obtain a place in the abode of torments that Divinity prepares for the unfortunate victims of His eternal fury. Those who find the idea of another life so flattering and so sweet, have they then forgotten that this other life, according to them, is to be accompanied by torments for the majority of mortals? Is not the idea of total annihilation infinitely preferable to the idea of an eternal existence accompanied with suffering and gnashing of teeth? The fear of ceasing to exist, is it more afflicting than the thought of having not always been? The fear of ceasing to be is but an evil for the imagination, which alone brought forth the dogma of another life.

You say, O Christian philosophers, that the idea of a happier life is delightful; we agree; there is no one who would not desire a more agreeable and a more durable existence than the one we enjoy here below. But, if Paradise is tempting, you will admit, also, that hell is frightful. It is very difficult to merit heaven, and very easy to gain hell. Do you not say that one straight and narrow path leads to the happy regions, and that a broad road leads to the regions of the unhappy? Do you not constantly tell us that the number of the chosen ones is very small, and that of the damned is very large? Do we not need, in order to be saved, such grace as your God grants to but few? Well! I tell you that these ideas are by no means consoling; I prefer to be annihilated at once rather than to burn forever; I will tell you that the fate of beasts appears to me more desirable than the fate of the damned; I will tell you that the belief which delivers me from overwhelming fears in this world, appears to me more desirable than the uncertainty in which I am left through belief in a God who, master of His favors, gives them but to His favorites, and who permits all the others to render themselves worthy of eternal punishments. It can be but blind enthusiasm or folly that can prefer a system which evidently encourages improbable conjectures, accompanied by uncertainty and desolating fear.

CIX.

ALL RELIGIOUS PRINCIPLES ARE IMAGINARY. INNATE SENSE IS BUT THE EFFECT OF A ROOTED HABIT. GOD IS AN IDLE FANCY, AND THE QUALITIES WHICH ARE LAVISHED UPON HIM DESTROY EACH OTHER.

All religious principles are a thing of imagination, in which experience and reason have nothing to do. We find much difficulty in conquering them, because imagination, when once occupied in creating chimeras which astonish or excite it, is incapable of reasoning. He who combats religion and its phantasies by the arms of reason, is like a man who uses a sword to kill flies: as soon as the blow is struck, the flies and the fancies return to the minds from which we thought to have banished them.

As soon as we refuse the proofs which theology pretends to give of the existence of a God, they oppose to the arguments which destroy them, an innate conviction, a profound persuasion, an invincible inclination inherent in every man, which brings to him, in spite of himself, the idea of an Almighty being which he can not altogether expel from his mind, and which he is compelled to recognize in spite of the strongest reasons that we can give him. But if we wish to analyze this innate conviction, upon which so much weight is placed, we will find that it is but the effect of a rooted habit, which, making them close their eyes against the most demonstrative proofs, leads the majority of men, and often the most enlightened ones, back to the prejudices of childhood. What can this innate sense or this ill-founded persuasion prove against the evidence which shows us that what implies contradiction can not exist?

We are told, very gravely, that it is not demonstrated that God does not exist. However, nothing is better demonstrated, notwithstanding all that men have told us so far, than that this God is an idle fancy, whose existence is totally impossible, as nothing is more evident or more clearly demonstrated than that a being can not combine qualities so dissimilar, so contradictory, so irreconcilable as those which all the religions of the earth ascribe to Divinity. The theologian's God, as well as the God of the theist, is He not evidently a cause incompatible with the effects attributed to Him? In whatever light we may look upon it, we must either invent another God, or conclude that the one which, for so many centuries, has been revealed to mortals, is at the same time very good and very wicked, very powerful and very weak, immutable and changeable, perfectly intelligent and perfectly destitute of reason, of plan, and of means; the friend of order and permitting disorder; very just and very unjust; very skillful and very awkward. Finally, are we not obliged to admit that it is impossible to reconcile the discordant attributes which are heaped upon a being of whom we can not say a single word without falling into the most palpable contradictions? Let us attempt to attribute but a single quality to Divinity, and what is said of it will be contradicted immediately by the effects we assign to this cause.

CX.

EVERY RELIGION IS BUT A SYSTEM IMAGINED FOR THE PURPOSE OF RECONCILING CONTRADICTIONS BY THE AID OF MYSTERIES.

Theology could very properly be defined as the science of contradictions. Every religion is but a system imagined for the purpose of reconciling irreconcilable ideas. By the aid of habitude and terror, we come to persist in the greatest absurdities, even when they are the most clearly exposed. All religions are easy to combat, but very difficult to eradicate. Reason can do nothing against habit, which becomes, as is said, a second nature. There are many persons otherwise sensible, who, even after having examined the ruinous foundations of their belief, return to it in spite of the most striking arguments.

As soon as we complain of not understanding religion, finding in it at every step absurdities which are repulsive, seeing in it but impossibilities, we are told that we are not made to conceive the truths of the religion which is proposed to us; that wandering reason is but an unfaithful guide, only capable of conducting us to perdition; and what is more, we are assured that what is folly in the eyes of man, is wisdom in the eyes of God, to whom nothing is impossible. Finally, in order to decide by a single word the most insurmountable difficulties which theology presents to us on all sides, they simply cry out: "Mysteries!"

CXI.

ABSURDITY AND INUTILITY OF THE MYSTERIES FORGED IN THE SOLE INTEREST OF THE PRIESTS.

What is a mystery? If I examine the thing closely, I discover very soon that a mystery is nothing but a contradiction, a palpable absurdity, a notorious impossibility, on which theologians wish to compel men to humbly close the eyes; in a word, a mystery is whatever our spiritual guides can not explain to us.

It is advantageous for the ministers of religion that the people should not comprehend what they are taught. It is impossible for us to examine what we do not comprehend. Every time that we can not see clearly, we are obliged to be guided. If religion was comprehensible, priests would not have so many charges here below.

No religion is without mysteries; mystery is its essence; a religion destitute of mysteries would be a contradiction of terms. The God which serves as a foundation to natural religion, to theism or to deism, is Himself the greatest mystery to a mind wishing to dwell upon Him.

CXII.

CONTINUATION.

All the revealed religions which we see in the world are filled with mysterious dogmas, unintelligible principles, of incredible miracles, of astonishing tales which seem imagined but to confound reason. Every religion announces a concealed God, whose essence is a mystery; consequently, it is just as difficult to conceive of His conduct as of the essence of this God Himself. Divinity has never spoken to us but in an enigmatical and mysterious way in the various religions which have been founded in the different regions of our globe. It has revealed itself everywhere but to announce mysteries, that is to say, to warn mortals that it designs that they should believe in contradictions, in impossibilities, or in things of which they were incapable of forming any positive idea.

The more mysteries a religion has, the more incredible objects it presents to the mind, the better fitted it is to please the imagination of men, who find in it a continual pasturage to feed upon. The more obscure a religion is, the more it appears divine, that is to say, in conformity to the nature of an invisible being, of whom we have no idea.

It is the peculiarity of ignorance to prefer the unknown, the concealed, the fabulous, the wonderful, the incredible, even the terrible, to that which is clear, simple, and true. Truth does not give to the imagination such lively play as fiction, which each one may arrange as he pleases. The vulgar ask nothing better than to listen to fables; priests and legislators, by inventing religions and forging mysteries from them, have served them to their taste. In this way they have attracted enthusiasts, women, and the illiterate generally. Beings of this kind resign easily to reasons which they are incapable of examining; the love of the simple and the true is found but in the small number of those whose imagination is regulated by study and by reflection. The inhabitants of a village are never more pleased with their pastor than when he mixes a good deal of Latin in his sermon. Ignorant men always imagine that he who speaks to them of things which they do not understand, is a very wise and learned man. This is the true principle of the credulity of nations, and of the authority of those who pretend to guide them.

CXIII.

CONTINUATION.

To speak to men to announce to them mysteries, is to give and retain, it is to speak not to be understood. He who talks but by enigmas, either seeks to amuse himself by the embarrassment which he causes, or finds it to his advantage not to explain himself too clearly. Every secret betrays suspicion, weakness, and fear. Princes and their ministers make a mystery of their projects for fear that their enemies in penetrating them would cause them to fail. Can a good God amuse Himself by the embarrassment of His creatures? A God who enjoys a power which nothing in the world can resist, can He apprehend that His intentions could be thwarted? What interest would He have in putting upon us enigmas and mysteries? We are told that man, by the weakness of his nature, is not capable of comprehending the Divine economy which can be to him but a tissue of mysteries; that God can not unveil secrets to him which are beyond his reach. In this case, I reply, that man is not made to trouble himself with Divine economy, that this economy can not interest him in the least, that he has no need of mysteries which he can not understand; finally, that a mysterious religion is not made for him, any more than an eloquent discourse is made for a flock of sheep.

CXIV.

A UNIVERSAL GOD SHOULD HAVE REVEALED A UNIVERSAL RELIGION.

Divinity has revealed itself in the different parts of our globe in a manner of such little uniformity, that in matters of religion men look upon each other with hatred and disdain. The partisans of the different sects see each other very ridiculous and foolish. The most respected mysteries in one religion are laughable for another. God, having revealed Himself to men, ought at least to speak in the same language to all, and relieve their weak minds of the embarrassment of seeking what can be the religion which truly emanated from Him, or what is the most agreeable form of worship in His eyes.

A universal God ought to have revealed a universal religion. By what fatality are so many different religions found on the earth? Which is the true one amongst the great number of those of which each one pretends to be the right one, to the exclusion of all the others? We have every reason to believe that not one of them enjoys this advantage. The divisions and the disputes about opinions are indubitable signs of the uncertainty and of the obscurity of the principles which they profess.

CXV.

THE PROOF THAT RELIGION IS NOT NECESSARY, IS THAT IT IS UNINTELLIGIBLE.

If religion was necessary to all men, it ought to be intelligible to all men. If this religion was the most important thing for them, the goodness of God, it seems, ought to make it for them the clearest, the most evident, and the best demonstrated of all things. Is it not astonishing to see that this matter, so essential to the salvation of mortals, is precisely the one which they understand the least, and about which, during so many centuries, their doctors have disputed the most? Never have priests, of even the same sect, come to an agreement among themselves about the manner of understanding the wishes of a God who has truly revealed Himself to them. The world which we inhabit can be compared to a public place, in whose different parts several charlatans are placed, each one straining himself to attract customers by depreciating the remedies offered by his competitors. Each stand has its purchasers, who are persuaded that their empiric alone possesses the good remedies; notwithstanding the continual use which they make of them, they do not perceive that they are no better, or that they are just as sick as those who run after the charlatans of another stand. Devotion is a disease of the imagination, contracted in infancy; the devotee is a hypochondriac, who increases his disease by the use of remedies. The wise man takes none of it; he follows a good regimen and leaves the rest to nature.

CXVI.

ALL RELIGIONS ARE RIDICULED BY THOSE OF OPPOSITE THOUGH EQUALLY INSANE BELIEF.

Nothing appears more ridiculous in the eyes of a sensible man than for one denomination to criticize another whose creed is equally foolish. A Christian thinks that the Koran, the Divine revelation announced by Mohammed, is but a tissue of impertinent dreams and impostures injurious to Divinity. The Mohammedan, on his side, treats the Christian as an idolater and a dog; he sees but absurdities in his religion; he imagines he has the right to conquer his country and force him, sword in hand, to accept the faith of his Divine prophet; he believes especially that nothing is more impious or more unreasonable than to worship a man or to believe in the Trinity. The Protestant Christian, who without scruple worships a man, and who believes firmly in the inconceivable mystery of the Trinity, ridicules the Catholic Christian because the latter believes in the mystery of the transubstantiation. He treats him as a fool, as ungodly and idolatrous, because he kneels to worship the bread in which he believes he sees the God of the universe. All the Christian denominations agree in considering as folly the incarnation of the God of the Indies, Vishnu. They contend that the only true incarnation is that of Jesus, Son of the God of the universe and of the wife of a carpenter. The theist, who calls himself a votary of natural religion, is satisfied to acknowledge a God of whom he has no conception; indulges himself in jesting upon other mysteries taught by all the religions of the world.

CXVII.

OPINION OF A CELEBRATED THEOLOGIAN.

Did not a famous theologian recognize the absurdity of admitting the existence of a God and arresting His course? "To us," he said, "who believe through faith in a true God, an individual substance, there ought to be no trouble in believing everything else. This first mystery, which is no small matter of itself, once admitted, our reason can not suffer violence in admitting all the rest. As for myself, it is no more trouble to accept a million of things that I do not understand, than to believe the first one."

Is there anything more contradictory, more impossible, or more mysterious, than the creation of matter by an immaterial Being, who Himself immutable, causes the continual changes that we see in the world? Is there anything more incompatible with all the ideas of common sense than to believe that a good, wise, equitable, and powerful Being presides over nature and directs Himself the movements of a world which is filled with follies, miseries, crimes, and disorders, which He could have foreseen, and by a single word could have prevented or made to disappear? Finally, as soon as we admit a Being so contradictory as the theological God, what right have we to refuse to accept the most improbable fables, the most astonishing miracles, the most profound mysteries?

CXVIII.

THE DEIST'S GOD IS NO LESS CONTRADICTORY, NO LESS FANCIFUL, THAN THE THEOLOGIAN'S GOD.

The theist exclaims, "Be careful not to worship the ferocious and strange God of theology; mine is much wiser and better; He is the Father of men; He is the mildest of Sovereigns; it is He who fills the universe with His benefactions!" But I will tell him, do you not see that everything in this world contradicts the good qualities which you attribute to your God? In the numerous family of this mild Father I see but unfortunate ones. Under the empire of this just Sovereign I see crime victorious and virtue in distress. Among these benefactions, which you boast of, and which your enthusiasm alone sees, I see a multitude of evils of all kinds, upon which you obstinately close your eyes.

Compelled to acknowledge that your good God, in contradiction with Himself, distributes with the same hand good and evil, you will find yourself obliged, in order to justify Him, to send me, as the priests would, to the other life. Invent, then, another God than the one of theology, because your God is as contradictory as its God is. A good God who does evil or who permits it to be done, a God full of equity and in an empire where innocence is so often oppressed; a perfect God who produces but imperfect and wretched works; such a God and His conduct, are they not as great mysteries as that of the incarnation? You blush, you say, for your fellow beings who are persuaded that the

God of the universe could change Himself into a man and die upon a cross in a corner of Asia. You consider the ineffable mystery of the Trinity very absurd Nothing appears more ridiculous to you than a God who changes Himself into bread and who is eaten every day in a thousand different places.

Well! are all these mysteries any more shocking to reason than a God who punishes and rewards men's actions? Man, according to your views, is he free or not? In either case your God, if He has the shadow of justice, can neither punish him nor reward him. If man is free, it is God who made him free to act or not to act; it is God, then, who is the primitive cause of all his actions; in punishing man for his faults, He would punish him for having done that which He gave him the liberty to do. If man is not free to act otherwise than he does, would not God be the most unjust of beings to punish him for the faults which he could not help committing? Many persons are struck with the detail of absurdities with which all religions of the world are filled; but they have not the courage to seek for the source whence these absurdities necessarily sprung. They do not see that a God full of contradictions, of oddities, of incompatible qualities, either inflaming or nursing the imagination of men, could create but a long line of idle fancies.

CXIX.

WE DO NOT PROVE AT ALL THE EXISTENCE OF A GOD BY SAYING THAT IN ALL AGES EVERY NATION HAS ACKNOWLEDGED SOME KIND OF DIVINITY.

They believe, to silence those who deny the existence of a God, by telling them that all men, in all ages and in all centuries, have believed in some kind of a God; that there is no people on the earth who have not believed in an invisible and powerful being, whom they made the object of their worship and of their veneration; finally, that there is no nation, no matter how benighted we may suppose it to be, that is not persuaded of the existence of some intelligence superior to human nature. But can the belief of all men change an error into truth? A celebrated philosopher has said with all reason: "Neither general tradition nor the unanimous consent of all men could place any injunction upon truth." [Bayle.] Another wise man said before him, that "an army of philosophers would not be sufficient to change the nature of error and to make it truth." [Averroës]

There was a time when all men believed that the sun revolved around the earth, while the latter remained motionless in the center of the whole system of the universe; it is scarcely more than two hundred years since this error was refuted. There was a time when nobody would believe in the existence of antipodes, and when they persecuted those who had the courage to sustain it; to-day no learned man dares to doubt it. All nations of the world, except some men less credulous than others, still believe in sorcerers, ghosts, apparitions, spirits; no sensible man imagines himself obliged to adopt these follies; but the most sensible people feel obliged to believe in a universal Spirit!

CXX.

ALL THE GODS ARE OF A BARBAROUS ORIGIN; ALL RELIGIONS ARE ANTIQUE MONUMENTS OF IGNORANCE, SUPERSTITION, AND FEROCITY; AND MODERN RELIGIONS ARE BUT ANCIENT FOLLIES REVIVED.

All the Gods worshiped by men have a barbarous origin; they were visibly imagined by stupid nations, or were presented by ambitious and cunning legislators to simple and benighted people, who had neither the capacity nor the courage to examine properly the object which, by means of terrors, they were made to worship. In examining closely the God which we see adored still in our days by the most civilized nations, we are compelled to acknowledge that He has evidently barbarous features. To be barbarous is to recognize no right but force; it is being cruel to excess; it is but following one's own caprice; it is a lack of foresight, of prudence, and reason. Nations, who believe yourselves civilized! do you not perceive this frightful character of the God to whom you offer your incense? The pictures which are drawn of Divinity, are they not visibly borrowed from the implacable, jealous, vindictive, blood-thirsty, capricious, inconsiderate humor of man, who has not yet cultivated his reason? Oh, men! you worship but a great savage, whom you consider as a model to follow, as an amiable master, as a perfect sovereign.

The religious opinions of men in every country are antique and durable monuments of ignorance credulity, of the terrors and the ferocity of their ancestors. Every barbarian is a child thirsting for the wonderful, which he imbibes with pleasure, and who never reasons upon that which he finds proper to excite his imagination; his ignorance of the ways of nature makes him attribute to spirits, to enchantments, to magic, all that appears to him extraordinary; in his eyes his priests are sorcerers, in whom he supposes an Almighty power; before whom his confused reason humiliates itself, whose oracles are for him infallible decrees, to contradict which would be dangerous. In matters of religion the majority of men have remained in their primitive barbarity. Modern religions are but follies of old times rejuvenated or presented in some new form. If the ancient barbarians have worshiped mountains, rivers, serpents, trees, fetishes of every kind; if the wise Egyptians worshiped crocodiles, rats, onions, do we not see nations who believe themselves wiser than they, worship with reverence a bread, into which they imagine that the enchantments of their priests cause the Divinity to descend? Is not the God-bread the fetish of many Christian nations, as little rational in this point as that of the most barbarous nations?

CXXI.

ALL RELIGIOUS CEREMONIES BEAR THE SEAL OF STUPIDITY OR BARBARITY.

In all times the ferocity, the stupidity, the folly of savage men were shown in religious customs which were often cruel and extravagant. A spirit of barbarity has come down to our days; it intrudes itself into the religions which are followed by the most civilized nations. Do we not still see human victims offered to Divinity? In order to appease the wrath of a God whom we suppose as ferocious, as jealous, as vindictive, as a savage, do not sanguinary laws cause the destruction of those who are believed to have displeased Him by their way of thinking?

Modern nations, at the instigation of their priests, have even excelled the atrocious folly of the most barbarous nations; at least do we not find that it never entered into a savage's mind to torment for the sake of opinions, to meddle in thought, to trouble men for the invisible actions of their brains? When we see polished and wise nations, such as the English, French, German, etc., notwithstanding all their enlightenment, continue to kneel before the barbarous God of the Jews, that is to say, of the most stupid, the most credulous, the most savage, the most unsocial nation which ever was on the earth; when we see these enlightened nations divide themselves into sects, tear one another, hate and despise each other for opinions, equally ridiculous, upon the conduct and the intentions of this irrational God; when we see intelligent persons occupy themselves foolishly in meditating on the wishes of this capricious and foolish God; we are tempted to exclaim,

"Oh, men! you are still savages! Oh, men! you are but children in the matter of religion!"

CXXII.

THE MORE ANCIENT AND GENERAL A RELIGIOUS OPINION IS, THE GREATER THE REASON FOR SUSPECTING IT.

Whoever has formed true ideas of the ignorance, credulity, negligence, and sottishness of common people, will always regard their religious opinions with the greater suspicion for their being generally established. The majority of men examine nothing; they allow themselves to be blindly led by custom and authority; their religious opinions are specially those which they have the least courage and capacity to examine; as they do not understand anything about them, they are compelled to be silent or put an end to their reasoning. Ask the common man if he believes in God. He will be surprised that you could doubt it. Then ask him what he understands by the word God. You will confuse him; you will perceive at once that he is incapable of forming any real idea of this word which he so often repeats; he will tell you that God is God, and you will find that he knows neither what he thinks of Him, nor the motives which he has for believing in Him.

All nations speak of a God; but do they agree upon this God? No! Well, difference of opinion does not serve as evidence, but is a sign of uncertainty and obscurity. Does the same man always agree with himself in his ideas of God? No! This idea varies with the vicissitudes of his life. This is another sign of uncertainty. Men always agree with other men and with themselves upon demonstrated truths, regardless of the position in which they find themselves;

except the insane, all agree that two and two make four, that the sun shines, that the whole is greater than any one of its parts, that Justice is a benefaction, that we must be benevolent to deserve the love of men, that injustice and cruelty are incompatible with goodness. Do they agree in the same way if they speak of God? All that they think or say of Him is immediately contradicted by the effects which they wish to attribute to Him. Tell several artists to paint a chimera, each of them will form different ideas of it, and will paint it differently; you will find no resemblance in the features each of them will have given to a portrait whose model exists nowhere. In painting God, do any of the theologians of the world represent Him otherwise than as a great chimera, upon whose features they never agree, each one arranging it according to his style, which has its origin but in his own brain? There are no two individuals in the world who have or can have the same ideas of their God.

CXXIII.

SKEPTICISM IN THE MATTER OF RELIGION, CAN BE THE EFFECT OF BUT A SUPERFICIAL EXAMINATION OF THEOLOGICAL PRINCIPLES.

Perhaps it would be more truthful to say, that all men are either skeptics or atheists, than to pretend that they are firmly convinced of the existence of a God. How can we be assured of the existence of a being whom we never have been able to examine, of whom it is impossible to form any permanent idea, whose different effects upon ourselves prevent us from forming an invariable judgment, of whom no idea can be uniform in two different brains? How can we claim to be completely persuaded of the existence of a being to whom we are constantly obliged to attribute a conduct opposed co the ideas which we had tried to form of it? Is it possible firmly to believe what we can not conceive? In believing thus, are we not adhering to the opinions of others without having one of our own? The priests regulate the belief of the vulgar; but do not these priests themselves acknowledge that God is incomprehensible to them? Let us conclude, then, that the conviction of the existence of a God is not as general as it is affirmed to be.

To be a skeptic, is to lack the motives necessary to establish a judgment. In view of the proofs which seem to establish, and of the arguments which combat the existence of a God, some persons prefer to doubt and to suspend their judgment; but at the bottom, this uncertainty is the result of an insufficient examination. Is it, then, possible to doubt evidence? Sensible people deride, and with reason, an absolute pyrrhonism, and even consider it impossible. A man who could doubt his own existence, or that of the sun, would appear very ridiculous, or would be suspected of reasoning in bad faith. Is it less extravagant to have uncertainties about the non-existence of an evidently impossible being? Is it more absurd to doubt of one's own existence, than to hesitate upon the impossibility of a being whose qualities destroy each other? Do we find more probabilities for believing in a spiritual being than for believing in the existence of a stick without two ends? Is the notion of an infinitely good and powerful being who permits an infinity of evils, less absurd or less impossible than that of a square triangle?

Let us conclude, then, that religious skepticism can be but the effect of a superficial examination of theological principles, which are in a perpetual contradiction of the clearest and best demonstrated principles! To doubt is to deliberate upon the judgment which we should pass. Skepticism is but a state of indecision which results from a superficial examination of subjects. Is it possible to be skeptical in the matter of religion when we design to return to its principles, and look closely into the idea of the God who serves as its foundation? Doubt arises ordinarily from laziness, weakness, indifference, or incapacity. To doubt, for many people, is to dread the trouble of examining things to which one attaches but little interest. Although religion is presented to men as the most important thing for them in this world as well as in the other, skepticism and doubt on this subject can be for the mind but a disagreeable state, and offers but a comfortable cushion. No man who has not the courage to contemplate without prejudice the God upon whom every religion is founded, can know what religion to accept; he does not know what to believe and what not to believe, to accept or to reject, what to hope or fear; finally, he is incompetent to judge for himself.

Indifference upon religion can not be confounded with skepticism; this indifference itself is founded upon the assurance or upon the probability which we find in believing that religion is not made to interest us. The persuasion which we have that a thing which is presented to us as very important, is not so, or is but indifferent, supposes a sufficient examination of the thing, without which it would be impossible to have this persuasion. Those who call themselves skeptics in regard to the fundamental points of religion, are generally but idle and lazy men, who are incapable of examining them.

CXXIV.

REVELATION REFUTED.

In all parts of the world, we are assured that God revealed Himself. What did He teach men? Does He prove to them evidently that He exists? Does He tell them where He resides? Does He teach them what He is, or of what His essence consists? Does He explain to them clearly His intentions and His plan? What He says of this plan, does it agree with the effects which we see? No! He informs us only that "He is the One that is," [I am that I am, saith the Lord] that He is an invincible God, that His ways are ineffable, that He becomes furious as soon as one has the temerity to penetrate His decrees, or to consult reason in order to judge of Him or His works. Does the revealed conduct of God correspond with the magnificent ideas which are given to us of His wisdom, goodness, justice, of His omnipotence? Not at all; in every revelation this conduct shows a partial, capricious being, at least, good to His favorite people, an enemy to all others. If He condescends to show Himself to some men, He takes care to keep all the others in invincible ignorance of His divine intentions. Does not every special revelation announce an unjust, partial, and malicious God?

Are the revealed wishes of a God capable of striking us by the sublime reason or the wisdom which they contain? Do they tend to the happiness of the people to whom Divinity has declared them? Examining the Divine wishes, I find in them, in all countries, but whimsical ordinances, ridiculous precepts, ceremonies of which we do not understand the aim, puerile practices, principles of conduct unworthy of the Monarch of Nature, offerings, sacrifices, expiations, useful, in fact, to the ministers of God, but very onerous to the rest of mankind. I find also, that they often have a tendency to render men unsocial, disdainful, intolerant, quarrelsome, unjust, inhuman toward all those who have not received either the same revelations as they, or the same ordinances, or the same favors from Heaven.

CXXV.

WHERE, THEN, IS THE PROOF THAT GOD DID EVER SHOW HIMSELF TO MEN OR SPEAK TO THEM?

Are the precepts of morality as announced by Divinity truly Divine, or superior to those which every rational man could imagine? They are Divine only because it is impossible for the human mind to see their utility. Their virtue consists in a total renunciation of human nature, in a voluntary oblivion of one's reason, in a holy hatred of self; finally, these sublime precepts show us perfection in a conduct cruel to ourselves and perfectly useless to others.

How did God show Himself? Did He Himself promulgate His laws? Did He speak to men with His own mouth? I am told that God did not show Himself to a whole nation, but that He employed always the organism of a few favored persons, who took the care to teach and to explain His intentions to the unlearned. It was never permitted to the people to go to the sanctuary; the ministers of the Gods always alone had the right to report to them what transpired.

CXXVI.

NOTHING ESTABLISHES THE TRUTH OF MIRACLES.

If, in the economy of all Divine revelations, I am unable to recognize either the wisdom, the goodness, or the equity of a God; if I suspect deceit, ambition, selfish designs in the great personages who have interposed between Heaven and us, I am assured that God has confirmed, by splendid miracles, the mission of those who have spoken for Him. But was it not much easier to show Himself, and to explain for Himself? On the other hand, if I have the curiosity to examine these miracles, I find that they are tales void of probability, related by suspicious people, who had the greatest interest in making others believe that they were sent from the Most High.

What witnesses are referred to in order to make us believe incredible miracles? They call as witnesses stupid people, who have ceased to exist for thousands of years, and who, even if they could attest the miracles in question, would be suspected of having been deceived by their own imagination, and of permitting themselves to be seduced by the illusions which skillful impostors performed before their eyes. But, you will say, these miracles are recorded in books which through constant tradition have been handed down to us. By whom were these books written? Who are the men who have transmitted and perpetuated them? They are either the same people who established these religions, or those who have become their adherents and their assistants. Thus, in the matter of religion, the testimony of interested parties is irrefragable and can not be contested!

CXXVII.

IF GOD HAD SPOKEN, IT WOULD BE STRANGE THAT HE HAD SPOKEN DIFFERENTLY TO ALL THE ADHERENTS OF THE DIFFERENT SECTS, WHO DAMN EACH OTHER, WHO ACCUSE EACH OTHER, WITH REASON, OF SUPERSTITION AND IMPIETY.

God has spoken differently to each nation of the globe which we inhabit. The Indian does not believe one word of what He said to the Chinaman; the Mohammedan considers what He has told to the Christian as fables; the Jew considers the Mohammedan and the Christian as sacrilegious corruptors of the Holy Law, which his God has given to his fathers. The Christian, proud of his more modern revelation, equally damns the Indian and the Chinaman, the Mohammedan, and even the Jew, whose holy books he holds. Who is wrong or right? Each one exclaims: "It is I!" Every one claims the same proofs; each one speaks of his miracles, his saints, his prophets, his martyrs. Sensible men answer, that they are all delirious; that God has not spoken, if it is true that He is a Spirit who has neither mouth nor tongue; that the God of the Universe could, without borrowing mortal organism, inspire His creatures with what He desired them to learn, and that, as they are all equally ignorant of what they ought to think about God, it is evident that God did not want to instruct them. The adherents of the different forms of worship which we see established in this world, accuse each other of superstition and of ungodliness. The Christians abhor the superstition of the heathen, of the Chinese, of the Mohammedans. The Roman Catholics treat the Protestant Christians as impious; the latter incessantly declaim against Roman superstition. They are all right. To be impious, is to have unjust opinions about the God who is adored; to be superstitious, is to have false ideas of Him. In accusing each other of superstition, the different religionists resemble humpbacks who taunt each other with their malformation.

CXXVIII.

OBSCURE AND SUSPICIOUS ORIGIN OF ORACLES.

The oracles which the Deity has revealed to the nations through His different mediums, are they clear? Alas! there are not two men who understand them alike. Those who explain them to others do not agree among themselves; in order to make them clear, they have recourse to interpretations, to commentaries, to allegories, to parables, in which is found a mystical sense very different from the literal one. Men are needed everywhere to explain the wishes of God, who could not or would not explain Himself clearly to those whom He desired to enlighten. God always prefers to use as mediums men who can be suspected of having been deceived themselves, or having reasons to deceive others.

CXXIX.

ABSURDITY OF PRETENDED MIRACLES.

The founders of all religions have usually proved their mission by miracles. But what is a miracle? It is an operation directly opposed to the laws of nature. But, according to you, who has made these laws? It is God. Thus your God, who, according to you, has foreseen everything, counteracts the laws which His wisdom had imposed upon nature! These laws were then defective, or at least in certain circumstances they were but in accordance with the views of this same God, for you tell us that He thought He ought to suspend or counteract them.

An attempt is made to persuade us that men who have been favored by the Most High have received from Him the power to perform miracles; but in order to perform a miracle, it is necessary to have the faculty of creating new causes capable of producing effects opposed to those which ordinary causes can produce. Can we realize how God can give to men the inconceivable power of creating causes out of nothing? Can it be believed that an unchangeable God can communicate to man the power to change or rectify His plan, a power which, according to His essence, an immutable being can not have himself? Miracles, far from doing much honor to God, far from proving the Divinity of religion, destroy evidently the idea which is given to us of God, of His immutability, of His incommunicable attributes, and even of His omnipotence. How can a theologian tell us that a God who embraced at once the whole of His plan, who could make but perfect laws, who can change nothing in them, should be obliged to employ miracles to make His projects successful, or grant to His creatures the faculty of performing prodigies, in order to execute His Divine will? Is it probable that a God needs the support of men? An Omnipotent Being, whose wishes are always gratified, a Being who holds in His hands the hearts and the minds of His creatures, needs but to wish, in order to make them believe all He desires.

CXXX.

REFUTATION OF PASCAL'S MANNER OF REASONING AS TO HOW WE SHOULD JUDGE MIRACLES.

What should we say of religions that based their Divinity upon miracles which they themselves cause to appear suspicious? How can we place any faith in the miracles related in the Holy Books of the Christians, where God Himself boasts of hardening hearts, of blinding those whom He wishes to ruin; where this God permits wicked spirits and magicians to perform as wonderful miracles as those of His servants; where it is prophesied that the Anti-Christ will have the power to perform miracles capable of destroying the faith even of the elect? This granted, how can we know whether God wants to instruct us or to lay a snare for us? How can we distinguish whether the wonders which we see, proceed from God or the Devil? Pascal, in order to disembarrass us, says very gravely, that we must judge the doctrine by miracles, and the miracles by the doctrine; that doctrine judges the miracles, and the miracles judge the doctrine. If there exists a defective and ridiculous circle, it is no doubt in this fine reasoning of one of the greatest defenders of the Christian religion. Which of all the religions in the world does not claim to possess the most admirable doctrine, and which does not bring to its aid a great number of miracles?

Is a miracle capable of destroying a demonstrated truth? Although a man should have the secret of curing all diseases, of making the lame to walk, of raising all the dead of a city, of floating in the air, of arresting the course of the sun and of the moon, will he be able to convince me by all this that two and two do not make four; that one makes three and that three makes but one; that a God who fills the universe with His immensity, could have transformed Himself into the body of a Jew; that the eternal can perish like man; that an immutable, foreseeing, and sensible God could have changed His opinion upon His religion, and reform His own work by a new revelation?

CXXXI.

EVEN ACCORDING TO THE PRINCIPLES OF THEOLOGY ITSELF, EVERY NEW REVELATION SHOULD BE REFUTED AS FALSE AND IMPIOUS.

According to the principles of theology itself, whether natural or revealed, every new revelation ought to be considered false; every change in a religion which had emanated from the Deity ought to be refuted as ungodly and blasphemous. Does not every reform suppose that God did not know how at the start to give His religion the required solidity and perfection? To say that God in giving a first law accommodated Himself to the gross ideas of a people whom He wished to enlighten, is to pretend that God neither could nor would make the people whom He enlightened at that time, as reasonable as they ought to be to please Him.

Christianity is an impiety, if it is true that Judaism as a religion really emanated from a Holy, Immutable, Almighty, grid Foreseeing God. Christ's religion implies either defects in the law that God Himself gave by Moses, or impotence or malice in this God who could not, or would not make the Jews as they ought to be to please Him. All religions, whether new, or ancient ones reformed, are evidently founded on the weakness, the inconstancy, the imprudence, and the malice of the Deity.

CXXXII.

EVEN THE BLOOD OF THE MARTYRS, TESTIFIES AGAINST THE TRUTH OF MIRACLES AND AGAINST THE DIVINE ORIGIN WHICH CHRISTIANITY CLAIMS.

If history informs me that the first apostles, founders or reformers of religions, performed great miracles, history teaches me also that these reforming apostles and their adherents have been usually despised, persecuted, and put to death as disturbers of the peace of nations. I am then tempted to believe that they have not performed the miracles attributed to them. Finally, these miracles should have procured to them a great number of disciples among those who witnessed them, who ought to have prevented the performers from being maltreated. My incredulity increases if I am told that the performers of miracles have been cruelly tormented or slain. How can we believe that missionaries, protected by a God, invested with His Divine Power, and enjoying the gift of miracles, could not perform the simple miracle of escaping from the cruelty of their persecutors?

Persecutions themselves are considered as a convincing proof in favor of the religion of those who have suffered them; but a religion which boasts of having caused the death of many martyrs, and which informs us that its founders have suffered for its extension unheard-of torments, can not be the religion of a benevolent, equitable, and Almighty God. A good God would not permit that men charged with revealing His will should be misused. An omnipotent God desiring to found a religion, would have employed simpler and less fatal means for His most faithful servants. To say that God desired that His religion should be sealed by blood, is to say that this God is weak, unjust, ungrateful, and sanguinary, and that He sacrifices unworthily His missionaries to the interests of His ambition.

CXXXIII.

THE FANATICISM OF THE MARTYRS, THE INTERESTED ZEAL OF MISSIONARIES, PROVE IN NOWISE THE TRUTH OF RELIGION.

To die for a religion does not prove it true or Divine; this proves at most that we suppose it to be so. An enthusiast in dying proves nothing but that religious fanaticism is often stronger than the love of life. An impostor can sometimes die with courage; he makes then, as is said, "a virtue of necessity." We are often surprised and affected at the sight of the generous courage and the disinterested zeal which have led missionaries to preach their doctrine at the risk even of suffering the most rigorous torments. We draw from this love, which is exhibited for the salvation of men, deductions favorable to the religion which they have proclaimed; but in truth this disinterestedness is only apparent. "Nothing ventured, nothing gained!" A missionary seeks fortune by the aid of his doctrine; he knows that if he has the good fortune to retail his commodity, he will become the absolute master of those who accept him as their guide; he is sure to become the object of their care, of their respect, of their veneration; he has every reason to believe that he will be abundantly provided for. These are the true motives which kindle the zeal and the charity of so many preachers and missionaries who travel all over the world.

To die for an opinion, proves no more the truth or the soundness of this opinion than to die in a battle proves the right of the prince, for whose benefit so many people are foolish enough to sacrifice themselves. The courage of a martyr, animated by the idea of Paradise, is not any more supernatural than the courage of a warrior, inspired with the idea of glory or held to duty by the fear of disgrace. What difference do we find between an Iroquois who sings while he is burned by a slow fire, and the martyr St. Lawrence, who while upon the gridiron insults his tyrant?

The preachers of a new doctrine succumb because they are not the strongest; the apostles usually practice a perilous business, whose consequences they can foresee; their courageous death does not prove any more the truth of their principles or their own sincerity, than the violent death of an ambitious man or a brigand proves that they had the right to trouble society, or that they believed themselves authorized to do it. A missionary's profession has been always flattering to his ambition, and has enabled him to subsist at the expense of the common people; these advantages have been sufficient to make him forget the dangers which are connected with it.

CXXXIV.

THEOLOGY MAKES OF ITS GOD AN ENEMY OF COMMON SENSE AND OF ENLIGHTENMENT.

You tell us, O theologians! that "what is folly in the eyes of men, is wisdom before God, who is pleased to confound the wisdom of the wise." But do you not pretend that human wisdom is a gift from Heaven? In telling us that this wisdom displeases God, is but folly in His eyes, and that He wishes to confound it, you proclaim that your God is but the friend of unenlightened people, and that He makes to sensible people a fatal gift, for which this perfidious Tyrant promises to punish them cruelly some day. Is it not very strange that we can not be the friend of your God but by declaring ourselves the enemy of reason and common sense?

CXXXV.

FAITH IS IRRECONCILABLE WITH REASON, AND REASON IS PREFERABLE TO FAITH.

Faith, according to theologians, is consent without evidence. From this it follows that religion exacts that we should firmly believe, without evidence, in propositions which are often improbable or opposed to reason. But to challenge reason as a judge of faith, is it not acknowledging that reason can not agree with faith? As the ministers of religion have determined to banish reason, they must have felt the impossibility of reconciling reason with faith, which is visibly but a blind submission to those priests whose authority, in many minds, appears to be of a greater importance than evidence itself, and preferable to the testimony of the senses. "Sacrifice your reason; give up experience; distrust the testimony of your senses; submit without examination to all that is given to you as coming from Heaven." This is the usual language of all the priests of the world; they do not agree upon any point, except in the necessity of never reasoning when they present principles to us which they claim as the most important to our happiness.

I will not sacrifice my reason, because this reason alone enables me to distinguish good from evil, the true from the false. If, as you pretend, my reason comes from God, I will never believe that a God whom you call so good, had ever given me reason but as a snare, in order to lead me to perdition. Priests! in crying down reason, do you not see that you slander your God, who, as you assure us, has given us this reason?

I will not give up experience, because it is a much better guide than imagination, or than the authority of the guides whom they wish to give me. This experience teaches me that enthusiasm and interest can blind and mislead them, and that the authority of experience ought to have more weight upon my mind than the suspicious testimony of many men whom I know to be capable of deceiving themselves, or very much interested in deceiving others.

I will not distrust my senses. I do not ignore the fact that they can sometimes lead me into error; but on the other hand, I know that they do not deceive me always. I know very well that the eye shows the sun much smaller than it really is; but experience, which is only the repeated application of the senses, teaches me that objects continually diminish by reason of their distance; it is by these means that I reach the conclusion that the sun is much larger than the earth; it is thus that my senses suffice to rectify the hasty judgments which they induced me to form. In warning me to doubt the testimony of my senses, you destroy for me the proofs of all religion. If men can be dupes of their imagination, if their senses are deceivers, why would you have me believe in the miracles which made an impression upon the deceiving senses of our ancestors? If my senses are faithless guides, I learn that I should not have faith even in the miracles which I might see performed under my own eyes.

CXXXVI.

HOW ABSURD AND RIDICULOUS IS THE SOPHISTRY OF THOSE WHO WISH TO SUBSTITUTE FAITH FOR REASON.

You tell me continually that the "truths of religion are beyond reason." Do you not admit, then, that these truths are not made for reasonable beings? To pretend that reason can deceive us, is to say that truth can be false, that usefulness can be injurious. Is reason anything else but the knowledge of the useful and the true? Besides, as we have but our reason, which is more or less exercised, and our senses, such as they are, to lead us in this life, to claim that reason is an unsafe guide, and that our senses are deceivers, is to tell us that our errors are necessary, that our ignorance is invincible, and that, without extreme injustice, God can not punish us for having followed the only guides which He desired to give us. To pretend that we are obliged to believe in things which are beyond our reason, is an assertion as ridiculous as to say that God would compel us to fly without wings. To claim that there are objects on which reason should not be consulted, is to say that in the most important affairs, we must consult but imagination, or act by chance.

Our Doctors of Divinity tell us that we ought to sacrifice our reason to God; but what motives can we have for sacrificing our reason to a being who gives us but useless gifts, which He does not intend that we should make use of? What confidence can we place in a God who, according to our Doctors themselves, is wicked enough to harden hearts, to strike us with blindness, to place snares in our way, to lead us into temptation? Finally, how can we place confidence in the ministers of this God, who, in order to guide us more conveniently, command us to close our eyes?

CXXXVII.

HOW PRETEND THAT MAN OUGHT TO BELIEVE VERBAL TESTIMONY ON WHAT IS CLAIMED TO BE THE MOST IMPORTANT THING FOR HIM?

Men persuade themselves that religion is the most serious affair in the world for them, while it is the very thing which they least examine for themselves. If the question arises in the purchase of land, of a house, of the investment of money, of a transaction, or of some kind of an agreement, you will see each one examine everything with care, take the greatest precautions, weigh all the words of a document, to beware of any surprise or imposition. It is not the same with religion; each one accepts it at hazard, and believes it upon verbal testimony, without taking the trouble to examine it. Two causes seem to concur in sustaining men in the negligence and the thoughtlessness which they exhibit when the question comes up of examining their religious opinions. The first one is, the hopelessness of penetrating the obscurity by which every religion is surrounded; even in its first principles, it has only a tendency to repel indolent minds, who see in it but chaos, to penetrate which, they judge impossible. The second is, that each one is afraid to incommode himself by the severe precepts which everybody admires in the theory, and which few persons take the trouble of practicing. Many people preserve their religion like old family titles which they have never taken the trouble to examine minutely, but which they place in their archives in case they need them.

CXXXVIII.

FAITH TAKES ROOT BUT IN WEAK, IGNORANT, OR INDOLENT MINDS.

The disciples of Pythagoras had an implicit faith in their Master's doctrine: "HE HAS SAID IT!" was for them the solution of all problems. The majority of men act with as little reason. A curate, a priest, an ignorant monk, will become in the matter of religion the master of one's thoughts. Faith relieves the weakness of the human mind, for whom application is commonly a very painful work; it is much easier to rely upon others than to examine for one's self; examination being slow and difficult, it is usually unpleasant to ignorant and stupid minds as well as to very ardent ones; this is, no doubt, why faith finds so many partisans.

The less enlightenment and reason men possess, the more zeal they exhibit for their religion. In all the religious factions, women, aroused by their directors, exhibit very great zeal in opinions of which it is evident they have not the least idea. In theological quarrels people rush like a ferocious beast upon all those against whom their priest wishes to excite them. Profound ignorance, unlimited credulity, a very weak head, an irritated imagination, these are the materials of which devotees, zealots, fanatics, and saints are made. How can we make those people understand reason who allow themselves to be guided without examining anything? The devotees and common people are, in the hands of their guides, only automatons which they move at their fancy.

CXXXIX.

TO TEACH THAT THERE EXISTS ONE TRUE RELIGION IS AN ABSURDITY, AND A CAUSE OF MUCH TROUBLE AMONG THE NATIONS.

Religion is a thing of custom and fashion; we must do as others do. But, among the many religions in the world, which one ought we to choose? This examination would be too long and too painful; we must then hold to the faith of our fathers, to that of our country, or to that of the prince, who, possessing power, must be the best. Chance alone decides the religion of a man and of a people. The French would be to-day as good Mussulmen as they are Christians, if their ancestors had not repulsed the efforts of the Saracens. If we judge of the intentions of Providence by the events and the revolutions of this world, we are compelled to believe that it is quite indifferent about the different religions which exist on earth. During thousands of years Paganism, Polytheism, and Idolatry have been the religions of the world; we are assured today, that during this period the most flourishing nations had not the least idea of the Deity, an idea which is claimed, however, to be so important to all men. The Christians pretend that, with the exception of the Jewish people, that is to say, a handful of unfortunate beings, the whole human race lived in utter ignorance of its duties toward God, and had but imperfect ideas of Divine majesty. Christianity, offshoot of Judaism, which was very humble in its obscure origin, became powerful and cruel under the Christian emperors, who, driven by a holy zeal, spread it marvelously in their empire by sword and fire, and founded it upon the ruins of overthrown Paganism. Mohammed and his successors, aided by Providence, or by their victorious arms, succeeded in a short time in expelling the Christian religion from a part of Asia, Africa, and even of Europe itself; the Gospel was compelled to surrender to the Koran. In all the factions or sects which during a great number of centuries have lacerated the Christians, "THE REASON OF THE STRONGEST WAS ALWAYS THE BEST;" the arms and the will of the princes alone decided upon the most useful doctrine for the salvation of the nations. Could we not conclude by this, either that the Deity takes but little interest in the religion of men, or that He declares Himself always in favor of opinions which best suit the Authorities of the earth, in order that He can change His systems as soon as they take a notion to change?

A king of Macassar, tired of the idolatry of his fathers, took a notion one day to leave it. The monarch's council deliberated for a long time to know whether they should consult Christian or Mohammedan Doctors. In the impossibility of finding out which was the better of the two religions, it was resolved to send at the same time for the missionaries of both, and to accept the doctrine of those who would have the advantage of arriving first. They did not doubt that God, who disposes of events, would thus Himself explain His will. Mohammed's missionaries having been more diligent, the king with his people submitted to the law which he had imposed upon himself; the missionaries of Christ were dismissed by default of their God, who did not permit them to arrive early enough. God evidently consents that chance should decide the religion of nations.

Those who govern, always decide the religion of the people. The true religion is but the religion of the prince;

the true God is the God whom the prince wishes them to worship; the will of the priests who govern the prince, always becomes the will of God. A jester once said, with reason, that "the true faith is always the one which has on its side 'the prince and the executioner.'"

Emperors and executioners for a long time sustained the Gods of Rome against the God of the Christians; the latter having won over to their side the emperors, their soldiers and their executioners succeeded in suppressing the worship of the Roman Gods. Mohammed's God succeeded in expelling the Christian's God from a large part of the countries which He formerly occupied. In the eastern part of Asia, there is a large country which is very flourishing, very productive, thickly populated, and governed by such wise laws, that the most savage conquerors adopted them with respect. It is China! With the exception of Christianity, which was banished as dangerous, they followed their own superstitious ideas; while the mandarins or magistrates, undeceived long ago about the popular religion, do not trouble themselves in regard to it, except to watch over it, that the bonzes or priests do not use this religion to disturb the peace of the State. However, we do not see that Providence withholds its benefactions from a nation whose chiefs take so little interest in the worship which is offered to it. The Chinese enjoy, on the contrary, blessings and a peace worthy of being envied by many nations which religion divides, ravages, and often destroys. We can not reasonably expect to deprive a people of its follies; but we can hope to cure of their follies those who govern the people; these will then prevent the follies of the people from becoming dangerous. Superstition is never to be feared except when it has the support of princes and soldiers; it is only then that it becomes cruel and sanguinary. Every sovereign who assumes the protection of a sect or of a religious faction, usually becomes the tyrant of other sects, and makes himself the must cruel perturbator in his kingdom.

CXL.

RELIGION IS NOT NECESSARY TO MORALITY AND TO VIRTUE.

We are constantly told, and a good many sensible persons come to believe it, that religion is necessary to restrain men; that without it there would be no check upon the people; that morality and virtue are intimately connected with it: "The fear of the Lord is," we are told, "the beginning of wisdom." The terrors of another life are salutary terrors, and calculated to subdue men's passions. To disabuse us in regard to the utility of religious notions, it is sufficient to open the eyes and to consider what are the morals of the most religious people. We see haughty tyrants, oppressive ministers, perfidious courtiers, countless extortioners, unscrupulous magistrates, impostors, adulterers, libertines, prostitutes, thieves, and rogues of all kinds, who have never doubted the existence of a vindictive God, or the punishments of hell, or the joys of Paradise.

Although very useless for the majority of men, the ministers of religion have tried to make death appear terrible to the eyes of their votaries. If the most devoted Christians could be consistent, they would pass their whole lives in tears, and would finally die in the most terrible alarms. What is more frightful than death to those unfortunate ones who are constantly reminded that "it is a fearful thing to fall into the hands of a living God;" that they should "seek salvation with fear and trembling!" However, we are assured that the Christian's death has great consolations, of which the unbeliever is deprived. The good Christian, we are told, dies with the firm hope of enjoying eternal happiness, which he has tried to deserve.

But this firm assurance, is it not a punishable presumption in the eyes of a severe God? The greatest saints, are they not to be in doubt whether they are worthy of the love or of the hatred of God Priests who console us with the hope of the joys of Paradise, and close your eyes to the torments of hell, have you then had the advantage of seeing your names and ours inscribed in the book of life?

CXLI.

RELIGION IS THE WEAKEST RESTRAINT THAT CAN BE OPPOSED TO THE PASSIONS.

To oppose to the passions and present interests of men the obscure notions about a metaphysical God whom no one can conceive of; the incredible punishments of another life; the pleasures of Heaven, of which we can not form an idea, is it not combating realities with chimeras? Men have always but confused ideas of their God; they see Him only in the clouds; they never think of Him when they wish to do wrong. Whenever ambition, fortune, or pleasure entices them or leads them away, God, and His menaces, and His promises weigh nothing in the balance. The things of this life have for men a degree of certainty, which the most lively faith can never give to the objects of another life.

Every religion, in its origin, was a restraint invented by legislators who wished to subjugate the minds of the common people. Like nurses who frighten children in order to put them to sleep, ambitious men use the name of the gods to inspire fear in savages; terror seems well suited to compel them to submit quietly to the yoke which is to be imposed upon them. Are the ghost stories of childhood fit for mature age? Man in his maturity no longer believes in them, or if he does, he is troubled but little by it, and he keeps on his road.

CXLII.

HONOR IS A MORE SALUTARY AND A STRONGER CHECK THAN RELIGION.

There is scarcely a man who does not fear more what he sees than what he does not see; the judgments of men, of which he experiences the effects, than the judgments of God, of whom he has but floating ideas. The desire to please the world, the current of custom, the fear of being ridiculed, and of "WHAT WILL THEY SAY?" have more power than all religious opinions. A warrior with the fear of dishonor, does he not hazard his life in battles every day, even at the risk of incurring eternal damnation?

The most religious persons sometimes show more respect for a servant than for God. A man that firmly believes that God sees everything, knows everything, is everywhere, will, when he is alone, commit actions which he never would do in the presence of the meanest of mortals. Those even who claim to be the most firmly convinced of the existence of a God, act every instant as if they did not believe anything about it.

CXLIII.

RELIGION IS CERTAINLY NOT A POWERFUL CHECK UPON THE PASSIONS OF KINGS, WHO ARE ALMOST ALWAYS CRUEL AND FANTASTIC TYRANTS BY THE EXAMPLE OF THIS SAME GOD, OF WHOM THEY CLAIM TO BE THE REPRESENTATIVES; THEY USE RELIGION BUT TO BRUTALIZE THEIR SLAVES SO MUCH THE MORE, TO LULL THEM TO SLEEP IN THEIR FETTERS, AND TO PREY UPON THEM WITH THE GREATER FACILITY.

"Let us tolerate at least," we are told, "the idea of a God, which alone can be a restraint upon the passions of kings." But, in good faith, can we admire the marvelous effects which the fear of this God produces generally upon the mind of the princes who claim to be His images? What idea can we form of the original, if we judge it by its duplicates? Sovereigns, it is true, call, themselves the representatives of God, His lieutenants upon earth. But does the fear of a more powerful master than themselves make them attend to the welfare of the peoples that Providence has confided to their care? The idea of an invisible Judge, to whom alone they pretend to be accountable for their actions, should inspire them with terror! But does this terror render them more equitable, more humane, less avaricious of the blood and the goods of their subjects, more moderate in their pleasures, more attentive to their duties? Finally, does this God, by whom we are assured that kings reign, prevent them from vexing in a thousand ways the peoples of whom they ought to be the leaders, the protectors, and fathers? Let us open our eyes, let us turn our regards upon all the earth, and we shall see, almost everywhere, men governed by tyrants, who make use of religion but to brutalize their slaves, whom they oppress by the weight of their vices, or whom they sacrifice without mercy to their fatal extravagances. Far from being a restraint to the passions of kings, religion, by its very principles, gives them a loose rein. It transforms them into Divinities, whose caprices the nations never dare to resist. At the same time that it unchains princes and breaks for them the ties of the social pact, it enchains the minds and the hands of their oppressed subjects. Is it surprising, then, that the gods of the earth believe that all is permitted to them, and consider their subjects as vile instruments of their caprices or of their ambition?

Religion, in every country, has made of the Monarch of Nature a cruel, fantastic, partial tyrant, whose caprice is the rule. The God-monarch is but too well imitated by His representatives upon the earth. Everywhere religion seems invented but to lull to sleep the people in fetters, in order to furnish their masters the facility of devouring them, or to render them miserable with impunity.

CXLIV.

ORIGIN OF THE MOST ABSURD, THE MOST RIDICULOUS, AND THE MOST ODIOUS USURPATION, CALLED THE DIVINE RIGHT OF KINGS. WISE COUNSELS TO KINGS.

In order to guard themselves against the enterprises of a haughty Pontiff who desired to reign over kings, and in order to protect their persons from the attacks of the credulous people excited by their priests, several princes of Europe pretended to have received their crowns and their rights from God alone, and that they should account to Him only for their actions. Civil power in its battles against spiritual power, having at length gained the advantage, and the priests being compelled to yield, recognized the Divine right of kings and preached it to the people, reserving to themselves the right to change opinions and to preach revolution, every time that the divine rights of kings did not agree with the divine rights of the clergy. It was always at the expense of the people that peace was restored between the kings and the priests, but the latter maintained their pretensions notwithstanding all treaties.

Many tyrants and wicked princes, whose conscience reproaches them for their negligence or their perversity, far from fearing their God, rather like to bargain with this invisible Judge, who never refuses anything, or with His priests, who are accommodating to the masters of the earth rather than to their subjects. The people, when reduced to despair, consider the divine rights of their chiefs as an abuse. When men become exasperated, the divine rights of tyrants are compelled to yield to the natural rights of their subjects; they have better market with the gods than with men. Kings are responsible for their actions but to God, the priests but to themselves; there is reason to believe that both of them have more faith in the indulgence of Heaven than in that of earth. It is much easier to escape the judgments of the gods, who can be appeased at little expense, than the judgments of men whose patience is exhausted. If you take away from the sovereigns the fear of an invisible power, what restraint will you oppose to their misconduct? Let them learn how to govern, how to be just, how to respect the rights of the people, to recognize the benefactions of the nations from whom they obtain their grandeur and power; let them learn to fear men, to submit to the laws of equity, that no one can violate without danger; let these laws restrain equally the powerful and the weak, the great and the small, the sovereign and the subjects.

The fear of the Gods, religion, the terrors of another life— these are the metaphysical and supernatural barriers which are opposed to the furious passions of princes! Are these barriers sufficient? We leave it to experience to solve the question! To oppose religion to the wickedness of tyrants, is to wish that vague speculations should be more powerful than inclinations which conspire to fortify them in it from day to day.

CXLV.

RELIGION IS FATAL TO POLITICS; IT FORMS BUT LICENTIOUS AND PERVERSE DESPOTS, AS WELL AS ABJECT AND UNHAPPY SUBJECTS.

We are told constantly of the immense advantages which religion secures to politics; but if we reflect a moment, we will see without trouble that religious opinions blind and lead astray equally the rulers and the people, and never enlighten them either in regard to their true duties or their real interests. Religion but too often forms licentious, immoral tyrants, obeyed by slaves who are obliged to conform to their views. From lack of the knowledge of the true principles of administration, the aim and the rights of social life, the real interests of men, and the duties which unite them, the princes are become, in almost every land, licentious, absolute, and perverse; and their subjects abject unhappy, and wicked. It was to avoid the trouble of studying these important subjects, that they felt themselves obliged to have recourse to chimeras, which so far, instead of being a remedy, have but increased the evils of the human race and withdrawn their attention from the most interesting things. Does not the unjust and cruel manner in which so many nations are governed here below, furnish the most visible proofs, not only of the non-effect produced by the fear of another life, but of the non-existence of a Providence interested in the fate of the human race? If there existed a good God, would we not be forced to admit that He strangely neglects the majority of men in this life? It would appear that this God created the nations but to be toys for the passions and follies of His representatives upon earth.

CXLVI.

CHRISTIANITY EXTENDED ITSELF BUT BY ENCOURAGING DESPOTISM, OF WHICH IT, LIKE ALL RELIGION, IS THE STRONGEST SUPPORT.

If we read history with some attention, we shall see that Christianity, fawning at first, insinuated itself among the savage and free nations of Europe but by showing their chiefs that its principles would favor despotism and place absolute power in their hands. We see, consequently, barbarous kings converting themselves with a miraculous promptitude; that is to say, adopting without examination a system so favorable to their ambition, and exerting themselves to have it adopted by their subjects. If the ministers of this religion have since often moderated their servile principles, it is because the theory has no influence upon the conduct of the Lord's ministers, except when it suits their temporal interests.

Christianity boasts of having brought to men a happiness unknown to preceding centuries. It is true that the Grecians have not known the Divine right of tyrants or usurpers over their native country. Under the reign of Paganism it never entered the brain of anybody that Heaven did not want a nation to defend itself against a ferocious beast which insolently ravaged it. The Christian religion, devised for the benefit of tyrants, was established on the principle that the nations should renounce the legitimate defense of themselves. Thus Christian nations are deprived of the first law of nature, which decrees that man should resist evil and disarm all who attempt to destroy him. If the ministers of the Church have often permitted nations to revolt for Heaven's cause, they never allowed them to revolt against real evils or known violences.

It is from Heaven that the chains have come to fetter the minds of mortals. Why is the Mohammedan everywhere a slave? It is because his Prophet subdued him in the name of the Deity, just as Moses before him subjugated the Jews. In all parts of the world we see that priests were the first law-givers and the first sovereigns of the savages whom they governed. Religion seems to have been invented but to exalt princes above their nations, and to deliver the people to their discretion. As soon as the latter find themselves unhappy here below, they are silenced by menacing them with God's wrath; their eyes are fixed on Heaven, in order to prevent them from perceiving the real causes of their sufferings and from applying the remedies which nature offers them.

CXLVII.

THE ONLY AIM OF RELIGIOUS PRINCIPLES IS TO PERPETUATE THE TYRANNY OF KINGS AND TO SACRIFICE THE NATIONS TO THEM.

By incessantly repeating to men that the earth is not their true country; that the present life is but a passage; that they were not made to be happy in this world; that their sovereigns hold their authority but from God, and are responsible to Him alone for the misuse of it; that it is never permitted to them to resist, the priesthood succeeded in perpetuating the misconduct of the kings and the misfortunes of the people; the interests of the nations have been cowardly sacrificed to their chiefs. The more we consider the dogmas and the principles of religion, the more we shall be convinced that their only aim is to give advantage to tyrants and priests; not having the least regard for the good of society. In order to mask the powerlessness of these deaf Gods, religion has succeeded in making mortals believe that it is always iniquity which excites the wrath of Heaven. The people blame themselves for the disasters and the adversities which they endure continually. If disturbed nature sometimes causes the people to feel its blows, their bad governments are but too often the immediate and permanent causes from which spring the continual calamities that they are obliged to endure. Is it not the ambition of kings and of the great, their negligence, their vices, their oppression, to which are generally due sterility, mendacity, wars, contagions, bad morals, and all the multiplied scourges which desolate the earth?

In continually directing the eyes of men toward Heaven, making them believe that all their evils are due to Divine wrath, in furnishing them but inefficient and futile means of lessening their troubles, it would appear that the only object of the priests is to prevent the nations from dreaming of the true sources of their miseries, and to perpetuate them. The ministers of religion act like those indigent mothers, who, in need of bread, put their hungry children to sleep by songs, or who present them toys to make them forget the want which torments them.

Blinded from childhood by error, held by the invincible ties of opinion, crushed by panic terrors, stupefied at the bosom of ignorance, how could the people understand the true causes of their troubles? They think to remedy them by invoking the gods. Alas! do they not see that it is it the name of these gods that they are ordered to present their throat to the sword of their pitiless tyrants, in whom they would find the most visible cause of the evils under which they groan, and for which they uselessly implore the assistance of Heaven? Credulous people! in your adversities redouble your prayers, your offerings, your sacrifices; besiege your temples, strangle countless victims, fast in sackcloth and in ashes, drink your own tears; finally, exhaust yourselves to enrich your gods: you will do nothing but enrich their priests; the gods of Heaven will not be propitious to you, except when the gods of the earth will recognize that they are men like yourselves, and will give to your welfare the care which is your due.

CXLVIII.

HOW FATAL IT IS TO PERSUADE KINGS THAT THEY HAVE ONLY GOD TO FEAR IF THEY INJURE THE PEOPLE.

Negligent, ambitious, and perverse princes are the real causes of public adversities, of useless and unjust wars continually depopulating the earth, of greedy and despotic governments, destroying the benefactions of nature for men. The rapacity of the courts discourages agriculture, blots out industry, causes famine, contagion, misery; Heaven is neither cruel nor favorable to the wishes of the people; it is their haughty chiefs, who always have a heart of brass.

It is a notion destructive to wholesome politics and to the morals of princes, to persuade them that God alone is to be feared by them, when they injure their subjects or when they neglect to render them happy. Sovereigns! It is not the Gods, but your people whom you offend when you do evil. It is to these people, and by retroaction, to yourselves, that you do harm when you govern unjustly.

Nothing is more common in history than to see religious tyrants; nothing more rare than to find equitable, vigilant, enlightened princes. A monarch can be pious, very strict in fulfilling servilely the duties of his religion, very submissive to his priests, liberal in their behalf, and at the same time destitute of all the virtues and talents necessary for governing. Religion for the princes is but an instrument intended to keep the people more firmly under the yoke.

According to the beautiful principles of religious morality, a tyrant who, during a long reign, will have done nothing but oppress his subjects, rob them of the fruits of their labor, sacrifice them without pity to his insatiable ambition; a conqueror who will have usurped the provinces of others, who will have slaughtered whole nations, who will have been all his life a real scourge of the human race, imagines that his conscience can be tranquillized, if, in order to expiate so many crimes, he will have wept at the feet of a priest, who will have the cowardly complaisance to console and reassure a brigand, whom the most frightful despair would punish too little for the evil which he has done upon earth.

CLXIX.

A RELIGIOUS KING IS A SCOURGE TO HIS KINGDOM.

A sincerely religious sovereign is generally a very dangerous chief for a State; credulity always indicates a narrow mind; devotion generally absorbs the attention which the prince ought to give to the ruling of his people. Docile to the suggestions of his priests, he constantly becomes the toy of their caprices, the abettor of their quarrels, the instrument and the accomplice of their follies, to which he attaches the greatest importance. Among the most fatal gifts which religion has bestowed upon the world, we must consider above all, these devoted and zealous monarchs, who, with the idea of working for the salvation of their subjects, have made it their sacred duty to torment, to persecute, to destroy those whose conscience made them think otherwise than they do. A religious bigot at the head of an empire, is one of the greatest scourges which Heaven in its fury could have sent upon earth. One fanatical or deceitful priest who has the ear of a credulous and powerful prince, suffices to put a State into disorder and the universe into combustion.

In almost all countries, priests and devout persons are charged with forming the mind and the heart of the young princes destined to govern the nations. What enlightenment can teachers of this stamp give? Filled themselves with prejudices, they will hold up to their pupil superstition as the most important and the most sacred thing, its chimerical duties as the most holy obligations, intolerance, and the spirit of persecution, as the true foundations of his future authority; they will try to make him a chief of party, a turbulent fanatic, and a tyrant; they will suppress at an early period his reason; they will premonish him against it; they will prevent truth from reaching him; they will prejudice him against true talents, and prepossess him in favor of despicable talents; finally they will make of him an imbecile devotee, who will have no idea of justice or of injustice, of true glory or of true greatness, and who will be devoid of the intelligence and virtue necessary to the government of a great kingdom. Here, in brief, is the plan of education for a child destined to make, one day, the happiness or the misery of several millions of men.

CL.

THE SHIELD OF RELIGION IS FOR TYRANNY, A WEAK RAMPART AGAINST THE DESPAIR OF THE PEOPLE. A DESPOT IS A MADMAN, WHO INJURES HIMSELF AND SLEEPS UPON THE EDGE OF A PRECIPICE.

Priests in all times have shown themselves supporters of despotism, and the enemies of public liberty. Their profession requires vile and submissive slaves, who never have the audacity to reason. In an absolute government, their great object is to secure control of the mind of a weak and stupid prince, in order to make themselves masters of the people. Instead of leading the people to salvation, priests have always led them to servitude.

For the sake of the supernatural titles which religion has forged for the most wicked princes, the latter have generally united with the priests, who, sure of governing by controlling the opinion of the sovereign himself, have charge of tying the hands of the people and of keeping them under their yoke. But it is vain that the tyrant, protected by the shield of religion, flatters himself with being sheltered from all the blows of fate. Opinion is a weak rampart against the despair of the people. Besides, the priest is the friend of the tyrant only so long as he finds his profit by the tyranny; he preaches sedition and demolishes the idol which he has made, when he considers it no longer in conformity with the interests of Heaven, which he speaks of as he pleases, and which never speaks but in behalf of his interests. No doubt it will be said, that the sovereigns, knowing all the advantages which religion procures for them, are truly interested in upholding it with all their strength. If religious opinions are useful to tyrants, it is evident that they are useless to those who govern according to the laws of reason and of equity. Is there any advantage in exercising tyranny? Does not tyranny deprive princes of true power, the love of the people, in which is safety? Should not every rational prince perceive that the despot is but an insane man who injures himself? Will not every enlightened prince beware of his flatterers, whose object is to put him to sleep at the edge of the precipice to which they lead him?

CLI.

RELIGION FAVORS THE ERRORS OF PRINCES, BY DELIVERING THEM FROM FEAR AND REMORSE.

If the sacerdotal flatteries succeed in perverting princes and changing them into tyrants, the latter on their side necessarily corrupt the great men and the people. Under an unjust master, without goodness, without virtue, who knows no law but his caprice, a nation must become necessarily depraved. Will this master wish to have honest, enlightened, and virtuous men near him? No! he needs flatterers in those who approach him, imitators, slaves, base and servile minds, who give themselves up to his taste; his court will spread the contagion of vice to the inferior classes. By degrees all will be necessarily corrupted, in a State whose chief is corrupt himself. It was said a long time ago that the princes seem ordained to do all they do themselves. Religion, far from being a restraint upon the sovereigns, entitles them, without fear and without remorse, to the errors which are as fatal to themselves as to the nations which they govern. Men are never deceived with impunity. Tell a prince that he is a God, and very soon he will believe that he owes nothing to anybody. As long as he is feared, he will not care much for love; he will recognize no rights, no relations with his subjects, nor obligations in their behalf. Tell this prince that he is responsible for his actions to God alone, and very soon he will act as if he was responsible to nobody.

CLII.

WHAT IS AN ENLIGHTENED SOVEREIGN?

An enlightened sovereign is he who understands his true interests; he knows they are united to those of his nation; he knows that a prince can be neither great, nor powerful, nor beloved, nor respected, so long as he will command but miserable slaves; he knows that equity, benevolence, and vigilance will give him more real rights over men than fabulous titles which claim to come from Heaven. He will feel that religion is useful but to the priests; that it is useless to society, which is often troubled by it; that it must be limited to prevent it from doing injury; finally, he will understand that, in order to reign with glory, he must make good laws, possess virtues, and not base his power on impositions and chimeras.

CLIII.

THE DOMINANT PASSIONS AND CRIMES OF PRIESTCRAFT. WITH THE ASSISTANCE OF ITS PRETENDED GOD AND OF RELIGION, IT ASSERTS ITS PASSIONS AND COMMITS ITS CRIMES.

The ministers of religion have taken great care to make of their God a terrible, capricious, and changeable tyrant; it was necessary for them that He should be thus in order that He might lend Himself to their various interests. A God who would be just and good, without a mixture of caprice and perversity; a God who would constantly have the qualities of an honest man or of a compliant sovereign, would not suit His ministers. It is necessary to the priests that we tremble before their God, in order that we have recourse to them to obtain the means to be quieted. No man is a hero to his valet de chambre. It is not surprising that a God clothed by His priests in such a way as to cause others to fear Him, should rarely impose upon those priests themselves, or exert but little influence upon their conduct. Consequently we see them behave themselves in a uniform way in every land; everywhere they devour nations, debase souls, discourage industry, and sow discord under the pretext of the glory of their God. Ambition and avarice were at all times the dominating passions of the priesthood; everywhere the priest places himself above the sovereign and the laws; everywhere we see him occupied but with the interests of his pride, his cupidity, his despotic and vindictive mood; everywhere he substitutes expiations, sacrifices, ceremonies, and mysterious practices; in a word, inventions lucrative to himself for useful and social virtues. The mind is confounded and reason interdicted with the view of ridiculous practices and pitiable means which the ministers of the gods invented in every country to purify souls and render Heaven favorable to nations. Here, they practice circumcision upon a child to procure it Divine benevolence; there, they pour water upon his head to wash away the crimes which he could not yet have committed; in other places he is told to plunge himself into a river whose waters have the power to wash away all his impurities; in other places certain food is forbidden to him, whose use would not fail to excite celestial indignation; in other countries they order the sinful man to come periodically for the confession of his faults to a priest, who is often a greater sinner than he.

CLIV.

CHARLATANRY OF THE PRIESTS.

What would we say of a crowd of quacks, who every day would exhibit in a public place, selling their remedies and recommending them as infallible, while we should find them afflicted with the same infirmities which they pretend to cure? Would we have much confidence in the recipes of these charlatans, who would bawl out: "Take our remedies, their effects are infallible—they cure everybody except us?" What would we think to see these same charlatans pass their lives in complaining that their remedies never produce any effect upon the patients who take them? Finally, what idea would we form of the foolishness of the common man who, in spite of this confession, would continue to pay very high for remedies which will not be beneficial to him? The priests resemble alchemists, who boldly assert that they have the secret of making gold, while they scarcely have clothing enough to cover their nudity.

The ministers of religion incessantly declaim against the corruption of the age, and complain loudly of the little success of their teachings, at the same time they assure us that religion is the universal remedy, the true panacea for all human evils. These priests are sick themselves; however, men continue to frequent their stands and to have faith in their Divine antidotes, which, according to their own confession, cure nobody!

CLV.

COUNTLESS CALAMITIES ARE PRODUCED BY RELIGION, WHICH HAS TAINTED MORALITY AND DISTURBED ALL JUST IDEAS AND ALL SOUND DOCTRINES.

Religion, especially among modern people, in taking possession of morality, totally obscured its principles; it has rendered men unsocial from a sense of duty; it has forced them to be inhuman toward all those who did not think as they did. Theological disputes, equally unintelligible for the parties already irritated against each other, have unsettled empires, caused revolutions, ruined sovereigns, devastated the whole of Europe; these despicable quarrels could not be extinguished even in rivers of blood. After the extinction of Paganism the people established a religious principle of going into a frenzy, every time that an opinion was brought forth which their priests considered contrary to the holy doctrine. The votaries of a religion which preaches externally but charity, harmony, and peace, have shown themselves more ferocious than cannibals or savages every time that their instructors have excited them to the destruction of their brethren. There is no crime which men have not committed in the idea of pleasing the Deity or of appeasing His wrath. The idea of a terrible God who was represented as a despot, must necessarily have rendered His subjects wicked. Fear makes but slaves, and slaves are cowardly, low, cruel, and think they have a right to do anything when it is the question of gaining the good-will or of escaping the punishments of the master whom they fear. Liberty of thought can alone give to men humanity and grandeur of soul. The notion of a tyrant God can create but abject, angry, quarrelsome, intolerant slaves. Every religion which supposes a God easily irritated, jealous, vindictive, punctilious about His rights or His title, a God small enough to be offended at opinions which we have of Him, a God unjust enough to exact uniform ideas in regard to Him, such a religion becomes necessarily turbulent, unsocial, sanguinary; the worshipers of such a God never believe they can, without crime, dispense with hating and even destroying all those whom they designate as adversaries of this God; they would believe themselves traitors to the cause of their celestial Monarch, if they should live on good terms with rebellious fellow-citizens. To love what God hates, would it not be exposing one's self to His implacable hatred? Infamous persecutors, and you, religious cannibals! will you never feel the folly and injustice of your intolerant disposition? Do you not see that man is no more the master of his religious opinions, of his credulity or incredulity, than of the language which he learns in childhood, and which he can not change? To tell men to think as you do, is it not asking a foreigner to express his thoughts in your language? To punish a man for his erroneous opinions, is it not punishing him for having been educated differently from yourself? If I am incredulous, is it possible for me to banish from my mind the reasons which have unsettled my faith? If God allows men the freedom to damn themselves, is it your business? Are you wiser and more prudent than this God whose rights you wish to avenge?

CLVI.

EVERY RELIGION IS INTOLERANT, AND CONSEQUENTLY DESTRUCTIVE OF BENEFICENCE.

There is no religious person who, according to his temperament, does not hate, despise, or pity the adherents of a sect different from his own. The dominant religion (which is never but that of the sovereign and the armies) always makes its superiority felt in a very cruel and injurious manner toward the weaker sects. There does not exist yet upon earth a true tolerance; everywhere a jealous God is worshiped, and each nation believes itself His friend to the exclusion of all others.

Every nation boasts itself of worshiping the true God, the universal God, the Sovereign of Nature; but when we come to examine this Monarch of the world, we perceive that each organization, each sect, each religious party, makes of this powerful God but an inferior sovereign, whose cares and kindness extend themselves but over a small number of His subjects who pretend to have the exclusive advantage of His favors, and that He does not trouble Himself about the others.

The founders of religions, and the priests who maintain them, have intended to separate the nations which they indoctrinated, from other nations; they desired to separate their own flock by distinctive features; they gave to their votaries Gods inimical to other Gods as well as the forms of worship, dogmas, ceremonies, separately; they persuaded them especially that the religions of others were ungodly and abominable. By this infamous contrivance, these ambitious impostors took exclusive possession of the minds of their votaries, rendered them unsocial, and made them consider as outcasts all those who had not the same ideas and form of worship as their own. This is the way religion succeeded in closing the heart, and in banishing from it that affection which man ought to have for his fellow-being. Sociability, tolerance, humanity, these first virtues of all morality are totally in compatible with religious prejudices.

CLVII.

ABUSE OF A STATE RELIGION.

Every national religion has a tendency to make man vain, unsocial, and wicked; the first step toward humanity is to permit each one to follow peacefully the worship and the opinions which suit him. But such a conduct can not please the ministers of religion, who wish to have the right to tyrannize over even the thoughts of men. Blind and bigoted princes, you hate, you persecute, you devote heretics to torture, because you are persuaded that these unfortunate ones displease God. But do you not claim that your God is full of kindness? How can you hope to please Him by such barbarous actions which He can not help disapproving of? Besides, who told you that their opinions displease your God? Your priests told you! But who guarantees that your priests are not deceived themselves or that they do not wish to deceive you? It is these same priests! Princes! it is upon the perilous word of your priests that you commit the most atrocious and the most unheard-of crimes, with the idea of pleasing the Deity!

CLVIII.

RELIGION GIVES LICENSE TO THE FEROCITY OF THE PEOPLE BY LEGITIMIZING IT, AND AUTHORIZES CRIME BY TEACHING THAT IT CAN BE USEFUL TO THE DESIGNS OF GOD.

"Never," says Pascal, "do we do evil so thoroughly and so willingly as when we do it through a false principle of conscience." Nothing is more dangerous than a religion which licenses the ferocity of the people, and justifies in their eyes the blackest crimes; it puts no limits to their wickedness as soon as they believe it authorized by their God, whose interests, as they are told, can justify all their actions. If there is a question of religion, immediately the most civilized nations become true savages, and believe everything is permitted to them. The more cruel they are, the more agreeable they suppose themselves to be to their God, whose cause they imagine can not be sustained by too much zeal. All religions of the world have authorized countless crimes. The Jews, excited by the promises of their God, arrogated to themselves the right of exterminating whole nations; the Romans, whose faith was founded upon the oracles of their Gods, became real brigands, and conquered and ravaged the world; the Arabians, encouraged by their Divine preceptor, carried the sword and the flame among Christians and idolaters. The Christians, under pretext of spreading their holy religion, covered the two hemispheres a hundred times with blood.

In all events favorable to their own interests, which they always call the cause of God, the priests show us the finger of God. According to these principles, religious bigots have the luck of seeing the finger of God in revolts, in revolutions, massacres, regicides, prostitutions, infamies, and, if these things contribute to the advantage of religion, we can say, then, that God uses all sorts of means to secure His ends. Is there anything better calculated to annihilate every idea of morality in the minds of men, than to make them understand that their God, who is so powerful and so perfect, is often compelled to use crime to accomplish His designs?

CLIX.

REFUTATION OF THE ARGUMENT, THAT THE EVILS ATTRIBUTED TO RELIGION ARE BUT THE SAD EFFECTS OF THE PASSIONS OF MEN.

When we complain about the violence and evils which generally religion causes upon earth, we are answered at once, that these excesses are not due to religion, but that they are the sad effect of men's passions. I would ask, however, what unchained these passions? It is evidently religion; it is a zeal which renders inhuman, and which serves to cover the greatest infamy. Do not these disorders prove that religion, instead of restraining the passions of men, does but cover them with a cloak that sanctifies them; and that nothing would be more beneficial than to tear away this sacred cloak of which men make such a bad use? What horrors would be banished from society, if the wicked were deprived of a pretext so plausible for disturbing it!

Instead of cherishing peace among men, the priests stirred up hatred and strife. They pleaded their conscience, and pretended to have received from Heaven the right to be quarrelsome, turbulent, and rebellious. Do not the ministers of God consider themselves to be wronged, do they not pretend that His Divine Majesty is injured every time that the sovereigns have the temerity to try to prevent them from doing injury? The priests resemble that irritable woman, who cried out fire! murder! assassins! while her husband was holding her hands to prevent her from beating him.

CLX.

ALL MORALITY IS INCOMPATIBLE WITH RELIGIOUS OPINIONS.

Notwithstanding the bloody tragedies which religion has so often caused in this world, we are constantly told that there can be no morality without religion. If we judge theological opinions by their effects, we would be right in assuming that all morality is perfectly incompatible with the religious opinions of men. "Imitate God," is constantly repeated to us. Ah! what morals would we have if we should imitate this God! Which God should we imitate? Is it the deist's God? But even this God can not be a model of goodness for us. If He is the author of all, He is equally the author of the good and of the bad we see in this world; if He is the author of order, He is also the author of disorder, which would not exist without His permission; if He produces, He destroys; if He gives life, He also causes death; if He grants abundance, riches, prosperity, and peace, He permits or sends famines, poverty, calamities, and wars. How can you accept as a model of permanent beneficence the God of theism or of natural religion, whose favorable intentions are at every moment contradicted by everything that transpires in the world? Morality needs a firmer basis than the example of a God whose conduct varies, and whom we can not call good but by obstinately closing the eyes to the evil which He causes, or permits to be done in this world.

Shall we imitate the good and great Jupiter of ancient Paganism? To imitate such a God would be to take as a model a rebellious son, who wrests his father's throne from him and then mutilates his body; it is imitating a debauchee and adulterer, an incestuous, intemperate man, whose conduct would cause any reasonable mortal to blush. What would have become of men under the control of Paganism if they had imagined, according to Plato, that virtue consisted in imitating the gods?

Must we imitate the God of the Jews? Will we find a model for our conduct in Jehovah? He is truly a savage God, really created for an ignorant, cruel, and immoral people; He is a God who is constantly enraged, breathing only vengeance; who is without pity, who commands carnage and robbery; in a word, He is a God whose conduct can not serve as a model to an honest man, and who can be imitated but by a chief of brigands.

Shall we imitate, then, the Jesus of the Christians? Can this God, who died to appease the implacable fury of His Father, serve as an example which men ought to follow? Alas! we will see in Him but a God, or rather a fanatic, a misanthrope, who being plunged Himself into misery, and preaching to the wretched, advises them to be poor, to combat and extinguish nature, to hate pleasure, to seek sufferings, and to despise themselves; He tells them to leave father, mother, all the ties of life, in order to follow Him. What beautiful morality! you will say. It is admirable, no doubt; it must be Divine, because it is impracticable for men. But does not this sublime morality tend to render virtue despicable? According to this boasted morality of the man-God of the Christians, His disciples in this lower world are, like Tantalus, tormented with burning thirst, which they are not permitted to quench. Do not such morals give us a wonderful idea of nature's Author? If He has, as we are assured, created everything for the use of His creatures, by what strange caprice does He forbid the use of the good things which He has created for them? Is the pleasure which man constantly desires but a snare that God has maliciously laid in his path to entrap him?

CLXI.

THE MORALS OF THE GOSPEL ARE IMPRACTICABLE.

The votaries of Christ would like to make us regard as a miracle the establishment of their religion, which is in every respect contrary to nature, opposed to all the inclinations of the heart, an enemy to physical pleasures. But the austerity of a doctrine has a tendency to render it more wonderful to the ignorant. The same reason which makes us respect, as Divine and supernatural, inconceivable mysteries, causes us to admire, as Divine and supernatural, a morality impracticable and beyond the power of man. To admire morals and to practice them, are two very different things. All the Christians continually admire the morals of the Gospel, but it is practiced but by a small number of saints; admired by people who themselves avoid imitating their conduct, under the pretext that they are lacking either the power or the grace.

The whole universe is infected more or less with a religious morality which is founded upon the opinion that to please the Deity it is necessary to render one's self unhappy upon earth. We see in all parts of our globe penitents, hermits, fakirs, fanatics, who seem to have studied profoundly the means of tormenting themselves for the glory of a Being whose goodness they all agree in celebrating. Religion, by its essence, is the enemy of joy and of the welfare of men. "Blessed are those who suffer!" Woe to those who have abundance and joy! These are the rare revelations which Christianity teaches!

CLXII.

A SOCIETY OF SAINTS WOULD BE IMPOSSIBLE.

In what consists the saint of all religions? It is a man who prays, fasts, who torments himself, who avoids the world, who, like an owl, is pleased but in solitude, who abstains from all pleasure, who seems frightened at every object which turns him a moment from his fanatical meditations. Is this virtue? Is a being of this stamp of any use to himself or to others? Would not society be dissolved, and would not men retrograde into barbarism, if each one should be fool enough to wish to be a saint?

It is evident that the literal and rigorous practice of the Divine morality of the Christians would lead nations to ruin. A Christian who would attain perfection, ought to drive away from his mind all that can alienate him from heaven—his true country. He sees upon earth but temptations, snares, and opportunities to go astray; he must fear science as injurious to faith; he must avoid industry, as it is a means of obtaining riches, which are fatal to salvation; he must renounce preferments and honors, as things capable of exciting his pride and calling his attention away from his soul; in a word, the sublime morality of Christ, if it were not impracticable, would sever all the ties of society.

A saint in the world is no more useful than a saint in the desert; the saint has an unhappy, discontented, and often irritable, turbulent disposition; his zeal often obliges him, conscientiously, to disturb society by opinions or dreams which his vanity makes him accept as inspirations from

Heaven. The annals of all religions are filled with accounts of anxious, intractable, seditious saints, who have distinguished themselves by ravages that, for the greater glory of God, they have scattered throughout the universe. If the saints who live in solitude are useless, those who live in the world are very often dangerous. The vanity of performing a role, the desire of distinguishing themselves in the eyes of the stupid vulgar by a strange conduct, constitute usually the distinctive characteristics of great saints; pride persuades them that they are extraordinary men, far above human nature; beings who are more perfect than others; chosen ones, which God looks upon with more complaisance than the rest of mortals. Humility in a saint is, is a general rule, but a pride more refined than that of common men. It must be a very ridiculous vanity which can determine a man to continually war with his own nature!

CLXIII.

HUMAN NATURE IS NOT DEPRAVED; AND A MORALITY WHICH CONTRADICTS THIS FACT IS NOT MADE FOR MAN.

A morality which contradicts the nature of man is not made for him. But you will say that man's nature is depraved. In what consists this pretended depravity? Is it because he has passions? But are not passions the very essence of man? Must he not seek, desire, love that which is, or that which he believes to be, essential to his happiness? Must he not fear and avoid that which he judges injurious or fatal to him? Excite his passions by useful objects; let him attach himself to these same objects, divert him by sensible and known motives from that which can do him or others harm, and you will make of him a reasonable and virtuous being. A man without passions would be equally indifferent to vice and to virtue.

Holy doctors! you constantly tell us that man's nature is perverted; you tell us that the way of all flesh is corrupt; you tell us that nature gives us but inordinate inclinations. In this case you accuse your God, who has not been able or willing to keep this nature in its original perfection. If this nature became corrupted, why did not this God repair it? The Christian assures me that human nature is repaired, that the death of his God has reestablished it in its integrity. How comes it then, that human nature, notwithstanding the death of a God, is still depraved? Is it, then, a pure loss that your God died? What becomes of His omnipotence and His victory over the Devil, if it is true that the Devil still holds the empire which, according to you, he has always exercised in the world?

Death, according to Christian theology, is the penalty of sin. This opinion agrees with that of some savage Negro nations, who imagine that the death of a man is always the supernatural effect of the wrath of the Gods. The Christians firmly believe that Christ has delivered them from sin, while they see that, in their religion as in the others, man is subject to death. To say that Jesus Christ has delivered us from sin, is it not claiming that a judge has granted pardon to a guilty man, while we see him sent to torture?

CLXIV.

OF JESUS CHRIST, THE PRIEST'S GOD.

If, closing our eyes upon all that transpires in this world, we should rely upon the votaries of the Christian religion, we would believe that the coming of our Divine Saviour has produced the most wonderful revolution and the most complete reform in the morals of nations. The Messiah, according to Pascal, [See Thoughts of Pascal] ought of Himself alone to produce a great, select, and holy people; conducting and nourishing it, and introducing it into the place of repose and sanctity, rendering it holy to God, making it the temple of God, saving it from the wrath of God, delivering it from the servitude of sin, giving laws to this people, engraving these laws upon their hearts, offering Himself to God for them, crushing the head of the serpent, etc. This great man has forgotten to show us the people upon whom His Divine Messiah has produced the miraculous effects of which He speaks with so much emphasis; so far, it seems, they do not exist upon the earth!

If we examine ever so little the morals of the Christian nations, and listen to the clamors of their priests, we will be obliged to conclude that their God, Jesus Christ, preached without fruit, without success; that His Almighty will still finds in men a resistance, over which this God either can not or does not wish to triumph. The morality of this Divine Doctor which His disciples admire so much, and practice so little, is followed during a whole century but by half a dozen of obscure saints, fanatical and ignorant monks, who alone will have the glory of shining in the celestial court;

all the remainder of mortals, although redeemed by the blood of this God, will be the prey of eternal flames.

CLXV.

THE DOGMA OF THE REMISSION OF SINS HAS BEEN INVENTED IN THE INTEREST OF THE PRIESTS.

When a man has a great desire to sin, he thinks very little about his God; more than this, whatever crimes he may have committed, he always flatters himself that this God will mitigate the severity of his punishments. No mortal seriously believes that his conduct can damn him. Although he fears a terrible God, who often makes him tremble, every time he is strongly tempted he succumbs and sees but a God of mercy, the idea of whom quiets him. Does he do evil? He hopes to have the time to correct himself, and promises earnestly to repent some day.

There are in the religious pharmacy infallible receipts for calming the conscience; the priests in every country possess sovereign secrets for disarming the wrath of Heaven. However true it may be that the anger of Deity is appeased by prayers, by offerings, by sacrifices, by penitential tears, we have no right to say that religion holds in check the irregularities of men; they will first sin, and afterward seek the means to reconcile God. Every religion which expiates, and which promises the remission of crimes, if it restrains any, it encourages the great number to commit evil. Notwithstanding His immutability, God is, in all the religions of this world, a veritable Proteus. His priests show Him now armed with severity, and then full of clemency and gentleness; now cruel and pitiless, and then easily reconciled by the repentance and the tears of the sinners.

Consequently, men face the Deity in the manner which conforms the most to their present interests. An always wrathful God would repel His worshipers, or cast them into despair. Men need a God who becomes angry and who can be appeased; if His anger alarms a few timid souls, His clemency reassures the determined wicked ones who intend to have recourse sooner or later to the means of reconciling themselves with Him; if the judgments of God frighten a few faint-hearted devotees who already by temperament and by habitude are not inclined to evil, the treasures of Divine mercy reassure the greatest criminals, who have reason to hope that they will participate in them with the others.

CLXVI.

THE FEAR OF GOD IS POWERLESS AGAINST HUMAN PASSIONS.

The majority of men rarely think of God, or, at least, do not occupy themselves much with Him. The idea of God has so little stability, it is so afflicting, that it can not hold the imagination for a long time, except in some sad and melancholy visionists who do not constitute the majority of the inhabitants of this world. The common man has no conception of it; his weak brain becomes perplexed the moment he attempts to think of Him. The business man thinks of nothing but his affairs; the courtier of his intrigues; worldly men, women, youth, of their pleasures; dissipation soon dispels the wearisome notions of religion. The ambitious, the avaricious, and the debauchee sedulously lay aside speculations too feeble to counterbalance their diverse passions.

Whom does the idea of God overawe? A few weak men disappointed and disgusted with this world; some persons whose passions are already extinguished by age, by infirmities, or by reverses of fortune. Religion is a restraint but for those whose temperament or circumstances have already subjected them to reason. The fear of God does not prevent any from committing sin but those who do not wish to sin very much, or who are no longer in a condition to sin. To tell men that Divinity punishes crime in this world, is to claim as a fact that which experience contradicts constantly The most wicked men are usually the arbiters of the world, and those whom fortune blesses with its favors. To convince us of the judgments of God by sending us to the other life, is to make us accept conjectures in order to destroy facts which we can not dispute.

CLXVII.

THE INVENTION OF HELL IS TOO ABSURD TO PREVENT EVIL.

No one dreams about another life when he is very much absorbed in objects which he meets on earth. In the eyes of a passionate lover, the presence of his mistress extinguishes the fires of hell, and her charms blot out all the pleasures of Paradise. Woman! you leave, you say, your lover for your God? It is that your lover is no longer the same in your estimation; or your lover leaves you, and you must fill the void which is made in your heart. Nothing is more common than to see ambitious, perverse, corrupt, and immoral men who are religious, and who sometimes exhibit even zeal in its behalf; if they do not practice religion, they promise themselves they will practice it some day; they keep it in reserve as a remedy which, sooner or later, will be necessary to quiet the conscience for the evil which they intend yet to do. Besides, devotees and priests being a very numerous, active, and powerful party, it is not astonishing to see impostors and thieves seek for its support in order to gain their ends. We will be told, no doubt, that many honest people are sincerely religious without profit; but is uprightness of heart always accompanied with intelligence? We are cited to a great number of learned men, men of genius, who are very religious. This proves that men of genius can have prejudices, can be pusillanimous, can have an imagination which seduces them and prevents them from examining objects coolly. Pascal proves nothing in favor of religion, except that a man of genius can possess a grain of weakness, and is but a child when he is weak enough to listen to prejudices. Pascal himself tells us "that the mind can be strong and narrow, and just as extended as it is weak." He says more: "We can have our senses all right, and not be equally able in all things; because there are men who, being right in a certain sphere of things, lose themselves in others."

CLXVIII.

ABSURDITY OF THE MORALITY AND OF THE RELIGIOUS VIRTUES ESTABLISHED SOLELY IN THE INTEREST OF THE PRIESTS.

What is virtue according to theology? It is, we are told, the conformity of men's actions with the will of God. But who is God? He is a being whom no one is able to conceive of, and whom, consequently, each one modifies in his own way. What is the will of God? It is what men who have seen God, or whom God has inspired, have told us. Who are those who have seen God? They are either fanatics, or scoundrels, or ambitious men, whose word we can not rely upon. To found morality upon a God that each man represents differently, that each one composes by his own idea, whom everybody arranges according to his own temperament and his own interest, is evidently founding morality upon the caprice and upon the imagination of men; it is basing it upon the whims of a sect, faction, or party, who, excluding all others, claim to have the advantage of worshiping the true God.

To establish morality, or the duties of man, upon the Divine will, is founding it upon the wishes, the reveries, or the interests of those who make God talk without fear of contradiction. In every religion the priests alone have the right to decide upon what pleases or displeases their God; we may rest assured that they will decide upon what pleases or displeases themselves.

The dogmas, ceremonies, the morality and the virtues which all religions of the world prescribe, are visibly calculated only to extend the power or to increase the emoluments of the founders and of the ministers of these religions; the dogmas are obscure, inconceivable, frightful, and, thereby, very liable to cause the imagination to wander, and to render the common man more docile to those who wish to domineer over him; the ceremonies and practices procure fortune or consideration to the priests; the religious morals and virtues consist in a submissive faith, which prevents reasoning; in a devout humility, which assures to the priests the submission of their slaves; in an ardent zeal, when the question of religion is agitated; that is to say, when the interest of these priests is considered, all religious virtues having evidently for their object the advantage of the priests.

CLXIX.

WHAT DOES THAT CHRISTIAN CHARITY AMOUNT TO, SUCH AS THEOLOGIANS TEACH AND PRACTICE?

When we reproach the theologians with the sterility of their religious virtues, they praise, with emphasis, charity, that tender love of our neighbor which Christianity makes an essential duty for its disciples. But, alas! what becomes of this pretended charity as soon as we examine the actions of the Lord's ministers? Ask if you must love your neighbor if he is impious, heretical, and incredulous, that is to say, if he does not think as they do? Ask them if you must tolerate opinions contrary to those which they profess? Ask them if the Lord can show indulgence to those who are in error? Immediately their charity disappears, and the dominating clergy will tell you that the prince carries the sword but to sustain the interests of the Most High; they will tell you that for love of the neighbor, you must persecute, imprison, exile, or burn him. You will find tolerance among a few priests who are persecuted themselves, but who put aside Christian charity as soon as they have the power to persecute in their turn.

The Christian religion which was originally preached by beggars and by very wretched men, strongly recommends alms-giving under the name of charity; the faith of Mohammed equally makes it an indispensable duty. Nothing, no doubt, is better suited to humanity than to assist the unfortunate, to clothe the naked, to lend a charitable hand to whoever needs it. But would it not be more humane and more charitable to foresee the misery and to prevent the poor from increasing? If religion, instead of deifying princes, had but taught them to respect the property of their subjects, to be just, and to exercise but their legitimate rights, we should not see such a great number of mendicants in their realms. A greedy, unjust, tyrannical government multiplies misery; the rigor of taxes produces discouragement, idleness, indigence, which, on their part, produce robbery, murders, and all kinds of crime. If the sovereigns had more humanity, charity, and justice, their States would not be peopled by so many unfortunate ones whose misery becomes impossible to soothe.

The Christian and Mohammedan States are filled with vast and richly endowed hospitals, in which we admire the pious charity of the kings and of the sultans who erected them. Would it not have been more humane to govern the people well, to procure them ease, to excite and to favor industry and trade, to permit them to enjoy in safety the fruits of their labors, than to oppress them under a despotic yoke, to impoverish them by senseless wars, to reduce them to mendicity in order to gratify an immoderate luxury, and afterward build sumptuous monuments which can contain but a very small portion of those whom they have rendered miserable? Religion, by its virtues, has but given a change to men; instead of foreseeing evils, it applies but insufficient remedies. The ministers of Heaven have always known how to benefit themselves by the calamities of others; public misery became their element; they made themselves the administrators of the goods of the poor, the distributors of alms, the depositaries of charities; thereby they extended and sustained at all times their power over the unfortunates who usually compose the most numerous, the most anxious, the most seditious part of society. Thus the greatest evils are made profitable to the ministers of the Lord.

The Christian priests tell us that the goods which they possess are the goods of the poor, and pretend by this title that their possessions are sacred; consequently, the sovereigns and the people press themselves to accumulate lands, revenues, treasures for them; under pretext of charity, our spiritual guides have become very opulent, and enjoy, in the sight of the impoverished nations, goods which were destined but for the miserable; the latter, far from murmuring about it, applaud a deceitful generosity which enriches the Church, but which very rarely alleviates the sufferings of the poor.

According to the principles of Christianity, poverty itself is a virtue, and it is this virtue which the sovereigns and the priests make their slaves observe the most. According to these ideas, a great number of pious Christians have renounced with good-will the perishable riches of the earth; have distributed their patrimony to the poor, and have retired into a desert to live a life of voluntary indigence. But very soon this enthusiasm, this supernatural taste for misery, must surrender to nature. The successors to these voluntary poor, sold to the religious people their prayers and their powerful intercession with the Deity; they became rich and powerful; thus, monks and hermits lived in idleness, and, under the pretext of charity, devoured insultingly the substance of the poor. Poverty of spirit was that of which religion made always the greatest use. The fundamental virtue of all religion, that is to say, the most useful one to its ministers, is faith. It consists in an unlimited credulity, which causes men to believe, without examination, all that which the interpreters of the Deity wish them to believe. With the aid of this wonderful virtue, the priests became the arbiters of justice and of injustice; of good and of evil; they found it easy to commit crimes when crimes became necessary to their interests. Implicit faith has been the source of the greatest outrages which have been committed upon the earth.

CLXX.

CONFESSION, THAT GOLDEN MINE FOR THE PRIESTS, HAS DESTROYED THE TRUE PRINCIPLES OF MORALITY.

He who first proclaimed to the nations that, when man had wronged man, he must ask God's pardon, appease His wrath by presents, and offer Him sacrifices, obviously subverted the true principles of morality. According to these ideas, men imagine that they can obtain from the King of Heaven, as well as from the kings of the earth, permission to be unjust and wicked, or at least pardon for the evil which they might commit.

Morality is founded upon the relations, the needs, and the constant interests of the inhabitants of the earth; the relations which subsist between men and God are either entirely unknown or imaginary. The religion associating God with men has visibly weakened or destroyed the ties which unite men.

Mortals imagine that they can, with impunity, injure each other by making a suitable reparation to the Almighty Being, who is supposed to have the right to remit all the injuries done to His creatures. Is there anything more liable to encourage wickedness and to embolden to crime, than to persuade men that there exists an invisible being who has the right to pardon injustice, rapine, perfidy, and all the outrages they can inflict upon society? Encouraged by these fatal ideas, we see the most perverse men abandon themselves to the greatest crimes, and expect to repair them by imploring Divine mercy; their conscience rests in peace when a priest assures them that Heaven is quieted by sincere repentance, which is very useless to the world; this priest consoles them in the name of Deity, if they consent in reparation of their faults to divide with His ministers the fruits of their plunderings, of their frauds, and of their wickedness. Morality united to religion, becomes necessarily subordinate to it. In the mind of a religious person, God must be preferred to His creatures; "It is better to obey Him than men!" The interests of the Celestial Monarch must be above those of weak mortals. But the interests of Heaven are evidently the interests of the ministers of Heaven; from which it follows evidently, that in all religions, the priests, under pretext of Heaven's interest's, or of God's glory, will be able to dispense with the duties of human morals when they do not agree with the duties which God is entitled to impose.

Besides, He who has the power to pardon crimes, has He not the right to order them committed?

CLXXI.

THE SUPPOSITION OF THE EXISTENCE OF A GOD IS NOT NECESSARY TO MORALITY.

We are constantly told that without a God, there can be no moral obligation; that it is necessary for men and for the sovereigns themselves to have a lawgiver sufficiently powerful to compel them to be moral; moral obligation implies a law; but this law arises from the eternal and necessary relations of things among themselves, which have nothing in common with the existence of a God. The rules which govern men's conduct spring from their own nature, which they are supposed to know, and not from the Divine nature, of which they have no conception; these rules compel us to render ourselves estimable or contemptible, amiable or hateful, worthy of reward or of punishments, happy or unhappy, according to the extent to which we observe them. The law that compels man not to harm himself, is inherent in the nature of a sensible being, who, no matter how he came into this world, or what can be his fate in another, is compelled by his very nature to seek his welfare and to shun evil, to love pleasure and to fear pain. The law which compels a man not to harm others and to do good, is inherent in the nature of sensible beings living in society, who, by their nature, are compelled to despise those who do them no good, and to detest those who oppose their happiness. Whether there exists a God or not, whether this God has spoken or not, men's moral duties will always be the same so long as they possess their own nature; that is to say, so long as they are sensible beings. Do men need a God whom they do not know, or an invisible lawgiver, or a mysterious religion, or chimerical fears in order to comprehend that all excess tends ultimately to destroy them, and that in order to preserve themselves they must abstain from it; that in order to be loved by others, they must do good; that doing evil is a sure means of incurring their hatred and vengeance? "Before the law there was no sin." Nothing is more false than this maxim. It is enough for a man to be what he is, to be a sensible being in order to distinguish that which pleases or displeases him. It is enough that a man knows that another man is a sensible being like himself, in order for him to know what is useful or injurious to him. It is enough that man needs his fellow-creature, in order that he should fear that he might produce unfavorable impressions upon him. Thus a sentient and thinking being needs but to feel and to think, in order to discover that which is due to him and to others. I feel, and another feels, like myself; this is the foundation of all morality.

CLXXII.

RELIGION AND ITS SUPERNATURAL MORALITY ARE FATAL TO THE PEOPLE, AND OPPOSED TO MAN'S NATURE.

We can judge of the merit of a system of morals but by its conformity with man's nature. According to this comparison, we have a right to reject it, if we find it detrimental to the welfare of mankind. Whoever has seriously meditated upon religion and its supernatural morality, whoever has weighed its advantages and disadvantages, will become convinced that they are both injurious to the interests of the human race, or directly opposed to man's nature.

"People, to arms! Your God's cause is at stake! Heaven is outraged! Faith is in danger! Down upon infidelity, blasphemy, and heresy!"

By the magical power of these valiant words, which the people never understand, the priests in all ages were the leaders in the revolts of nations, in dethroning kings, in kindling civil wars, and in imprisoning men. When we chance to examine the important objects which have excited the Celestial wrath and produced so many ravages upon the earth, it is found that the foolish reveries and the strange conjectures of some theologian who did not understand himself, or, the pretensions of the clergy, have severed all ties of society and inundated the human race in its own blood and tears.

CLXXIII.

HOW THE UNION OF RELIGION AND POLITICS IS FATAL TO THE PEOPLE AND TO THE KINGS.

The sovereigns of this world in associating the Deity in the government of their realms, in pretending to be His lieutenants and His representatives upon earth, in admitting that they hold their power from Him, must necessarily accept His ministers as rivals or as masters. Is it, then, astonishing that the priests have often made the kings feel the superiority of the Celestial Monarch? Have they not more than once made the temporal princes understand that the greatest physical power is compelled to surrender to the spiritual power of opinion? Nothing is more difficult than to serve two masters, especially when they do not agree upon what they demand of their subjects. The anion of religion with politics has necessarily caused a double legislation in the States. The law of God, interpreted by His priests, is often contrary to the law of the sovereign or to the interest of the State. When the princes are firm, and sure of the love of their subjects, God's law is sometimes obliged to comply with the wise intentions of the temporal sovereign; but more often the sovereign authority is obliged to retreat before the Divine authority, that is to say, before the interests of the clergy. Nothing is more dangerous for a prince, than to meddle with ecclesiastical affairs (to put his hands into the holy-water pot), that is to say, to attempt the reform of abuses consecrated by religion. God is never more angry than when the Divine rights, the privileges, the possessions, and the immunities of His priests are interfered with.

Metaphysical speculations or the religious opinions of men, never influence their conduct except when they believe them conformed to their interests. Nothing proves this truth more forcibly than the conduct of a great number of princes in regard to the spiritual power, which we see them very often resist. Should not a sovereign who is persuaded of the importance and the rights of religion, conscientiously feel himself obliged to receive with respect the orders of his priests, and consider them as commandments of the Deity? There was a time when the kings and the people, more conformable, and convinced of the rights of the spiritual power, became its slaves, surrendered to it on all occasions, and were but docile instruments in its hands; this happy time is no more. By a strange inconsistency, we sometimes see the most religious monarchs oppose the enterprises of those whom they regard as God's ministers. A sovereign who is filled with religion or respect for his God, ought to be constantly prostrate before his priests, and regard them as his true sovereigns. Is there a power upon the earth which has the right to measure itself with that of the Most High?

CLXXIV.

CREEDS ARE BURDENSOME AND RUINOUS TO THE MAJORITY OF NATIONS.

Have the princes who believe themselves interested in propagating the prejudices of their subjects, reflected well upon the effects which are produced by privileged demagogues, who have the right to speak when they choose, and excite in the name of Heaven the passions of many millions of their subjects? What ravages would not these holy haranguers cause should they conspire to disturb a State, as they have so often done?

Nothing is more onerous and more ruinous for the greatest part of the nations than the worship of their Gods! Everywhere their ministers not only rank as the first order in the State, but also enjoy the greater portion of society's benefits, and have the right to levy continual taxes upon their fellow-citizens. What real advantages do these organs of the Most High procure for the people in exchange for the immense profits which they draw from them? Do they give them in exchange for their wealth and their courtesies anything but mysteries, hypotheses, ceremonies, subtle questions, interminable quarrels, which very often their States must pay for with their blood?

CLXXV.

RELIGION PARALYZES MORALITY.

Religion, which claims to be the firmest support of morality, evidently deprives it of its true motor, to substitute imaginary motors, inconceivable chimeras, which, being obviously contrary to common sense, can not be firmly believed by any one. Everybody assures us that he believes firmly in a God who rewards and punishes; everybody claims to be persuaded of the existence of a hell and of a Paradise; however, do we see that these ideas render men better or counterbalance in the minds of the greatest number of them the slightest interest? Each one assures us that he is afraid of God's judgments, although each one gives vent to his passions when he believes himself sure of escaping the judgments of men. The fear of invisible powers is rarely as great as the fear of visible powers. Unknown or distant sufferings make less impression upon people than the erected gallows, or the example of a hanged man. There is scarcely any courtier who fears God's anger more than the displeasure of his master. A pension, a title, a ribbon, are sufficient to make one forget the torments of hell and the pleasures of the celestial court. A woman's caresses expose him every day to the displeasure of the Most High. A joke, a banter, a bon-mot, make more impression upon the man of the world than all the grave notions of his religion. Are we not assured that a true repentance is sufficient to appease Divinity? However, we do not see that this true repentance is sincerely expressed; at least, we very rarely see great thieves, even in the hour of death, restore the goods which they know they have unjustly acquired. Men persuade themselves, no doubt, that they will submit to the eternal fire, if they can not guarantee themselves against it. But as settlements can be made with Heaven by giving the Church a portion of their fortunes, there are very few religious thieves who do not die perfectly quieted about the manner in which they gained their riches in this world.

CLXXVI.

FATAL CONSEQUENCES OF PIETY.

Even by the confession of the most ardent defenders of religion and of its usefulness, nothing is more rare than sincere conversions; to which we might add, nothing is more useless to society. Men do not become disgusted with the world until the world is disgusted with them; a woman gives herself to God only when the world no longer wants her. Her vanity finds in religious devotion a role which occupies her and consoles her for the ruin of her charms. She passes her time in the most trifling practices, parties, intrigues, invectives, and slander; zeal furnishes her the means of distinguishing herself and becoming an object of consideration in the religious circle. If the bigots have the talent to please God and His priests, they rarely possess that of pleasing society or of rendering themselves useful to it. Religion for a devotee is a veil which covers and justifies all his passions, his pride, his bad humor, his anger, his vengeance, his impatience, his bitterness. Religion arrogates to itself a tyrannical superiority which banishes from commerce all gentleness, gaiety, and joy; it gives the right to censure others; to capture and to exterminate the infidels for the glory of God; it is very common to be religious and to have none of the virtues or the qualities necessary to social life.

CLXXVII.

THE SUPPOSITION OF ANOTHER LIFE IS NEITHER CONSOLING TO MAN NOR NECESSARY TO MORALITY.

We are assured that the dogma of another life is of the greatest importance to the peace of society; it is imagined that without it men would have no motives for doing good. Why do we need terrors and fables to teach any reasonable man how he ought to conduct himself upon earth? Does not each one of us see that he has the greatest interest in deserving the approbation, esteem, and kindness of the beings which surround him, and in avoiding all that can cause the censure, the contempt, and the resentment of society? No matter how short the duration of a festival, of a conversation, or of a visit may be, does not each one of us wish to act a befitting part in it, agreeable to himself and to others? If life is but a passage, let us try to make it easy; it can not be so if we lack the regards of those who travel with us.

Religion, which is so sadly occupied with its gloomy reveries, represents man to us as but a pilgrim upon earth; it concludes that in order to travel with more safety, he should travel alone; renounce the pleasures which he meets and deprive himself of the amusements which could console him for the fatigues and the weariness of the road. A stoical and morose philosophy sometimes gives us counsels as senseless as religion; but a more rational philosophy inspires us to strew flowers on life's pathway; to dispel melancholy and panic terrors; to link our interests with those of our traveling companions; to divert ourselves by gaiety and honest pleasures from the pains and the crosses to which we are so often exposed. We are made to feel, that in order to travel pleasantly, we should abstain from that which could become injurious to ourselves, and to avoid with great care that which could make us odious to our associates.

CLXXVIII.

AN ATHEIST HAS MORE MOTIVES FOR ACTING UPRIGHTLY, MORE CONSCIENCE, THAN A RELIGIOUS PERSON.

It is asked what motives has an atheist for doing right. He can have the motive of pleasing himself and his fellow-creatures; of living happily and tranquilly; of making himself loved and respected by men, whose existence and whose dispositions are better known than those of a being impossible to understand. Can he who fears not the Gods, fear anything? He can fear men, their contempt, their disrespect, and the punishments which the laws inflict; finally, he can fear himself; he can be afraid of the remorse that all those experience whose conscience reproaches them for having deserved the hatred of their fellow-beings. Conscience is the inward testimony which we render to ourselves for having acted in such a manner as to deserve the esteem or the censure of those with whom we associate. This conscience is based upon the knowledge which we have of men, and of the sentiments which our actions must awaken in them. A religious person's conscience persuades him that he has pleased or displeased his God, of whom he has no idea, and whose obscure and doubtful intentions are explained to him only by suspicious men, who know no more of the essence of Divinity than he does, and who do not agree upon what can please or displease God. In a word, the conscience of a credulous man is guided by men whose own conscience is in error, or whose interest extinguishes intelligence.

Can an atheist have conscience? What are his motives for abstaining from secret vices and crimes of which other men are ignorant, and which are beyond the reach of laws? He can be assured by constant experience that there is no vice which, in the nature of things, does not bring its own punishment. If he wishes to preserve himself, he will avoid all those excesses which can be injurious to his health; he would not desire to live and linger, thus becoming a burden to himself and others. In regard to secret crimes, he would avoid them through fear of being ashamed of himself, from whom he can not hide. If he has reason, he will know the price of the esteem that an honest man should have for himself. He will know, besides, that unexpected circumstances can unveil to the eyes of others the conduct which he feels interested in concealing. The other world gives no motive for doing well to him who finds no motive for it here.

CLXXIX.

AN ATHEISTICAL KING WOULD BE PREFERABLE TO ONE WHO IS RELIGIOUS AND WICKED, AS WE OFTEN SEE THEM.

The speculating atheist, the theist will tell us, may be an honest man, but his writings will cause atheism in politics. Princes and ministers, being no longer restrained by the fear of God, will give themselves up without scruple to the most frightful excesses. But no matter what we can suppose of the depravity of an atheist on a throne, can it ever be any greater or more injurious than that of so many conquerors, tyrants, persecutors, of ambitious and perverse courtiers, who, without being atheists, but who, being very often religious, do not cease to make humanity groan under the weight of their crimes? Can an atheistical king inflict more evil on the world than a Louis XI., a Philip II., a Richelieu, who have all allied religion with crime? Nothing is rarer than atheistical princes, and nothing more common than very bad and very religious tyrants.

CLXXX.

THE MORALITY ACQUIRED BY PHILOSOPHY IS SUFFICIENT TO VIRTUE.

Any man who reflects can not fail of knowing his duties, of discovering the relations which subsist between men, of meditating upon his own nature, of discerning his needs, his inclinations, and his desires, and of perceiving what he owes to the beings necessary to his own happiness. These reflections naturally lead to the knowledge of the morality which is the most essential for society. Every man who loves to retire within himself in order to study and seek for the principles of things, has no very dangerous passions; his greatest passion will be to know the truth, and his greatest ambition to show it to others. Philosophy is beneficial in cultivating the heart and the mind. In regard to morals, has not he who reflects and reasons the advantage over him who does not reason?

If ignorance is useful to priests and to the oppressors of humanity, it is very fatal to society. Man, deprived of intelligence, does not enjoy the use of his reason; man, deprived of reason and intelligence, is a savage, who is liable at any moment to be led into crime. Morality, or the science of moral duties, is acquired but by the study of man and his relations. He who does not reflect for himself does not know true morals, and can not walk the road of virtue. The less men reason, the more wicked they are. The barbarians, the princes, the great, and the dregs of society, are generally the most wicked because they are those who reason the least. The religious man never reflects, and avoids reasoning; he fears examination; he follows authority; and very often an erroneous conscience makes him consider it a holy duty to commit evil. The incredulous man reasons, consults experience, and prefers it to prejudice. If he has reasoned justly, his conscience becomes clear; he finds more real motives for right-doing than the religious man, who has no motives but his chimeras, and who never listens to reason. Are not the motives of the incredulous man strong enough to counterbalance his passions? Is he blind enough not to recognize the interests which should restrain him? Well! he will be vicious and wicked; but even then he will be no worse and no better than many credulous men who, notwithstanding religion and its sublime precepts, continue to lead a life which this very religion condemns. Is a credulous murderer less to be feared than a murderer who does not believe anything? Is a religious tyrant any less a tyrant than an irreligious one?

CLXXXI.

OPINIONS RARELY INFLUENCE CONDUCT.

There is nothing more rare in the world than consistent men. Their opinions do not influence their conduct, except when they conform to their temperament, their passions, and to their interests. Religious opinions, according to daily experience, produce much more evil than good; they are injurious, because they very often agree with the passions of tyrants, fanatics, and priests; they produce no effect, because they have not the power to balance the present interests of the majority of men. Religious principles are always put aside when they are opposed to ardent desires; without being incredulous, they act as if they believed nothing. We risk being deceived when we judge the opinions of men by their conduct or their conduct by their opinions. A very religious man, notwithstanding the austere and cruel principles of a bloody religion, will sometimes be, by a fortunate inconsistency, humane, tolerant, moderate; in this case the principles of his religion do not agree with the mildness of his disposition. A libertine, a debauchee, a hypocrite, an adulterer, or a thief will often show us that he has the clearest ideas of morals. Why do they not practice them? It is because neither their temperament, their interests, nor their habits agree with their sublime theories. The rigid principles of Christian morality, which so many attempt to pass off as Divine, have but very little influence upon the conduct of those who preach them to others. Do they not tell us every day to do what they preach, and not what they practice?

The religious partisans generally designate the incredulous as libertines. It may be that many incredulous people are immoral; this immorality is due to their temperament, and not to their opinions. But what has their conduct to do with these opinions? Can not an immoral man be a good physician, a good architect, a good geometer, a good logician, a good metaphysician? With an irreproachable conduct, one can be ignorant upon many things, and reason very badly. When truth is presented, it matters not from whom it comes. Let us not judge men by their opinions, or opinions by men; let us judge men by their conduct; and their opinions by their conformity with experience, reason, and their usefulness for mankind.

CLXXXII.

REASON LEADS MEN TO IRRELIGION AND TO ATHEISM, BECAUSE RELIGION IS ABSURD, AND THE GOD OF THE PRIESTS IS A MALICIOUS AND FEROCIOUS BEING.

Every man who reasons soon becomes incredulous, because reasoning proves to him that theology is but a tissue of falsehoods; that religion is contrary to all principles of common sense; that it gives a false color to all human knowledge. The rational man becomes incredulous, because he sees that religion, far from rendering men happier, is the first cause of the greatest disorders, and of the permanent calamities with which the human race is afflicted. The man who seeks his well-being and his own tranquillity, examines his religion and is undeceived, because he finds it inconvenient and useless to pass his life in trembling at phantoms which are made but to intimidate silly women or children. If, sometimes, libertinage, which reasons but little, leads to irreligion, the man who is regular in his morals can have very legitimate motives for examining his religion, and for banishing it from his mind. Too weak to intimidate the wicked, in whom vice has become deeply rooted, religious terrors afflict, torment, and burden imaginative minds. If souls have courage and elasticity, they shake off a yoke which they bear unwillingly. If weak or timorous, they wear the yoke during their whole life, and they grow old, trembling, or at least they live under burdensome uncertainty.

The priests have made of God such a malicious, ferocious being, so ready to be vexed, that there are few men in the world who do not wish at the bottom of their hearts that this God did not exist. We can not live happy if we are always in fear. You worship a terrible God, O religious people! Alas! And yet you hate Him; you wish that He was not. Can we avoid wishing the absence or the destruction of a master, the idea of whom can but torment the mind? It is the dark colors in which the priests paint the Deity which revolt men, moving them to hate and reject Him.

CLXXXIII.

FEAR ALONE CREATES THEISTS AND BIGOTS.

If fear has created the Gods, fear still holds their empire in the mind of mortals; they have been so early accustomed to tremble even at the name of the Deity, that it has become for them a specter, a goblin, a were-wolf which torments them, and whose idea deprives them even of the courage to attempt to reassure themselves. They are afraid that this invisible specter will strike them if they cease to be afraid. The religious people fear their God too much to love Him sincerely; they serve Him as slaves, who can not escape His power, and take the part of flattering their Master; and who, by continually lying, persuade themselves that they love Him. They make a virtue of necessity. The love of religious bigots for their God, and of slaves for their despots, is but a servile and simulated homage which they render by compulsion, in which the heart has no part.

CLXXXIV.

CAN WE, OR SHOULD WE, LOVE OR NOT LOVE GOD?

The Christian Doctors have made their God so little worthy of love, that several among them have thought it their duty not to love Him; this is a blasphemy which makes less sincere doctors tremble. Saint Thomas, having asserted that we are under obligation to love God as soon as we can use our reason, the Jesuit Sirmond replied to him that that was very soon; the Jesuit Vasquez claims that it is sufficient to love God in the hour of death; Hurtado says that we should love God at all times; Henriquez is content with loving Him every five years; Sotus, every Sunday. "Upon what shall we rely?" asks Father Sirmond, who adds: "that Suarez desires that we should love God sometimes. But at what time? He allows you to judge of it; he knows nothing about it himself; for he adds: 'What a learned doctor does not know, who can know?'" The same Jesuit Sirmond continues, by saying: "that God does not command us to love Him with human affection, and does not promise us salvation but on condition of giving Him our hearts; it is enough to obey Him and to love Him, by fulfilling His commandments; that this is the only love which we owe Him, and He has not commanded so much to love Him as not to hate Him." [See "Apology, Des Lettres Provinciales," Tome II.] This doctrine appears heretical, ungodly, and abominable to the Jansenists, who, by the revolting severity which they attribute to their God, render Him still less lovable than their adversaries, the Jesuits. The latter, in order to make converts, represent God in such a light as to give confidence to the most perverse mortals. Thus, nothing is less established among the Christians than the important question, whether we can or should love or not love God. Among their spiritual guides some pretend that we must love God with all the heart, notwithstanding all His severity; others, like the Father Daniel, think that an act of pure love of God is the most heroic act of Christian virtue, and that human weakness can scarcely reach so high. The Jesuit Pintereau goes still further; he says: "The deliverance from the grievous yoke of Divine love is a privilege of the new alliance."

CLXXXV.

THE VARIOUS AND CONTRADICTORY IDEAS WHICH EXIST EVERYWHERE UPON GOD AND RELIGION, PROVE THAT THEY ARE BUT IDLE FANCIES.

It is always the character of man which decides upon the character of his God; each one creates a God for himself, and in his own image. The cheerful man who indulges in pleasures and dissipation, can not imagine God to be an austere and rebukeful being; he requires a facile God with whom he can make an agreement. The severe, sour, bilious man wants a God like himself; one who inspires fear; and regards as perverse those that accept only a God who is yielding and easily won over. Heresies, quarrels, and schisms are necessary. Can men differently organized and modified by diverse circumstances, agree in regard to an imaginary being which exists but in their own brains? The cruel and interminable disputes continually arising among the ministers of the Lord, have not a tendency to attract the confidence of those who take an impartial view of them. How can we help our incredulity, when we see principles about which those who teach them to others, never agree? How can we avoid doubting the existence of a God, the idea of whom varies in such a remarkable way in the mind of His ministers? How can we avoid rejecting totally a God who is full of contradictions? How can we rely upon priests whom we see continually contending, accusing each other of being infidels and heretics, rending and persecuting each other without mercy, about the way in which they understand the pretended truths which they reveal to the world?

CLXXXVI.

THE EXISTENCE OF GOD, WHICH IS THE BASIS OF ALL RELIGION, HAS NOT YET BEEN DEMONSTRATED.

However, so far, this important truth has not yet been demonstrated, not only to the incredulous, but in a satisfactory way to theologians themselves. In all times, we have seen profound thinkers who thought they had new proofs of the truth most important to men. What have been the fruits of their meditations and of their arguments? They left the thing at the same point; they have demonstrated nothing; nearly always they have excited the clamors of their colleagues, who accuse them of having badly defended the best of causes.

CLXXXVII.

PRIESTS, MORE THAN UNBELIEVERS, ACT FROM INTEREST.

The apologists of religion repeat to us every day that the passions alone create unbelievers. "It is," they say, "pride, and a desire to distinguish themselves, that make atheists; they seek also to efface the idea of God from their minds, because they have reason to fear His rigorous judgments." Whatever may be the motives which cause men to be irreligious, the thing in question is whether they have found truth. No man acts without motives; let us first examine the arguments—we shall examine the motives afterward—and we shall find that they are more legitimate, and more sensible, than those of many credulous devotees who allow themselves to be guided by masters little worthy of men's confidence.

You say, O priests of the Lord! that the passions cause unbelievers; you pretend that they renounce religion through interest, or because it interferes with their irregular inclinations; you assert that they attack your Gods because they fear their punishments. Ah! yourselves in defending this religion and its chimeras, are you, then, really exempt from passions and interests? Who receive the fees of this religion, on whose behalf the priests are so zealous? It is the priests. To whom does religion procure power, credit, honors, wealth? To the priests! In all countries, who make war upon reason, science, truth, and philosophy and render them odious to the sovereigns and to the people? Who profit by the ignorance of men and their vain prejudices? The priests! You are, O priests, rewarded, honored, and paid for deceiving mortals, and you punish those who undeceive them. The follies of men procure you blessings, offerings, expiations; the most useful truths bring to those who announce them, chains, sufferings, stakes. Let the world judge between us.

CLXXXVIII.

PRIDE, PRESUMPTION, AND CORRUPTION OF THE HEART ARE MORE OFTEN FOUND AMONG PRIESTS THAN AMONG ATHEISTS AND UNBELIEVERS.

Pride and vanity always were and always will be the inherent vices of the priesthood. Is there anything that has a tendency to render men haughty and vain more than the assumption of exercising Heavenly power, of possessing a sacred character, of being the messengers of the Most High? Are not these dispositions continually increased by the credulity of the people, by the deference and the respect of the sovereigns, by the immunities, the privileges, and the distinctions which the clergy enjoy? The common man is, in every country, more devoted to his spiritual guides, whom he considers as Divine men, than to his temporal superiors, whom he considers as ordinary men. Village priests enjoy more honor than the lord or the judge. A Christian priest believes himself far above a king or an emperor. A Spanish grandee having spoken hastily to a monk, the latter said to him, arrogantly, "Learn to respect a man who has every day your God in his hands and your queen at his feet."

Have the priests any right to accuse the unbelievers of pride? Do they distinguish themselves by a rare modesty or profound humility? Is it not evident that the desire to domineer over men is the essence of their profession? If the Lord's ministers were truly modest, would we see them so greedy of respect, so easily irritated by contradictions, so prompt and so cruel in revenging themselves upon those whose opinions offend them? Does not modest science impress us with the difficulty of unraveling truth? What other passion than frenzied pride can render men so ferocious, so vindictive, so devoid of toleration and gentleness? What is more presumptuous than to arm nations and cause rivers of blood, in order to establish or to defend futile conjectures?

You say, O Doctors of Divinity! that it is presumption alone which makes atheists. Teach them, then, what your God is; instruct them about His essence; speak of Him in an intelligible way; tell of Him reasonable things, which are not contradictory or impossible! If you are not in the condition to satisfy them; if, so far, none of you have been able to demonstrate the existence of a God in a clear and convincing way; if, according to your own confession, His essence is as much hidden from you as from the rest of mortals, pardon those who can not admit that which they can neither understand nor reconcile. Do not accuse of presumption and vanity those who have the sincerity to confess their ignorance; accuse not of folly those who find it impossible to believe in contradictions. You should blush at the thought of exciting the hatred of the people and the vengeance of the sovereigns against men who do not think as you do upon a Being of whom you have no idea yourselves. Is there anything more audacious and more extravagant than to reason about an object which it is impossible to conceive of?

You tell us it is corruption of the heart which produces atheists; that they shake off the yoke of the Deity because they fear His terrible judgments. But why do you paint your God in such black colors? Why does this powerful God permit that such corrupt hearts should exist? Why should we not make efforts to break the yoke of a Tyrant who, being able to make of the hearts of men what He pleases, allows them to become perverted and hardened; blinds them; refuses them His grace, in order to have the satisfaction of punishing them eternally for having been hardened, blinded, and not having received the grace which He refused them? The theologians and the priests must feel themselves very sure of Heaven's grace and of a happy future, in order not to detest a Master so capricious as the God whom they announce to us. A God who damns eternally must be the most odious Being that the human mind could imagine.

CLXXXIX.

PREJUDICES ARE BUT FOR A TIME, AND NO POWER IS DURABLE EXCEPT IT IS BASED UPON TRUTH, REASON, AND EQUITY.

No man on earth is truly interested in sustaining error; sooner or later it is compelled to surrender to truth. General interest tends to the enlightenment of mortals; even the passions sometimes contribute to the breaking of some of the chains of prejudice. Have not the passions of some sovereigns destroyed, within the past two centuries in some countries of Europe, the tyrannical power which a haughty Pontiff formerly exercised over all the princes of his sect? Politics, becoming more enlightened, has despoiled the clergy of an immense amount of property which credulity had accumulated in their hands. Should not this memorable example make even the priests realize that prejudices are but for a time, and that truth alone is capable of assuring a substantial well-being?

Have not the ministers of the Lord seen that in pampering the sovereigns, in forging Divine rights for them, and in delivering to them the people, bound hand and foot, they were making tyrants of them? Have they not reason to fear that these gigantic idols, whom they have raised to the skies, will crush them also some day? Do not a thousand examples prove that they ought to fear that these unchained lions, after having devoured nations, will in turn devour them?

We will respect the priests when they become citizens. Let them make use, if they can, of Heaven's authority to create fear in those princes who incessantly desolate the earth; let them deprive them of the right of being unjust; let them recognize that no subject of a State enjoys living under tyranny; let them make the sovereigns feel that they themselves are not interested in exercising a power which, rendering them odious, injures their own safety, their own power, their own grandeur; finally, let the priests and the undeceived kings recognize that no power is safe that is not based upon truth, reason, and equity.

CXC.

HOW MUCH POWER AND CONSIDERATION THE MINISTERS OF THE GODS WOULD HAVE, IF THEY BECAME THE APOSTLES OF REASON AND THE DEFENDERS OF LIBERTY!

The ministers of the Gods, in warring against human reason, which they ought to develop, act against their own interest. What would be their power, their consideration, their empire over the wisest men; what would be the gratitude of the people toward them if, instead of occupying themselves with their vain quarrels, they had applied themselves to the useful sciences; if they had sought the true principles of physics, of government, and of morals. Who would dare reproach the opulence and credit of a corporation which, consecrating its leisure and its authority to the public good, should use the one for studying and meditating, and the other for enlightening equally the minds of the sovereigns and the subjects?

Priests! lay aside your idle fancies, your unintelligible dogmas, your despicable quarrels; banish to imaginary regions these phantoms, which could be of use to you only in the infancy of nations; take the tone of reason, instead of sounding the tocsin of persecution against your adversaries; instead of entertaining the people with foolish disputes, of preaching useless and fanatical virtues, preach to them humane and social morality; preach to them virtues which are really useful to the world; become the apostles of reason, the lights of the nations, the defenders of liberty, reformers of abuses, the friends of truth, and we will bless you, we will honor you, we will love you, and you will be sure of holding an eternal empire over the hearts of your fellow-beings.

CXCI.

WHAT A HAPPY AND GREAT REVOLUTION WOULD TAKE PLACE IN THE UNIVERSE, IF PHILOSOPHY WAS SUBSTITUTED FOR RELIGION!

Philosophers, in all ages, have taken the part that seemed destined for the ministers of religion. The hatred of the latter for philosophy was never more than professional jealousy. All men accustomed to think, instead of seeking to injure each other, should unite their efforts in combating errors, in seeking truth, and especially in dispelling the prejudices from which the sovereigns and subjects suffer alike, and whose upholders themselves finish, sooner or later, by becoming the victims.

In the hands of an enlightened government the priests would become the most useful of citizens. Could men with rich stipends from the State, and relieved of the care of providing for their own subsistence, do anything better than to instruct themselves in order to be able to instruct others? Would not their minds be better satisfied in discovering truth than in wandering in the labyrinths of darkness? Would it be any more difficult to unravel the principles of man's morals, than the imaginary principles of Divine and theological morals? Would ordinary men have as much trouble in understanding the simple notions of their duties, as in charging their memories with mysteries, unintelligible words, and obscure definitions which are impossible for them to understand? How much time and trouble is lost in trying to teach men things which are of no use to them.

What resources for the public benefit, for encouraging the progress of the sciences and the advancement of knowledge, for the education of youth, are presented to well-meaning sovereigns through so many monasteries, which, in a great number of countries devour the people's substance without an equivalent. But superstition, jealous of its exclusive empire, seems to have formed but useless beings. What advantage could not be drawn from a multitude of cenobites of both sexes whom we see in so many countries, and who are so well paid to do nothing. Instead of occupying them with sterile contemplations, with mechanical prayers, with monotonous practices; instead of burdening them with fasts and austerities, let there be excited among them a salutary emulation that would inspire them to seek the means of serving usefully the world, which their fatal vows oblige them to renounce. Instead of filling the youthful minds of their pupils with fables, dogmas, and puerilities, why not invite or oblige the priests to teach them true things, and so make of them citizens useful to their country? The way in which men are brought up makes them useful but to the clergy, who blind them, and to the tyrants, who plunder them.

CXCII.

THE RETRACTION OF AN UNBELIEVER AT THE HOUR OF DEATH, PROVES NOTHING AGAINST INCREDULITY.

The adherents of credulity often accuse the unbelievers of bad faith because they sometimes waver in their principles, changing opinions during sickness, and retracting them at the hour of death. When the body is diseased, the faculty of reasoning is generally disturbed also. The infirm and decrepit man, in approaching his end, sometimes perceives himself that reason is leaving him, he feels that prejudice returns. There are diseases which have a tendency to lessen courage, to make pusillanimous, and to enfeeble the brain; there are others which, in destroying the body, do not affect the reason. However, an unbeliever who retracts in sickness, is not more rare or more extraordinary than a devotionist who permits himself, while in health, to neglect the duties that his religion prescribes for him in the most formal manner.

Cleomenes, King of Sparta, having shown little respect for the Gods during his reign, became superstitious in his last days; with the view of interesting Heaven in his favor, he called around him a multitude of sacrificing priests. One of his friends expressing his surprise, Cleomenes said: "What are you astonished at? I am no longer what I was, and not being the same, I can not think in the same way."

The ministers of religion in their daily conduct, often belie the rigorous principles which they teach to others, so that the unbelievers in their turn think they have a right to accuse them of bad faith. If some unbelievers contradict, in sight of death or during sickness, the opinions which they entertained in health, do not the priests in health belie opinions of the religion which they hold? Do we see a great multitude of humble, generous prelates devoid of ambition, enemies of pomp and grandeur, the friends of poverty? In short, do we see the conduct of many Christian priests corresponding with the austere morality of Christ, their God and their model?

CXCIII.

IT IS NOT TRUE THAT ATHEISM SUNDERS ALL THE TIES OF SOCIETY.

Atheism, we are told, breaks all social ties. Without belief in God, what becomes of the sacredness of the oath? How can we bind an atheist who can not seriously attest the Deity? But does the oath place us under stronger obligations to the engagements which we make? Whoever dares to lie, will he not dare to perjure himself? He who is base enough to violate his word, or unjust enough to break his promises in contempt of the esteem of men, will not be more faithful for having taken all the Gods as witnesses to his oaths. Those who rank themselves above the judgments of men, will soon put themselves above the judgments of God. Are not princes, of all mortals, the most prompt in taking oaths, and the most prompt in violating them?

CXCIV.

REFUTATION OF THE ASSERTION THAT RELIGION IS NECESSARY FOR THE MASSES.

Religion, they tell us, is necessary for the masses; that though enlightened persons may not need restraint upon their opinions, it is necessary at least for the common people, in whom education has not developed reason. Is it true, then, that religion is a restraint for the people? Do we see that this religion prevents them from intemperance, drunkenness, brutality, violence, frauds, and all kinds of excesses?

Could a people who had no idea of the Deity, conduct itself in a more detestable manner than many believing people in whom we see dissolute habits, and the vices most unworthy of rational beings? Do we not see the artisan or the man of the people go from his church and plunge headlong into his usual excesses, persuading himself all the while that his periodical homage to God gives him the right to follow without remorse his vicious practices and habitual inclinations? If the people are gross and ignorant, is not their stupidity due to the negligence of the princes who do not attend to the public education, or who oppose the instruction of their subjects? Finally, is not the irrationality of the people plainly the work of the priests, who, instead of interesting them in a rational morality, do nothing but entertain them with fables, phantoms, intrigues, observances, idle fancies, and false virtues, upon which they claim that everything depends?

Religion is, for the people, but a vain attendance upon ceremonies, to which they cling from habit, which amuses their eyes, which enlivens temporarily their sleepy minds, without influencing the conduct, and without correcting their morals. By the confession even of the ministers at the altars, nothing is more rare than the interior and spiritual religion, which is alone capable of regulating the life of man, and of triumphing over his inclinations. In good faith, among the most numerous and the most devotional people, are there many capable of understanding the principles of their religious system, and who find them of sufficient strength to stifle their perverse inclinations?

Many people will tell us that it is better to have some kind of a restraint than none at all. They will pretend that if religion does not control the great mass, it serves at least to restrain some individuals, who, without it, would abandon themselves to crime without remorse. No doubt it is necessary for men to have a restraint; but they do not need an imaginary one; they need true and visible restraints; they need real fears, which are much better to restrain them than panic terrors and idle fancies. Religion frightens but a few pusillanimous minds, whose weakness of character already renders them little to be dreaded by their fellow-citizens. An equitable government, severe laws, a sound morality, will apply equally to everybody; every one would be forced to believe in it, and would feel the danger of not conforming to it.

CXCV.

EVERY RATIONAL SYSTEM IS NOT MADE FOR THE MULTITUDE.

We may be asked if atheism can suit the multitude? I reply, that every system which demands discussion is not for the multitude. What use is there, then, in preaching atheism? It can at least make those who reason, feel that nothing is more extravagant than to make ourselves uneasy, and nothing more unjust than to cause anxiety to others on account of conjectures, destitute of all foundation. As to the common man, who never reasons, the arguments of an atheist are no better suited to him than a philosopher's hypothesis, an astronomer's observations, a chemist's experiments, a geometer's calculations, a physician's examinations, an architect's designs, or a lawyer's pleadings, who all labor for the people without their knowledge.

The metaphysical arguments of theology, and the religious disputes which have occupied for so long many profound visionists, are they made any more for the common man than the arguments of an atheist? More than this, the principles of atheism, founded upon common sense, are they not more intelligible than those of a theology which we see bristling with insolvable difficulties, even for the most active minds? The people in every country have a religion which they do not understand, which they do not examine, and which they follow but by routine; their priests alone occupy themselves with the theology which is too sublime for them. If, by accident, the people should lose this unknown theology, they could console them selves for the loss of a thing which is not only entirely useless, but which produces among them very dangerous ebullitions.

It would be very foolish to write for the common man or to attempt to cure his prejudices all at once. We write but for those who read and reason; the people read but little, and reason less. Sensible and peaceable people enlighten themselves; their light spreads itself gradually, and in time reaches the people. On the other hand, those who deceive men, do they not often take the trouble themselves of undeceiving them?

CXCVI.

FUTILITY AND DANGER OF THEOLOGY. WISE COUNSELS TO PRINCES.

If theology is a branch of commerce useful to theologians, it has been demonstrated to be superfluous and injurious to the rest of society. The interests of men will succeed in opening their eyes sooner or later. The sovereigns and the people will some day discover the indifference and the contempt that a futile science deserves which serves but to trouble men without making them better. They will feel the uselessness of many expensive practices, which do not at all contribute to public welfare; they will blush at many pitiful quarrels, which will cease to disturb the tranquillity of the States as soon as they cease to attach any importance to them.

Princes! instead of taking part in the senseless contentions of your priests, instead of espousing foolishly their impertinent quarrels, instead of striving to bring all your subjects to uniform opinions, occupy yourselves with their happiness in this world, and do not trouble yourselves about the fate which awaits them in another. Govern them justly, give them good laws, respect their liberty and their property, superintend their education, encourage them in their labors, reward their talents and their virtues, repress their licentiousness, and do not trouble yourselves upon what they think about objects useless to them and to you. Then you will no longer need fictions to make yourselves obeyed; you will become the only guides of your subjects; their ideas will be uniform about the feelings of love and respect which will be your due. Theological fables are useful but to tyrants, who do not understand the art of ruling over reasonable beings.

CXCVII.

FATAL EFFECTS OF RELIGION UPON THE PEOPLE AND THE PRINCES.

Does it require the efforts of genius to comprehend that what is beyond man, is not made for men; that what is supernatural, is not made for natural beings; that impenetrable mysteries are not made for limited minds? If theologians are foolish enough to dispute about subjects which they acknowledge to be unintelligible to themselves, should society take a part in their foolish quarrels? Must human blood flow in order to give value to the conjectures of a few obstinate visionists? If it is very difficult to cure the theologians of their mania and the people of their prejudices, it is at least very easy to prevent the extravagances of the one and the folly of the other from producing pernicious effects. Let each one be allowed to think as he chooses, but let him not be allowed to annoy others for their mode of thinking. If the chiefs of nations were more just and more sensible, theological opinions would not disturb the public tranquillity any more than the disputes of philosophers, physicians, grammarians, and of critics. It is the tyranny of princes which makes theological quarrels have serious consequences. When kings shall cease to meddle with theology, theological quarrels will no longer be a thing to fear.

Those who boast so much upon the importance and usefulness of religion, ought to show us its beneficial results, and the advantages that the disputes and abstract speculations of theology can bring to porters, to artisans, to farmers, to fishmongers, to women, and to so many depraved servants, with whom the large cities are filled. People of this kind are all religious, they have implicit faith; their priests believe for them; they accept a faith unknown to their guides; they listen assiduously to sermons; they assist regularly in ceremonies; they think it a great crime to transgress the ordinances to which from childhood they have been taught to conform. What good to morality results from all this? None whatever; they have no idea of morality, and you see them indulge in all kinds of rogueries, frauds, rapine, and excesses which the law does not punish. The masses, in truth, have no idea of religion; what is called religion, is but a blind attachment to unknown opinions and mysterious dealings. In fact, to deprive the people of religion, is depriving them of nothing. If we should succeed in destroying their prejudices, we would but diminish or annihilate the dangerous confidence which they have in self-interested guides, and teach them to beware of those who, under the pretext of religion, very often lead them into fatal excesses.

CXCVIII.

CONTINUATION.

Under pretext of instructing and enlightening men, religion really holds them in ignorance, and deprives them even of the desire of understanding the objects which interest them the most. There exists for the people no other rule of conduct than that which their priests indicate to them. Religion takes the place of everything; but being in darkness itself, it has a greater tendency to misguide mortals, than to guide them in the way of science and happiness. Philosophy, morality, legislation, and politics are to them enigmas. Man, blinded by religious prejudices, finds it impossible to understand his own nature, to cultivate his reason, to make experiments; he fears truth as soon as it does not agree with his opinions. Everything tends to render the people devout, but all is opposed to their being humane, reasonable, and virtuous. Religion seems to have for its object only to blunt the feeling and to dull the intelligence of men.

The war which always existed between the priests and the best minds of all ages, comes from this, that the wise men perceived the fetters which superstition wished to place upon the human mind, which it fain would keep in eternal infancy, that it might be occupied with fables, burdened with terrors, and frightened by phantoms which would prevent it from progressing. Incapable of perfecting itself, theology opposed insurmountable barriers to the progress of true knowledge; it seemed to be occupied but with the care to keep the nations and their chiefs in the most profound ignorance of their true interests, of their relations, of their duties, of the real motives which can lead them to prosperity; it does but obscure morality; renders its principles arbitrary, subjects it to the caprices of the Gods, or of their ministers; it converts the art of governing men into a mysterious tyranny which becomes the scourge of nations; it changes the princes into unjust and licentious despots, and the people into ignorant slaves, who corrupt themselves in order to obtain the favor of their masters.

CXCIX.

HISTORY TEACHES US THAT ALL RELIGIONS WERE ESTABLISHED BY THE AID OF IGNORANCE, AND BY MEN WHO HAD THU EFFRONTERY TO STYLE THEMSELVES THE ENVOYS OF DIVINITY.

If we take the trouble to follow the history of the human mind, we will discover that theology took care not to extend its limits. It began by repeating fables, which it claimed to be sacred truths; it gave birth to poesy, which filled the people's imagination with puerile fictions; it entertained them but with its Gods and their incredible feats; in a word, religion always treated men like children, whom they put to sleep with tales that their ministers would like still to pass as incontestable truths. If the ministers of the Gods sometimes made useful discoveries, they always took care to hide them in enigmas and to envelope them in shadows of mystery. The Pythagorases and the Platos, in order to acquire some futile attainments, were obliged to crawl to the feet of the priests, to become initiated into their mysteries, to submit to the tests which they desired to impose upon them; it is at this cost that they were permitted to draw from the fountain-head their exalted ideas, so seducing still to all those who admire what is unintelligible. It was among Egyptian, Indian, Chaldean priests; it was in the schools of these dreamers, interested by profession in dethroning human reason, that philosophy was obliged to borrow its first rudiments. Obscure or false in its principles, mingled with fictions and fables, solely made to seduce imagination, this philosophy progressed but waveringly, and instead of enlightening the mind, it blinded it, and turned it away from useful objects. The theological speculations and mystical reveries of the ancients have, even in our days, the making of the law in a great part of the philosophical world. Adopted by modern theology, we can scarcely deviate from them without heresy; they entertain us with aerial beings, with spirits, angels, demons, genii, and other phantoms, which are the object of the meditations of our most profound thinkers, and which serve as a basis to metaphysics, an abstract and futile science, upon which the greatest geniuses have vainly exercised themselves for thousands of years. Thus hypotheses, invented by a few visionists of Memphis and of Babylon, continue to be the basis of a science revered for the obscurity which makes it pass as marvelous and Divine. The first legislators of nations were priests; the first mythologists and poets were priests; the first philosophers were priests; the first physicians were priests. In their hands science became a sacred thing, prohibited to the profane; they spoke only by allegories, emblems, enigmas, and ambiguous oracles—means well-suited to excite curiosity, to put to work the imagination, and especially to inspire in the ignorant man a holy respect for those whom he believed instructed by Heaven, capable of reading the destinies of earth, and who boldly pretended to be the organs of Divinity.

CC.

ALL RELIGIONS, ANCIENT AND MODERN, HAVE MUTUALLY BORROWED THEIR ABSTRACT REVERIES AND THEIR RIDICULOUS PRACTICES.

The religions of these ancient priests have disappeared, or, rather, they have changed their form. Although our modern theologians regard the ancient priests as impostors, they have taken care to gather up the scattered fragments of their religious systems, the whole of which does not exist any longer for us; we will find in our modern religions, not only the metaphysical dogmas which theology has but dressed in another form, but we still find remarkable remains of their superstitious practices, of their theurgy, of their magic, of their enchantments.

Christians are still commanded to regard with respect the monuments of the legislators, the priests, and the prophets of the Hebrew religion, which, according to appearances, has borrowed from Egypt the fantastic notions with which we see it filled. Thus the extravagances invented by frauds or idolatrous visionists, are still regarded as sacred opinions by the Christians!

If we but look at history, we see striking resemblances in all religions. Everywhere on earth we find religious ideas periodically afflicting and rejoicing the people; everywhere we see rites, practices often abominable, and formidable mysteries occupying the mind, and becoming objects of meditation. We see the different superstitions borrowing from each other their abstract reveries and their ceremonies. Religions are generally unformed rhapsodies combined by new Doctors of Divinity, who, in composing them, have used the materials of their predecessors, reserving the right of adding or subtracting what suits or does not suit their present views. The religion of Egypt served evidently as a basis for the religion of Moses, who expunged from it the worship of idols. Moses was but an Egyptian schismatic, Christianity is but a reformed Judaism. Mohammedanism is composed of Judaism, of Christianity, and of the ancient religion of Arabia.

CCI.

THEOLOGY HAS ALWAYS TURNED PHILOSOPHY FROM ITS TRUE COURSE.

From the most remote period theology alone regulated the march of philosophy. What aid has it lent it? It changed it into an unintelligible jargon, which only had a tendency to render the clearest truth uncertain; it converted the art of reasoning into a science of words; it threw the human mind into the aerial regions of metaphysics, where it unsuccessfully occupied itself in sounding useless and dangerous abysses. For physical and simple causes, this philosophy substituted supernatural causes, or, rather, causes truly occult; it explained difficult phenomena by agents more inconceivable than these phenomena; it filled discourse with words void of sense, incapable of giving the reason of things, better suited to obscure than to enlighten, and which seem invented but to discourage man, to guard him against the powers of his own mind, to make him distrust the principles of reason and evidence, and to surround the truth with an insurmountable barrier.

CCII.

THEOLOGY NEITHER EXPLAINS NOR ENLIGHTENS ANYTHING IN THE WORLD OR IN NATURE.

If we would believe the adherents of religion, nothing could be explicable in the world without it; nature would be a continual enigma; it would be impossible for man to comprehend himself. But, at the bottom, what does this religion explain to us? The more we examine it, the more we find that theological notions are fit but to perplex all our ideas; they change all into mysteries; they explain to us difficult things by impossible things. Is it, then, explaining things to attribute them to unknown agencies, to invisible powers, to immaterial causes? Is it really enlightening the human mind when, in its embarrassment, it is directed to the "depths of the treasures of Divine Wisdom," upon which they tell us it is in vain for us to turn our bold regards? Can the Divine Nature, which we know nothing about, make us understand man's nature, which we find so difficult to explain?

Ask a Christian philosopher what is the origin of the world. He will answer that God created the universe. What is God? We do not know anything about it. What is it to create? We have no idea of it! What is the cause of pestilences, famines, wars, sterility, inundations, earthquakes? It is God's wrath. What remedies can prevent these calamities? Prayers, sacrifices, processions, offerings, ceremonies, are, we are told, the true means to disarm Celestial fury. But why is Heaven angry? Because men are wicked. Why are men wicked? Because their nature is corrupt. What is the cause of this corruption? It is, a theologian of enlightened Europe will reply, because the first man was seduced by the first woman to eat of an apple which his God had forbidden him to touch. Who induced this woman to do such a folly? The Devil. Who created the Devil? God! Why did God create this Devil destined to pervert the human race? We know nothing about it; it is a mystery hidden in the bosom of the Deity.

Does the earth revolve around the sun? Two centuries ago a devout philosopher would have replied that such a thought was blasphemy, because such a system could not agree with the Holy Book, which every Christian reveres as inspired by the Deity Himself. What is the opinion to-day about it? Notwithstanding Divine Inspiration, the Christian philosophers finally concluded to rely upon evidence rather than upon the testimony of their inspired books.

What is the hidden principle of the actions and of the motions of the human body? It is the soul. What is a soul? It is a spirit. What is a spirit? It is a substance which has neither form, color, expansion, nor parts. How can we conceive of such a substance? How can it move a body? We know nothing about it. Have brutes souls? The Carthusian assures you that they are machines. But do we not see them act, feel, and think in a manner which resembles that of men? This is a pure illusion, you say. But why do you deprive the brutes of souls, which, without understanding it, you attribute to men? It is that the souls of the brutes would embarrass our theologians, who, content with the power of frightening and damning the immortal souls of men, do not take the same interest in damning those of the brutes. Such are the puerile solutions which philosophy, always guided by the leading-strings of theology, was obliged to bring forth to explain the problems of the physical and moral world.

CCIII.

HOW THEOLOGY HAS FETTERED HUMAN MORALS AND RETARDED THE PROGRESS OF ENLIGHTENMENT, OF REASON, AND OF TRUTH.

How many subterfuges and mental gymnastics all the ancient and modern thinkers have employed, in order to avoid falling out with the ministers of the Gods, who in all ages were the true tyrants of thought! How Descartes, Malebranche, Leibnitz, and many others have been compelled to invent hypotheses and evasions in order to reconcile their discoveries with the reveries and the blunders which religion had rendered sacred! With what prevarications have not the greatest philosophers guarded themselves even at the risk of being absurd, inconsistent, and unintelligible whenever their ideas did not correspond with the principles of theology! Vigilant priests were always ready to extinguish systems which could not be made to tally with their interests. Theology in every age has been the bed of Procrustes upon which this brigand extended his victims; he cut off the limbs when they were too long, or stretched them by horses when they were shorter than the bed upon which he placed them.

What sensible man who has a love for science, and is interested in the welfare of humanity, can reflect without sorrow and pain upon the loss of so many profound, laborious, and subtle heads, who, for many centuries, have foolishly exhausted themselves upon idle fancies that proved to be injurious to our race? What light could have been thrown into the minds of many famous thinkers, if, instead of occupying themselves with a useless theology, and its impertinent disputes, they had turned their attention upon intelligible and truly important objects. Half of the efforts that it cost the genius that was able to forge their religious opinions, half of the expense which their frivolous worship cost the nations, would have sufficed to enlighten them perfectly upon morality, politics, philosophy, medicine, agriculture, etc. Superstition nearly always absorbs the attention, the admiration, and the treasures of the people; they have a very expensive religion; but they have for their money, neither light, virtue, nor happiness.

CCIV.

CONTINUATION.

Some ancient and modern philosophers have had the courage to accept experience and reason as their guides, and to shake off the chains of superstition. Lucippe, Democritus, Epicurus, Straton, and some other Greeks, dared to tear away the thick veil of prejudice, and to deliver philosophy from theological fetters. But their systems, too simple, too sensible, and too stripped of wonders for the lovers of fancy, were obliged to surrender to the fabulous conjectures of Plato, Socrates, and Zeno. Among the moderns, Hobbes, Spinoza, Bayle, and others have followed the path of Epicurus, but their doctrine found but few votaries in a world still too much infatuated with fables to listen to reason.

In all ages one could not, without imminent danger, lay aside the prejudices which opinion had rendered sacred. No one was permitted to make discoveries of any kind; all that the most enlightened men could do was to speak and write with hidden meaning; and often, by a cowardly complaisance, to shamefully ally falsehood with truth. A few of them had a double doctrine—one public and the other secret. The key of this last having been lost, their true sentiments often became unintelligible and, consequently, useless to us. How could modern philosophers who, being threatened with the most cruel persecution, were called upon to renounce reason and to submit to faith—that is to say, to priestly authority—I say, how could men thus fettered give free flight to their genius, perfect reason, or hasten human progress? It was but in fear and trembling that the greatest men obtained glimpses of truth; they rarely had the courage to announce it; those who dared to do it have generally been punished for their temerity. Thanks to religion, it was never permitted to think aloud or to combat the prejudices of which man is everywhere the victim or the dupe.

CCV.

WE COULD NOT REPEAT TOO OFTEN HOW EXTRAVAGANT AND FATAL RELIGION IS.

Every man who has the boldness to announce truths to the world, is sure to receive the hatred of the priests; the latter loudly call upon the powers that be, for assistance; they need the assistance of kings to sustain their arguments and their Gods. These clamors show the weakness of their cause.

"They are in embarrassment when they cry for help."

It is not permitted to err in the matter of religion; on every other subject we can be deceived with impunity; we pity those who go astray, and we have some liking for the persons who discover truths new to us. But as soon as theology supposes itself concerned, be it in errors or discoveries, a holy zeal is kindled; the sovereigns exterminate; the people fly into frenzy; and the nations are all stirred up without knowing why. Is there anything more afflicting than to see public and individual welfare depend upon a futile science, which is void of principles, which has no standing ground but imagination, and which presents to the mind but words void of sense? What good is a religion which no one understands; which continually torments those who trouble themselves about it; which is incapable of rendering men better; and which often gives them the credit of being unjust and wicked? Is there a more deplorable folly, and one that ought more to be abated, than that which, far from doing any good to the human race, does but blind it, cause transports, and render it miserable, depriving it of truth, which alone can soften the rigor of fate?

CCVI.

RELIGION IS PANDORA'S BOX, AND THIS FATAL BOX IS OPEN.

Religion has in every age kept the human mind in darkness and held it in ignorance of its true relations, of its real duties and its true interests. It is but in removing its clouds and phantoms that we may find the sources of truth, reason, morality, and the actual motives which inspire virtue. This religion puts us on the wrong track for the causes of our evils, and the natural remedies which we can apply. Far from curing them, it can but multiply them and render them more durable.

Let us, then, say, with the celebrated Lord Bolingbroke, in his posthumous works: "Theology is the Box of Pandora; and if it is impossible to close it, it is at least useful to give warning that this fatal box is open."

I believe, my dear friends, that I have given you a sufficient preventative against all these follies. Your reason will do more than my discourses, and I sincerely wish that we had only to complain of being deceived! But human blood has flowed since the time of Constantine for the establishment of these horrible impositions. The Roman, the Greek, and the Protestant churches by vain, ambitious, and hypocritical disputes have ravaged Europe, Asia, and Africa. Add to these men, whom these quarrels murdered, the multitudes of monks and of nuns, who became sterile by their profession, and you will perceive that the Christian religion has destroyed half of the human race.

I conclude with the desire that we may return to Nature, whose declared enemy the Christian religion is, and which necessarily instructs us to do unto others as we would wish them to do unto us. Then the universe will be composed of good citizens, just fathers, obedient children, tender friends. Nature has given us this Religion, in giving us Reason. May fanaticism pervert it no more! I die filled with these desires more than with hope.

ETREPIGNY, March 15, 1732

JOHN MESLIER

ABSTRACT OF THE TESTAMENT OF JOHN MESLIER

By Voltaire;

OR, SENTIMENTS OF THE CURATE OF ETREPIGNY ADDRESSED TO HIS PARISHIONERS.

I.—OF RELIGIONS.

As there is no one religious denomination which does not pretend to be truly founded upon the authority of God, and entirely exempt from all the errors and impositions which are found in the others, it is for those who purpose to establish the truth of the faith of their sect, to show, by clear and convincing proofs, that it is of Divine origin; as this is lacking, we must conclude that it is but of human invention, and full of errors and deceptions; for it is incredible that an Omnipotent and Infinitely good God would have desired to give laws and ordinances to men, and not have wished them to bear better authenticated marks of truth, than those of the numerous impostors. Moreover, there is not one of our Christ-worshipers, of whatever sect he may be, who can make us see, by convincing proofs, that his religion is exclusively of Divine origin; and for want of such proof they have been for many centuries contesting this subject among themselves, even to persecuting each other by fire and sword to maintain their opinions; there is, however, not one sect of them all which could convince and persuade the others by such witnesses of truth; this certainly would not be, if they had, on one side or the other, convincing proofs of Divine origin. For, as no one of any religious sect, enlightened and of good faith, pretends to hold and to favor error and falsehood; and as, on the contrary, each, on his side, pretends to sustain truth, the true means of banishing all errors, and of uniting all men in peace in the same sentiments and in the same form of religion, would be to produce convincing proofs and testimonies of the truth; and thus show that such religion is of Divine origin, and not any of the others; then each one would accept this truth; and no person would dare to question these testimonies, or sustain the side of error and imposition, lest he should be, at the same time, confounded by contrary proofs: but, as these proofs are not found in any religion, it gives to impostors occasion to invent and boldly sustain all kinds of falsehoods.

Here are still other proofs, which will not be less evident, of the falsity of human religions, and especially of the falsity of our own. Every religion which relies upon mysteries as its foundation, and which takes, as a rule of its doctrine and its morals, a principle of errors, and which is at the same time a source of trouble and eternal divisions among men, can not be a true religion, nor a Divine Institution. Now, human religions, especially the Catholic, establish as the basis of their doctrine and of their morals, a principle of errors; then, it follows that these religions can not be true, or of Divine origin. I do not see that we can deny the first proposition of this argument; it is too clear and too evident to admit of a doubt. I pass to the proof of the second proposition, which is, that the Christian religion takes for the rule of its doctrine and its morals what they call faith, a blind trust, but yet firm, and secured by some laws or revelations of some Deity. We must necessarily suppose that it is thus, because it is this belief in some Deity and in some Divine Revelations, which gives all the credit and all the authority that it has in the world, and without which we could make no use of what it prescribes. This is why there is no religion which does not expressly recommend its votaries to be firm in their faith. ["Estate fortes in fide!"] This is the reason that all Christians accept as a maxim, that faith is the commencement and the basis of salvation, that it is the root of all justice and of all sanctification, as it is expressed at the Council of Trent.—Sess. 6, Ch. VIII.

Now it is evident that a blind faith in all which is proposed in the name and authority of God, is a principle of errors and falsehoods. As a proof, we see that there is no impostor in the matter of religion, who does not pretend to be clothed with the name and the authority of God, and who does not claim to be especially inspired and sent by God. Not only is this faith and blind belief which they accept as a basis of their doctrine, a principle of errors, etc., but it is also a source of trouble and division among men for the maintenance of their religion. There is no cruelty which they do not practice upon each other under this specious pretext.

Now then, it is not credible that an Almighty, All-Kind, and All-Wise God desired to use such means or such a deceitful way to inform men of His wishes; for this would be manifestly desiring to lead them into error and to lay snares in their way, in order to make them accept the side of falsehood. It is impossible to believe that a God who loved unity and peace, the welfare and the happiness of men, would ever have established as the basis of His religion, such a fatal source of trouble and of eternal divisions among them. Such religions can not be true, neither could they have been instituted by God. But I see that our Christ-worshipers will not fail to have recourse to their pretended motives for credulity, and that they will say, that although their faith and belief may be blind in one sense, they are nevertheless supported by such clear and convincing testimonies of truth, that it would be not only imprudence, but temerity and folly not to surrender one's self. They generally reduce these pretended motives to three or four leading features. The first, they draw from the pretended holiness of their religion, which condemns vice, and which recommends the practice of virtue. Its doctrine is so pure, so simple, according to what they say, that it is evident it could spring but from the sanctity of an infinitely good and wise God.

The second motive for credulity, they draw from the innocence and the holiness of life in those who embraced it with love, and defended it by suffering death and the most cruel torments, rather than forsake it: it not being credible that such great personages would allow themselves to be deceived in their belief, that they would renounce all the advantages of life, and expose themselves to such cruel torments and persecutions, in order to maintain errors and impositions. Their third motive for credulity, they draw from the oracles and prophecies which have so long been rendered in their favor, and which they pretend have been accomplished in a manner which permits no doubt. Finally, their fourth motive for credulity, which is the most important of all, is drawn from the grandeur and the multitude of the miracles performed, in all ages, and in every place, in favor of their religion.

But it is easy to refute all these useless reasonings and to show the falsity of all these evidences. For, firstly, the arguments which our Christ-worshipers draw from their pretended motives for credulity can serve to establish and confirm falsehood as well as truth; for we see that there is no religion, no matter how false it may be, which does not pretend to have a sound and true doctrine, and which, in its way, does not condemn all vices and recommend the practice of all virtues; there is not one which has not had firm and zealous defenders who have suffered persecution in order to maintain their religion; and, finally, there is none which does not pretend to have wonders and miracles that have been performed in their favor. The Mohammedans, the Indians, the heathen, as well as the Christians, claim miracles in their religions. If our Christ-worshipers make use of their miracles and their prophecies, they are found no less in the Pagan religions than in theirs. Thus the advantage we might draw from all these motives for credulity, is found about the same in all sorts of religions. This being established, as the history and practice of all religions demonstrate, it evidently follows that all these pretended motives for credulity, upon which our Christ-worshipers place so much value, are found equally in all religions; and, consequently, can not serve as reliable evidences of the truth of their religion more than of the truth of any other. The result is clear.

Secondly. In order to give an idea of the resemblance of the miracles of Paganism to those of Christianity, could we not say, for example, that there would be more reason to believe Philostratus in what he recites of the life of Apollonius than to believe all the evangelists in what they say of the miracles of Jesus Christ; because we know, at least that Philostratus was a man of intelligence, eloquence, and fluency; that he was the secretary of the Empress Julia, wife of the Emperor Severus, and that he was requested by this empress to write the life and the wonderful acts of Apollonius? It is evident that Apollonius rendered himself famous by great and extraordinary deeds, since an empress was sufficiently interested in them to desire a history of his life. This is what can not be said of Jesus Christ, nor of those who have furnished us His biography, for they were but ignorant men of the common people, poor workmen, fishermen, who had not even the sense to relate consistently the facts which they speak of, and which they mutually contradict very often. In regard to the One whose life and actions they describe, if He had really performed the miracles attributed to Him, He would have rendered Himself notable by His beautiful acts; every one would have admired Him, and there would be statues erected to Him as was done for the Gods; but instead of that, He was regarded as a man of no consequence, as a fanatic, etc. Josephus, the historian, after having spoken of the great miracles performed in favor of his nation and his religion, immediately diminishes their credibility and renders it suspicious by saying that he leaves to each one the liberty of believing what he chooses; this evidently shows that he had not much faith in them. It also gives occasion to the more judicious to regard the histories which speak of this kind of things as fabulous narrations. [See Montaigne, and the author of the "Apology for Great Men."] All that can be said upon this subject shows us clearly that pretended miracles can be invented to favor vice and falsehood as well as justice and truth.

I prove it by the evidence of what even our Christ-worshipers call the Word of God, and by the evidence of the One they adore; for their books, which they claim contain the Word of God, and Christ Himself, whom they adore as a God-made man, show us explicitly that there are not only false prophets—that is to say, impostors—who claim to be sent by God, and who speak in His name, but which show as explicitly that these false prophets can perform such great and prodigious miracles as shall deceive the very elect. [See Matthew, chapter xxiv., verses 5, 21-

27.] More than this, all these pretended performers of miracles wish us to put faith only in them, and not in those who belong to an opposite party.

On one occasion one of these pretended prophets, named Sedecias, being contradicted by another, named Michea, the former struck the latter and said to him, pleasantly, "By what way did the Spirit of God pass from me to you?"

But how can these pretended miracles be the evidences of truth? for it is clear that they were not performed. For it would be necessary to know: Firstly, If those who are said to be the first authors of these narrations truly are such. Secondly, If they were honest men, worthy of confidence, wise and enlightened; and to know if they were not prejudiced in favor of those of whom they speak so favorably. Thirdly, If they have examined all the circumstances of the facts which they relate; if they know them well; and if they make a faithful report of them. Fourthly, If the books or the ancient histories which relate all these great miracles have not been falsified and changed in course of time, as many others have been?

If we consult Tacitus and many other celebrated historians, in regard to Moses and his nation, we shall see that they are considered as a horde of thieves and bandits. Magic and astrology were in those days the only fashionable sciences; and as Moses was, it is said, instructed in the wisdom of the Egyptians, it was not difficult for him to inspire veneration and attachment for himself in the rustic and ignorant children of Jacob, and to induce them to accept, in their misery, the discipline he wished to give them. That is very different from what the Jews and our Christ-worshipers wish to make us believe. By what certain rule can we know that we should put faith in these rather than in the others? There is no sound reason for it. There is as little of certainty and even of probability in the miracles of the New Testament as in those of the Old.

It will serve no purpose to say that the histories which relate the facts contained in the Gospels have been regarded as true and sacred; that they have always been faithfully preserved without any alteration of the truths which they contain; since this is perhaps the very reason why they should be the more suspected, having been corrupted by those who drew profit from them, or who feared that they were not sufficiently favorable to them.

Generally, authors who transcribe this kind of histories, take the right to enlarge or to retrench all they please, in order to serve their own interests. This is what even our Christ-worshipers can not deny; for, without mentioning several other important personages who recognized the additions, the retrenchments, and the falsifications which have been made at different times in their Holy Scriptures, their saint Jerome, a famous philosopher among them, formally said in several passages of his "Prologues," that they had been corrupted and falsified; being, even in his day, in the hands of all kinds of persons, who added and suppressed whatever they pleased; so, "Thus there were," said he, "as many different models as different copies of the Gospels."

In regard to the books of the Old Testament, Esdras, a priest of the law, testifies himself to having corrected and completed wholly the pretended sacred books of his law, which had partly been lost and partly corrupted. He divided them into twenty-two books, according to the number of the Hebraic letters, and wrote several other books, whose doctrine was to be revealed to the learned men alone. If these books have been partly lost and partly corrupted, as Esdras and St. Jerome testify in so many passages, there is then no certainty in regard to what they contain; and as for Esdras saying he had corrected and compiled them by the inspiration of God Himself there is no certainty of that, since there is no impostor who would not make the same claim. All the books of the law of Moses and of the prophets which could be found, were burned in the days of Antiochus. The Talmud, considered by the Jews as a holy and sacred book, and which contains all the Divine laws, with the sentences and notable sayings of the Rabbins, of their interpretation of the Divine and of the human laws, and a prodigious number of other secrets and mysteries in the Hebraic language, is considered by the Christians as a book made up of reveries, fables, impositions, and ungodliness. In the year 1559 they burned in Rome, according to the command of the inquisitors of the faith, twelve hundred of these Talmuds, which were found in a library in the city of Cremona. The Pharisees, a famous sect among the Jews, accepted but the five books of Moses, and rejected all the prophets. Among the Christians, Marcion and his votaries rejected the books of Moses and the prophets, and introduced other fashionable Scriptures. Carpocrates and his followers did the same, and rejected the whole of the Old Testament, and contended that Jesus Christ was but a man like all others. The Marcionites repudiated as bad, the whole of the Old Testament, and rejected the greater part of the four Gospels and the Epistles of St. Paul. The Ebionites accepted but the Gospel of St. Matthew, rejecting the three others, and the Epistles of St. Paul. The Marcionites published a Gospel under the name of St. Matthias, in order to confirm their doctrine. The apostles introduced other Scriptures in order to maintain their errors; and to carry out this, they made use of certain Acts, which they attributed to St. Andrew and to St. Thomas.

The Manicheans wrote a gospel of their own style, and rejected the Scriptures of the prophets and the apostles. The Etzaites sold a certain book which they claimed to have come from Heaven; they cut up the other Scriptures according to their fancy. Origen himself, with all his great mind, corrupted the Scriptures and forged changes in the allegories which did not suit him, thus corrupting the sense of the prophets and apostles, and even some of the principal points of doctrine. His books are now mutilated and falsified; they are but fragments collected by others who have appeared since. The Ellogians attributed to the heretic Corinthus the Gospel and the Apocalypse of St. John; this is why they reject them. The heretics of our last centuries reject as apocryphal several books which the Roman Catholics consider as true and sacred—such as the books of Tobias, Judith, Esther, Baruch, the Song of the Three Children in the Furnace, the History of Susannah, and that of the Idol Bel, the Wisdom of Solomon, Ecclesiasticus, the first and second book of Maccabees; to which uncertain and doubtful books we could add several others that have been attributed to the other apostles; as, for example, the Acts of St. Thomas, his Circuits, his Gospel, and his Apocalypse; the Gospel of St. Bartholomew, that of St. Matthias, of St. Jacques, of St. Peter and of the Apostles, as also the Deeds of St. Peter, his book on Preaching, and that of his Apocalypse; that of the Judgment, that of the Childhood of the Saviour, and several others of the same kind, which are all rejected as apocryphal by the Roman Catholics, even by the Pope Gelasee, and by the S. S. F. F. of the Romish Communion. That which most confirms that there is no foundation of truth in regard to the authority given to these books, is that those who maintain their Divinity are compelled to acknowledge that they have no certainty as a basis, if their faith did not assure them and oblige them to believe it. Now, as faith is but a principle of error and imposture, how can faith, that is to say, a blind belief, render the books reliable which are themselves the foundation of this blind belief? What a pity and what insanity! But let us see if these books have of themselves any feature of truth; as, for example, of erudition, of wisdom, and of holiness, or some other perfections which are suited only to a God; and if the miracles which are cited agree with what we ought to think of the grandeur, goodness, justice, and infinite wisdom of an Omnipotent God.

There is no erudition, no sublime thought, nor any production which surpasses the ordinary capacities of the human mind. On the contrary, we shall see on one side fabulous tales similar to that of a woman formed of a man's rib; of the pretended terrestrial Paradise; of a serpent which spoke, which reasoned, and which was more cunning than man; of an ass which spoke, and reprimanded its master for ill-treating it; of a universal deluge, and of an ark where animals of all kinds were inclosed; of the confusion of languages and of the division of the nations, without speaking of numerous other useless narrations upon low and frivolous subjects which important authors would scorn to relate. All these narrations appear to be fables, as much as those invented about the industry of Prometheus, the box of Pandora, the war of the Giants against the Gods, and similar others which the poets have invented to amuse the men of their time.

On the other hand we will see a mixture of laws and ordinances, or superstitious practices concerning sacrifices, the purifications of the old law, the senseless distinctions in regard to animals, of which it supposes some to be pure and others to be impure. These laws are no more respectable than those of the most idolatrous nations. We shall see but simple stories, true or false, of several kings, princes, or individuals, who lived right or wrong, or who performed noble or mean actions, with other low and frivolous things also related.

From all this, it is evident that no great genius was required, nor Divine Revelations to produce these things. It would not be creditable to a God.

Finally, we see in these books but the discourses, the conduct, and the actions of those renowned prophets who proclaimed themselves especially inspired by God. We will see their way of acting and speaking, their dreams, their illusions, their reveries; and it will be easy to judge whether they do not resemble visionaries and fanatics much more than wise and enlightened persons.

There are, however, in a few of these books, several good teachings and beautiful maxims of morals, as in the Proverbs attributed to Solomon, in the book of Wisdom and of Ecclesiastes; but this same Solomon, the wisest of their writers, is also the most incredulous; he doubts even the immortality of the soul, and concludes his works by saying that there is nothing good but to enjoy in peace the fruits of one's labor, and to live with those whom we love.

How superior are the authors who are called profane, such as Xenophon, Plato, Cicero, the Emperor Antoninus, the Emperor Julian, Virgil, etc., to the books which we are told are inspired of God. I can truly say that the fables of Aesop, for example, are certainly more ingenious and more instructive than all these rough and poor parables which are related in the Gospels.

But what shows us that this kind of books is not of Divine Inspiration, is, that aside from the low order, coarseness of style, and the lack of system in the narrations of the different facts, which are very badly arranged, we do not see that the authors agree; they contradict each other in several things; they had not even sufficient enlightenment or natural talents to write a history.

Here are some examples of the contradictions which are found among them. The Evangelist Matthew claims that Jesus Christ descended from king David by his son Solomon through Joseph, reputed to be His father; and Luke claims that He is descended from the same David by his son Nathan through Joseph.

Matthew says, in speaking of Jesus, that, it being reported in Jerusalem that a new king of the Jews was born, and that the wise men had come to adore Him, the king Herod, fearing that this pretended new king would rob him of his crown some day, caused the murder of all the new-born children under two years, in all the neighborhood of Bethlehem, where he had been told that this new king was born; and that Joseph and the mother of Jesus, having been warned in a dream by an angel, of this wicked intention, took flight immediately to Egypt, where they stayed until the death of Herod, which happened many years afterward.

On the contrary, Luke asserts that Joseph and the mother of Jesus lived peaceably during six weeks in the place where their child Jesus was born; that He was circumcised according to the law of the Jews, eight days after His birth; and when the time prescribed by the law for the purification of His mother had arrived, she and Joseph, her husband, carried Him to Jerusalem in order to present Him to God in His temple, and to offer at the same time a sacrifice which was ordained by God's law; after which they returned to Galilee, into their town of Nazareth, where their child Jesus grew every day in grace and in wisdom. Luke goes on to say that His father and His mother went every year to Jerusalem on the solemn days of their Easter feast, but makes no mention of their flight into Egypt, nor of the cruelty of Herod toward the children of the province of Bethlehem. In regard to the cruelty of Herod, as neither the historians of that time speak of it, nor Josephus, the historian who wrote the life of this Herod, and as the other Evangelists do not mention it, it is evident that the journey of those wise men, guided by a star, this massacre of little children, and this flight to Egypt, were but absurd falsehoods. For it is not credible that Josephus, who blamed the vices of this king, could have been silent on such a dark and detestable action, if what the Evangelist said had been true.

In regard to the duration of the public life of Jesus Christ, according to what the first three Evangelists say, there could be scarcely more than three months from the time of His baptism until His death, supposing He was thirty years old when He was baptized by John, according to Luke, and that He was born on the 25th of December. For, from this baptism, which was in the year 15 of Tiberius Caesar, and in the year when Anne and Caiaphas were high-priests, to the first Easter following, which was in the month of March, there was but about three months; according to what the first three Evangelists say, He was crucified on the eve of the first Easter following His baptism, and the first time He went to Jerusalem with His disciples; because all that they say of His baptism, of His travels, of His miracles, of His preaching, of His death and passion, must have taken place in the same year of His baptism, for the Evangelists speak of no other year following, and it appears even by the narration of His acts that He performed them consecutively immediately after His baptism, and in a very short time, during which we see but an interval of six days before his Transfiguration; during these six days we do not see that He did anything. We see by this that He lived but about three months after His baptism, from which, if we subtract the forty days and forty nights which He passed in the desert immediately after His baptism, it would follow that the length of His public life from His first preaching till His death, would have lasted but about six weeks; and according to what John says, it would have lasted at least three years and three months, because it appears by the Gospel of this apostle, that, during the course of His public life He might have been three or four times at Jerusalem at the Easter feast which happened but once a year.

Now if it is true that He had been there three or four times after His baptism, as John testifies, it is false that He lived but three months after His baptism, and that He was crucified the first time He went to Jerusalem.

If it is said that these first three Evangelists really mean but one year, but that they do not indicate distinctly the others which elapsed since His baptism; or that John understood that there was but one Easter, although he speaks of several, and that he only anticipated the time when he repeatedly tells us that the Easter feast of the Jews was near at hand, and that Jesus went to Jerusalem, and, consequently, that there is but an apparent contradiction upon this subject between the Evangelists, I am willing to accept this; but it is certain that this apparent contradiction springs from the fact, that they do not explain themselves in all the circumstances that are noted in the narration which they make. Be that as it may, there will always be this inference made, that they were not inspired by God when they wrote their biographies of Christ.

Here is another contradiction in regard to the first thing which Jesus

Christ did immediately after His baptism; for the first three Evangelists state, that He was transported immediately by the Spirit into the desert, where He fasted forty days and forty nights, and where He was several times tempted by the Devil; and, according to what John says, He departed two days after His baptism to go into Galilee, where He performed His first miracle by changing water into wine at the wedding of Cana, where He found Himself three days after His arrival in Galilee, more than thirty leagues from the place in which He had been.

In regard to the place of His first retreat after His departure from the desert, Matthew says that He returned to Galilee, and that leaving the city of Nazareth, He went to live at Capernaum, a maritime city; and Luke says, that He came at first to Nazareth, and afterward went to Capernaum.

They contradict each other in regard to the time and manner in which the apostles followed Him; for the first three say that Jesus, passing on the shore of the Sea of Galilee, saw Simon and Andrew his brother, and that He saw at a little distance James and his brother John with their father, Zebedee. John, on the contrary, says that it was Andrew, brother of Simon Peter, who first followed Jesus with another disciple of John the Baptist, having seen Him pass before them, when they were with their Master on the shores of the Jordan.

In regard to the Lord's Supper, the first three Evangelists note that Jesus Christ instituted the Sacrament of His body and His blood, in the form of bread and wine, the same as our Roman Christ-worshipers say; and John does not mention this mysterious sacrament. John says that after this supper, Jesus washed His apostles' feet, and commanded them to do the same thing to each other, and relates a long discourse which He delivered then. But the other Evangelists do not speak of the washing of the feet, nor of the long discourse He gave them then. On the contrary, they testify that immediately after this supper, He went with His apostles upon the Mount of Olives, where He gave up His Spirit to sadness, and was in anguish while His apostles slept, at a short distance. They contradict each other upon the day on which they say the Lord's Supper took place; because on one side, they note that it took place Easter-eve, that is, the evening of the first day of Azymes, or of the feast of unleavened bread; as it is noted (1) in Exodus, (2) in Leviticus, and (3) in Numbers; and, on the other hand, they say that He was crucified the day following the Lord's Supper, about midday after the Jews had His trial during the whole night and morning. Now, according to what they say, the day after this supper took place, ought not to be Easter-eve. Therefore, if He died on the eve of Easter, toward midday, it was not on the eve of this feast that this supper took place. There is consequently a manifest error.

They contradict each other, also, in regard to the women who followed Jesus from Galilee, for the first three Evangelists say that these women, and those who knew Him, among whom were Mary Magdalene, and Mary, mother of James and Joseph, and the mother of Zebedee's children, were looking on at a distance when He was hanged and nailed upon the cross. John says, on the contrary, that the mother of Jesus and His mother's sister, and Mary Magdalene were standing near His cross with John, His apostle. The contradiction is manifest, for, if these women and this disciple were near Him, they were not at a distance, as the others say they were.

They contradict each other upon the pretended apparitions which they relate that Jesus made after His pretended resurrection; for Matthew speaks of but two apparitions: the one when He appeared to Mary Magdalene and to another woman, also named Mary, and when He appeared to His eleven disciples who had returned to Galilee upon the mountain where He had appointed to meet them. Mark speaks of three apparitions: The first, when He appeared to Mary Magdalene; the second, when He appeared to His two disciples, who went to Emmaus; and the third, when He appeared to His eleven disciples, whom He reproaches for their incredulity. Luke speaks of but two apparitions the same as Matthew; and John the Evangelist speaks of four apparitions, and adds to Mark's three, the one which He made to seven or eight of His disciples who were fishing upon the shores of the Tiberian Sea.

They contradict each other, also, in regard to the place of these apparitions; for Matthew says that it was in Galilee, upon a mountain; Mark says that it was when they were at table; Luke says that He brought them out of Jerusalem as far as Bethany, where He left them by rising to Heaven; and John says that it was in the city of Jerusalem, in a house of which they had closed the doors, and another time upon the borders of the Tiberian Sea.

Thus is much contradiction in the report of these pretended apparitions. They contradict each other in regard to His pretended ascension to heaven; for Luke and Mark say positively that He went to heaven in presence of the eleven apostles, but neither Matthew nor John mentions at all this pretended ascension. More than this, Matthew testifies sufficiently that He did not ascend to heaven; for he said positively that Jesus Christ assured His apostles that He would be and remain always with them until the end of the world. "Go ye," He said to them, in this pretended apparition, "and teach all nations, and be assured that I am with you always, even unto the end of the world." Luke contradicts himself upon the subject; for in his Gospel he says that it was in Bethany where He ascended to heaven in the presence of His apostles, and in his Acts of the Apostles (supposing him to have been the author) he says that it was upon the Mount of Olives. He contradicts himself again about this ascension; for he notes in his Gospel that it was the very day of His resurrection, or the first night following, that He ascended to heaven; and in the Acts of the Apostles he says that it was forty days after His resurrection; this certainly does not correspond. If all the apostles had really seen their Master gloriously rise to heaven, how could it be possible that Matthew and John, who would have seen it as well as the others, passed in silence such a glorious mystery, and which was so advantageous to their Master, considering that they relate many other circumstances of His life and of His actions which are much less important than this one? How is it that Matthew does not mention this ascension? And why does Christ not explain clearly how He would live with them always, although He left them visibly to ascend to heaven? It is not easy to comprehend by what secret He could live with those whom He left.

I pass in silence many other contradictions; what I have said is sufficient to show that these books are not of Divine Inspiration, nor even of human wisdom, and, consequently, do not deserve that we should put any faith in them.

II.

OF MIRACLES.

But by what privilege do these four Gospels, and some other similar books, pass for Holy and Divine more than several others, which bear no less the title of Gospels, and which have been published under the name of some other apostles? If it is said that the reputed Gospels are falsely attributed to the apostles, we can say the same of the first ones; if we suppose the first ones to be falsified and changed, we can think the same of the others. Thus there is no positive proof to make us discern the one from the other; in spite of the Church, which assumes to deride the matter, it is not credible.

In regard to the pretended miracles related in the Old Testament, they could have been performed but to indicate on the part of God an unjust and odious discrimination between nations and between individuals; purposely injuring the one in order to especially favor the other. The vocation and the choice which God made of the Patriarchs, Abraham, Isaac, and Jacob, in order to make for Himself of their posterity a people which He would sanctify and bless above all other peoples of the earth, is a proof of it. But it will be said God is the absolute master of His favors and of His benefits; He can grant them to whomsoever He pleases, without any one having the right to complain or to accuse Him of injustice. This reason is useless; for God, the Author of nature, the Father of all men, ought to love them all alike as His own work, and, consequently, He ought to be equally their protector and their benefactor; giving them life, He ought to give all that is necessary for the well-being of His creatures.

If all these pretended miracles of the Old and of the New Testament were true, we could say that God would have had more care in providing for the least good of men than for their greatest and principal good; that He would have punished more severely trifling faults in certain persons than He would have punished great crimes in others; and, finally, that He would not have desired to show Himself as beneficent in the most pressing needs as in the least. This is easy enough to show as much by the miracles which it is pretended that He performed, as by those which He did not perform, and which He would have performed rather than any other, if it is true that He performed any at all. For example, it is claimed that God had the kindness to send an angel to console and to assist a simple maid, while He left, and still leaves every day, a countless number of innocents to languish and starve to death; it is claimed that He miraculously preserved during forty years the clothes and the shoes of a few people, while He will not watch over the natural preservation of the vast quantities of goods which are useful and necessary for the subsistence of great nations, and that are lost every day by different accidents. It is claimed that He sent to the first beings of the human race, Adam and Eve, a devil, or a simple serpent, to seduce them, and by this means ruin all men. This is not credible! It is claimed, that by a special providence, He prevented the King of Gerais, a Pagan, from committing sin with a strange woman, although there would be no results to follow; and yet He did not prevent Adam and Eve from offending Him and falling into the sin of disobedience—a sin which, according to our Christ-worshipers was to be fatal, and cause the destruction of the human race. This is not credible!

Let us come to the pretended miracles of the New Testament. They consist, as is pretended, in this: that Jesus Christ and His apostles cured, through the Deity, all kinds of diseases and infirmities, giving sight to the blind, hearing to the deaf, speech to the dumb, making the lame to walk, curing the paralytics, driving the devils from those who were possessed, and bringing the dead to life.

We find several of these miracles in the Gospels, but we see a good many more of them in the books that our Christ-worshipers have written of the admirable lives of their saints; for in these lives we nearly everywhere read that these pretended blessed ones cured diseases and infirmities, expelled the devils wherever they encountered them, solely in the name of Jesus or by the sign of the cross; that they controlled the elements; that God favored them so much that He even preserved to them His Divine power after their death, and that this Divine power could be communicated even to the least of their clothing, even to their shadows, and even to the infamous instruments of their death. It is said that the shoe of St. Honorius raised a dead man on the sixth of January; that the staff of St. Peter, that of St. James, and that of St. Bernard performed miracles. The same is said of the cord of St. Francis, of the staff of St. John of God, and of the girdle of St. Melanie. It is said that St. Gracilien was divinely instructed as to what he ought to believe and to teach, and that he, by the influence of his prayer, removed a mountain which prevented him from building a church; that from the sepulchre of St. Andrew flowed incessantly a liquor which cured all sorts of diseases; that the soul of St. Benedict was seen ascending to Heaven clothed with a precious cloak and surrounded by burning lamps; that St. Dominic said that God never refused him anything he asked; that St. Francis commanded the swallows, swans, and other birds to obey him, and that often the fishes, rabbits, and the hares came and placed themselves on his hands and on his lap; that St. Paul and St. Pantaleon, having been beheaded, there flowed milk instead of blood; that the blessed Peter of Luxembourg, in the first two years after his death (1388 and 1389), performed two thousand four hundred miracles, among which forty-two dead were brought to life, not including more than three thousand other miracles which he has performed since; that the fifty philosophers whom St. Catherine converted, having all been thrown into a great fire, their whole bodies were afterward found and not a single hair was scorched; that the body of St. Catherine was carried off by angels after her death, and buried by them upon Mount Sinai; that the day of the canonization of St. Antoine de Padua, all the bells of the city of Lisbon rang of themselves, without any one knowing how it was done; that this saint being once near the sea-shore, and calling the fishes, they came to him in a great multitude, and raised their heads out of the water and listened to him attentively. We should never come to an end if we had to report all this idle talk; there is no subject, however vain, frivolous, and even ridiculous, on which the authors of these "LIVES OF THE SAINTS" do not take pleasure in heaping miracles upon miracles, for they are skillful in forging absurd falsehoods.

It is certainly not without reason that we consider these things as lies; for it is easy to see that all these pretended miracles have been invented but by imitating the fables of the Pagan poets. This is sufficiently obvious by the resemblance which they bear one to another.

III.

SIMILARITY BETWEEN ANCIENT AND MODERN MIRACLES.

If our Christ-worshipers claim that God endowed their saints with power to perform the miracles related in their lives, some of the Pagans claim also that the daughters of Anius, high-priest of Apollo, had really received from the god Bacchus the power to change all they desired into wheat, into wine, or into oil, etc.; that Jupiter gave to the nymphs who took care of his education, a horn of the goat which nursed him in his infancy, with this virtue, that it could give them an abundance of all they wished for.

If our Christ-worshipers assert that their saints had the power of raising the dead, and that they had Divine revelations, the Pagans had said before them that Athalide, son of Mercury, had obtained from his father the gift of living, dying, and coming to life whenever he wished, and that he had also the knowledge of all that transpired in this world as well as in the other; and that Esculapius, son of Apollo, had raised the dead, and, among others, he brought to life Hyppolites, son of Theseus, by Diana's request; and that Hercules, also, raised from the dead Alceste, wife of Admetus, King of Thessalia, to return her to her husband.

If our Christ-worshipers say that Christ was miraculously born of a virgin, the Pagans had said before them that Remus and Romulus, the founders of Rome, were miraculously born of a vestal virgin named Ilia, or Silvia, or Rhea Silvia; they had already said that Mars, Argus, Vulcan, and others were born of the goddess Juno without sexual union; and, also, that Minerva, goddess of the sciences, sprang from Jupiter's brain, and that she came out of it, all armed, by means of a blow which this god gave to his own head.

If our Christ-worshipers claim that their saints made water gush from rocks, the Pagans pretend also that Minerva made a fountain of oil spring forth from a rock as a recompense for a temple which had been dedicated to her.

If our Christ-worshipers boast of having received images from Heaven miraculously, as, for example, those of Notre-Dame de Loretto, and of Liesse and several other gifts from Heaven, as the pretended Holy Vial of Rheims, as the white Chasuble which St. Ildefonse received from the Virgin Mary, and other similar things: the Pagans boasted before them of having received a sacred shield as a mark of the preservation of their city of Rome, and the Trojans boasted before them of having received miraculously from Heaven their Palladium, or their Idol of Pallas, which came, they said, to takes its place in the temple which they had erected in honor of this Goddess.

If our Christ-worshipers pretend that Jesus Christ was seen by His apostles ascending to Heaven, and that several of their pretended saints were transported to Heaven by angels, the Roman Pagans had said before them, that Romulus, their founder, was seen after his death; that Ganymede, son of Troas, king of Troy, was transported to Heaven by Jupiter to serve him as cup-bearer that the hair of Berenice, being consecrated to the temple of Venus, was afterward carried to Heaven; they say the same thing of Cassiope and Andromedes, and even of the ass of Silenus.

If our Christ-worshipers pretend that several of their saints' bodies were miraculously saved from decomposition after death, and that they were found by Divine Revelations, after having been lost for a long time, the Pagans say the same of the holy of Orestes, which they pretend to have found through an oracle, etc.

If our Christ-worshipers say that the seven sleeping brothers slept during one hundred and seventy-seven years, while they were shut up in a cave, the Pagans claim that Epimenides, the philosopher, slept during fifty-seven years in a cave where he fell asleep.

If our Christ-worshipers claim that several of their saints continued to speak after losing the head, or having the tongue cut out, the Pagans claim that the head of Gambienus recited a long poem after separation from his body.

If our Christ-worshipers glorify themselves that their temples and churches are ornamented with several pictures and rich gifts which show miraculous cures performed by the intercession of their saints, we also see, or at least we formerly saw in the temple of Esculapius at Epidaurus, many paintings of miraculous cures which he had performed.

If our Christ-worshipers claim that several of their saints have been miraculously preserved in the flames without having received any injury to their bodies or their clothing, the Pagans claim that the Holy women of the temple of Diana walked upon burning coals barefooted without burning or hurting their feet, and that the priests of the Goddess Feronie and of Hirpicus walked in the same way upon burning coals in the fires which were made in honor of Apollo.

If the angels built a chapel for St. Clement at the bottom of the sea, the little house of Baucis and of Philemon was miraculously changed into a superb temple as a reward of their piety. If several of their saints, as St. James and St. Maurice, appeared several times in their armies, mounted and equipped in ancient style, and fought for them, Castor and Pollux appeared several times in battles and fought for the Romans against their enemies; if a ram was miraculously found to be offered as a sacrifice in the place of Isaac, whom his father Abraham was about to sacrifice, the Goddess Vesta also sent a heifer to be sacrificed in the place of Metella, daughter of Metellus: the Goddess Diana sent a hind in the place of Iphigenie when she was at the stake to be sacrificed to her, and by this means Iphigenie was saved.

If St. Joseph went into Egypt by the warning of an angel, Simonides, the poet, avoided several great dangers by miraculous warnings which had been given to him.

If Moses forced a stream of water to flow from a rock by striking it with his staff, the horse Pegasus did the same: by striking a rock with his foot a fountain issued.

If St. Vincent Ferrier brought to life a dead man hacked into pieces, whose body was already half roasted and half broiled, Pelops, son of Tantalus king of Phrygia, having been torn to pieces by his father to be sacrificed to the Gods, they gathered all the pieces, joined them, and brought them to life.

If several crucifixes and other images have miraculously spoken and answered, the Pagans say that their oracles have spoken and given answers to those who consulted them, and that the head of Orpheus and that of Policrates gave oracles after their death.

If God revealed by a voice from Heaven that Jesus Christ was His Son, as the Evangelists say, Vulcan showed by the apparition of a miraculous flame, that Coceculus was really his son.

If God has miraculously nourished some of His saints, the Pagan poets pretend that Triptolemus was miraculously nourished with Divine milk by Ceres, who gave him also a chariot drawn by two dragons, and that Phineus, son of Mars, being born after his mother's death, was nevertheless miraculously nourished by her milk.

If several saints miraculously tamed the ferocity of the most cruel beasts, it is said that Orpheus attracted to him, by the sweetness of his voice and by the harmony of his instruments, lions, bears, and tigers, and softened the ferocity of their nature; that he attracted rocks and trees, and that even the rivers stopped their course to listen to his song.

Finally, to abbreviate, because we could report many others, if our Christ-worshipers pretend that the walls of the city of Jericho fell by the sound of their trumpets, the Pagans say that the walls of the city of Thebes were built by the sound of the musical instruments of Amphion; the stones, as the poets say, arranging themselves to the sweetness of his harmony; this would be much more miraculous and more admirable than to see the walls demolished.

There is certainly a great similarity between the Pagan miracles and our own. As it would be great folly to give credence to these pretended miracles of Paganism, it is not any the less so to have faith in those of Christianity, because they all come from the same source of error. It was for this that the Manicheans and the Arians, who existed at the commencement of the Christian Era, derided these pretended miracles performed by the invocation of saints, and blamed those who invoked them after death and honored their relics.

Let us return at present to the principal end which God proposed to Himself, in sending His Son into the world to become man; it must have been, as they say, to redeem the world from sin and to destroy entirely the works of the pretended Devil, etc. This is what our Christ-worshipers claim also, that Jesus Christ died for them according to His Father's intention, which is plainly stated in all the pretended Holy Books. What! an Almighty God, who was willing to become a mortal man for the love of men, and to shed His blood to the last drop, to save them all, would yet have limited His power to only curing a few diseases and physical infirmities of a few individuals who were brought to Him; and would not have employed His Divine goodness in curing the infirmities of the soul! that is to say, in curing all men of their vices and their depravities, which are worse than the diseases of their bodies! This is not credible. What! such a good God would desire to preserve dead corpses from decay and corruption; and would not keep from the contagion and corruption of vice and sin the souls of a countless number of persons whom He sought to redeem at the price of His blood, and to sanctify by His grace! What a pitiful contradiction!

IV.

OF THE FALSITY OF THE CHRISTIAN RELIGION.

Let us proceed to the pretended visions and Divine Revelations, upon which our Christ-worshipers establish the truth and the certainty of their religion.

In order to give a just idea of it, I believe it is best to say in general, that they are such, that if any one should dare now to boast of similar ones, or wish to make them valued, he would certainly be regarded as a fool or a fanatic.

Here is what the pretended Visions and Divine Revelations are:

God, as these pretended Holy Books claim, having appeared for the first time to Abraham, said to him: "Get thee out of thy country, and from thy kindred and from thy father's house, into a land that I will show thee." Abraham, having gone there, God, says the Bible, appeared the second time to him, and said, "Unto thy seed will I give this land," and there built he an altar unto the Lord, who appeared unto him. After the death of Isaac, his son, Jacob going one day to Mesopotamia to look for a wife that would suit him, having walked all the day, and being tired from the long distance, desired to rest toward evening; lying upon the ground, with his head resting upon a few stones, he fell asleep, and during his sleep he saw a ladder set upon the earth, and the top of it reached to Heaven; and beheld the angels of God ascending and descending on it. And behold, the Lord stood above it, and said: "I am the Lord, God of Abraham thy father, and the God of Isaac; the land whereon thou liest, to thee will I give it, and to thy seed. And thy seed shall be as the dust of the earth, and thou shalt spread abroad to the west and to the east, and to the north and to the south and in thee and in thy seed shall all the nations of the earth be blessed. And behold, I am with thee and will keep thee in all places whither thou goest, and will bring thee again into this land: for I will not leave thee until I have done that which I have spoken to thee of." And Jacob awaked out of his sleep, and he said: "Surely the Lord is in this place, and I knew it not." And he was afraid, and said: "How dreadful is this place! this is none other than the house of God, and this is the gate of Heaven." And Jacob rose up early in the morning, and took the stone that he had put for his pillow, and set it up for a pillar, and poured oil on the top of it, and made at the same time a vow to God, that if he should return safe and sound, he would give Him a tithe of all he might possess.

Here is yet another vision. Watching the flocks of his father-in-law, Laban, who had promised him that all the speckled lambs produced by his sheep should be his recompense, he dreamed one night that he saw all the males leap upon the females, and all the lambs they brought forth were speckled. In this beautiful dream, God appeared to him, and said: "Lift up now thine eyes and see that the rams which leap upon the cattle are ring-streaked, speckled, and grizzled; for I have seen all that Laban does unto thee. Now arise, get thee out from this land, and return unto the land of thy kindred." As he was returning with his whole family, and with all he obtained from his father-in-law, he had, says the Bible, a wrestle with an unknown man during the whole night, until the breaking of the day, and as this man had not been able to subdue him, He asked him who he was. Jacob told Him his name; and He said: "Thy name shall be called no more Jacob, but Israel; for as a prince hast thou power with God and with men, and hast prevailed."

This is a specimen of the first of these pretended Visions and Divine Revelations. We can judge of the others by these. Now, what appearance of Divinity is there in dreams so gross and illusions so vain? As if some foreigners, Germans, for instance, should come into our France, and, after seeing all the beautiful provinces of our kingdom, should claim that God had appeared to them in their country, that He had told them to go into France, and that He would give to them and to their posterity all the beautiful lands, domains, and provinces of this kingdom which extend from the rivers Rhine and Rhone, even to the sea; that He would make an everlasting alliance with them, that He would multiply their race, that He would make their posterity as numerous as the stars of Heaven and as the sands of the sea, etc., who would not laugh at such folly, and consider these strangers as insane fools!

Now there is no reason to think otherwise of all that has been said by these pretended Holy Patriarchs, Abraham, Isaac, and Jacob, in regard to the Divine Revelations which they claim to have had. As to the institution of bloody sacrifices, the Holy Scriptures attribute it to God. As it would be too wearisome to go into the disgusting details of this kind of sacrifices, I refer the reader to Exodus. [See chapters xxv., xxvii., xxyiii., and xxix.]

Were not men insane and blind to believe they were honoring God by tearing into pieces, butchering, and burning His own creatures, under the pretext of offering them as sacrifices to Him? And even now, how is it that our Christ-worshipers are so extravagant as to expect to please God the Father, by offering up to Him the sacrifice of His Divine Son, in remembrance of His being shamefully nailed to a cross upon which He died? Certainly this can spring only from an obstinate blindness of mind.

In regard to the detail of the sacrifices of animals, it consists but in colored clothing, blood, plucks, livers, birds' crops, kidneys, claws, skins, in the dung, smoke, cakes, certain measures of oil and wine, the whole being offered and infected by dirty ceremonies as filthy and contemptible as the most extravagant performances of magic. What is most horrible of all this is, that the law of this detestable Jewish people commanded that even men should be offered up as sacrifices. The barbarians, whoever they were, who introduced this horrible law, commanded to put to death any man who had been consecrated to the God of the Jews, whom they called Adonai: and it is according to this execrable precept that Jephthah sacrificed his daughter, and that Saul wanted to sacrifice his son.

But here is yet another proof of the falsity of these revelations of which we have spoken. It is the lack of the fulfillment of the great and magnificent promises by which they were accompanied, for it is evident that these promises never have been fulfilled.

The proof of this consists in three principal points:

Firstly. Their posterity was to be more numerous than all the other nations of the world.

Secondly. The people who should spring from their race were to be the happiest, the holiest, and the most victorious of all the people of the earth.

Thirdly. His covenant was to be everlasting, and they should possess forever the country He should give them. Now it is plain that these promises-never were fulfilled.

Firstly. It is certain that the Jewish people, or the people of Israel—which is the only one that can be regarded as having descended from the Patriarchs Abraham, Isaac, and Jacob, and the only ones to whom these promises should have been fulfilled—have never been so numerous that it could be compared with the other nations of the earth, much less with the sands of the sea, etc., for we see that in the very time when it was the most numerous and the most flourishing, it never occupied more than the little sterile provinces of Palestine and its environs, which are almost nothing in comparison with the vast extent of a multitude of flourishing kingdoms which are on all sides of the earth.

Secondly. They have never been fulfilled concerning the great blessings with which they were to be favored; for, although they won a few small victories over some poor nations whom they plundered, this did not prevent them from being conquered and reduced to servitude; their kingdom destroyed as well as their nation, by the Roman army; and even now the remainder of this unfortunate nation is looked upon as the vilest and most contemptible of all the earth, having no country, no dominion, no superiority.

Finally, these promises have not been fulfilled in respect to this everlasting covenant, which God ought to have fulfilled to them; because we do not see now, and we have never seen, any evidence of this covenant; and, on the contrary, they have been for many centuries excluded from the possession of the small country they pretended God had promised that they should enjoy forever. Thus, since these pretended promises were never fulfilled, it is certain evidence of their falsity; which proves, plainly, that these pretended Holy Books which contain them were not of Divine inspiration. Therefore it is useless for our Christ-worshipers to pretend to make use of them as infallible testimony to prove the truth of their religion.

THE HOLY SCRIPTURES.

V.

(1) OF THE OLD TESTAMENT.

Our Christ-worshipers add to their reasons for credulity and to the proofs of the truth of their testimony, the prophecies which are, as they pretend, sure evidences of the truth of the revelations or inspirations of God, there being no one but God who could predict future events so long before they came to pass, as those which have been predicted by the prophets.

Let us see, then, who these pretended prophets are, and if we ought to consider them as important as our Christ-worshipers pretend they are. These men were but visionaries and fanatics, who acted and spoke according to the impulsions of their ruling passions, and who imagined that it was the Spirit of God by which they spoke and acted; or they were impostors who feigned to be prophets, and who, in order to more easily deceive the ignorant and simple-minded, boasted of acting and speaking by the Spirit of God. I would like to know how an Ezekiel would be received who should say that God made him eat for his breakfast a roll of parchment; commanded him to be tied like an insane man, and lie three hundred and ninety days upon his right side, and forty days upon his left, and commanded him to eat man's dung upon his bread, and afterward, as an accommodation, cow's dung? I ask how such a filthy statement would be received by the most stupid people of our provinces?

What can be yet a greater proof of the falsity of these pretended prophecies, than the violence with which these prophets reproach each other for speaking falsely in the name of God, reproaches which they claim to make in behalf of God. All of them say, "Beware of the false prophets!" as the quacks say, "Beware of the counterfeit pills!" How could these insane impostors tell the future? No prophecy in favor of their Jewish nation was ever fulfilled. The number of prophecies which predict the prosperity and the greatness of Jerusalem is almost innumerable; in explanation of this, it will be said that it is very natural that a subdued and captive people should comfort themselves in their real afflictions by imaginary hopes—as a year after King James was deposed, the Irish people of his party forged several prophecies in regard to him.

But if these promises made to the Jews had been really true, the Jewish nation long ago would have been, and would still be, the most numerous, the most powerful, the most blessed, and the most victorious of all nations.

VI.

(2) THE NEW TESTAMENT.

Let us examine the pretended prophecies which are contained in the Gospels.

Firstly. An angel having appeared in a dream to a man named Joseph, father, or at least so reputed, of Jesus, son of Mary, said unto him:

"Joseph, thou son of David fear not to take unto thee Mary thy wife, for that which is conceived in her is of the Holy Ghost. And she shall bring forth a Son, and thou shalt call His name JESUS; for He shall save His people from their sins." This angel said also to Mary:

"Fear not, Mary, for thou hast found favor with God. And behold, thou shalt conceive in thy womb and bring forth a Son, and shalt call His name Jesus. He shall be great, and shall be called the Son of the Highest: and the Lord God shall give unto Him the throne of His father David. And He shall reign over the house of Jacob forever; and of His kingdom there shall be no end!" Jesus began to preach and to say:

"Repent, for the kingdom of Heaven is at hand. Take no thought for your life, what ye shall eat, or what ye shall drink, nor yet for your body what ye shall put on. Is not the life more than meat, and the body than raiment, for your Heavenly Father knoweth that ye have need of all these things. But seek ye first the kingdom of God and His righteousness, and all these things shall be added unto you."

Now, let every man who has not lost common sense, examine if this Jesus ever was a king, or if His disciples had abundance of all things. This Jesus promised to deliver the world from sin. Is there any prophecy which is more false? Is not our age a striking proof of it? It is said that Jesus came to save His people. In what way did He save it? It is the greatest number which rules any party. For example, one dozen or two of Spaniards or Frenchmen do not constitute the French or Spanish people; and if an army of a hundred and twenty thousand men were taken prisoners of war by an army of enemies which was stronger, and if the chief of this army should redeem only a few men, as ten or twelve soldiers or officers, by paying their ransom, it could not be claimed that he had delivered or redeemed his army. Then, who is this God who has been sacrificed, who died to save the world, and leaves so many nations damned? What a pity! and what horror!

Jesus Christ says that we have but to ask and we shall receive, and to seek and we shall find. He assures us that all we ask of God in His name shall be granted, and that if we have faith as a grain of mustard-seed, we could by one word remove mountains. If this promise is true, nothing appears impossible to our Christ-worshipers who have faith in Jesus. However, the contrary happens. If Mohammed had made the promises to his votaries that Christ made to His, without success, what would not be said about it. They would cry out, "Ah, the cheat! ah, the impostor!" These Christ-worshipers are in the same condition: they have been blind, and have not even yet recovered from their blindness; on the contrary, they are so ingenious in deceiving themselves, that they pretend that these promises have been fulfilled from the beginning of Christianity; that at that time it was necessary to have miracles, in order to convince the incredulous of the truth of religion; but that this religion being sufficiently established, the miracles were no longer necessary. Where, then, is their proof of all this?

Besides, He who made these promises did not limit them to a certain time, or to certain places, or to certain persons; but He made them generally to everybody. The faith of those who believe, says He, shall be followed by these miracles; "They shall cast out devils in My name, they shall speak in divers tongues, they shall handle serpents," etc.

In regard to the removal of mountains, He positively says that "whoever shall say to a mountain: 'Be thou removed, and be thou cast into the sea;' it shall be done;" provided that he does not doubt in his heart, but believes all he commands will be done. Are not all these promises given in a general way, without restriction as to time, place, or persons?

It is said that all the sects which are founded in errors and imposture will come to a shameful end. But if Jesus Christ intends to say that He has established a society of followers who will not fall either into vice or error, these words are absolutely false, as there is in Christendom no sect, no society, and no church which is not full of errors and vices, especially the Roman Church, although it claims to be the purest and the holiest of all. It was born into error, or rather it was conceived and formed in error; and even now it is full of delusions which are contrary to the intentions, the sentiments, or the doctrine of its Founder, because it has, contrary to His intention, abolished the laws of the Jews, which He approved, and which He came Himself, as He said, to fulfill and not to destroy. It has fallen into the errors and idolatry of Paganism, as is seen by the idolatrous worship which is offered to its God of dough, to its saints, to their images, and to their relics.

I know well that our Christ-worshipers consider it a lack of intelligence to accept literally the promises and prophecies as they are expressed; they reject the literal and natural sense of the words, to give them a mystical and spiritual sense which they call allegorical and figurative; claiming, for example, that the people of Israel and Judea, to whom these promises were made, were not understood as the Israelites after the body, but the Israelites in spirit: that is to say, the Christians which are the Israel of God, the true chosen people that by the promise made to this enslaved people, to deliver it from captivity, it is understood to be not the corporal deliverance of a single captive people, but the spiritual deliverance of all men from the servitude of the Devil, which was to be accomplished by their Divine Saviour; that by the abundance of riches, and all the temporal blessings promised to this people, is meant the abundance of spiritual graces; and finally, that by the city of Jerusalem, is meant not the terrestrial Jerusalem, but the spiritual Jerusalem, which is the Christian Church.

But it is easy to see that these spiritual and allegorical meanings having only a strange, imaginary sense, being a subterfuge of the interpreters, can not serve to show the truth or the falsehood of a proposition, or of any promises whatever. It is ridiculous to forge such allegorical meanings, since it is only by the relations of the natural and true sense that we can judge of their truth or falsehood. A proposition, a promise, for example, which is considered true in the proper and natural sense of the terms in which it is expressed, will not become false in itself under cover of a strange sense, one which does not belong to it. By the same reasoning, that which is manifestly false in its proper and natural sense, will not become true in itself, although we give it a strange sense, one foreign to the true.

We can say that the prophecies of the Old Testament adjusted to the New, would be very absurd and puerile things. For example, Abraham had two wives, of which the one, who was but a servant, represented the synagogue, and the other one, his lawful wife, represented the Christian Church; and that this Abraham had two sons, of which the one born of Hagar, the servant, represented the Old Testament; and the other, born of Sarah, the wife, represented the New Testament. Who would not laugh at such a ridiculous doctrine?

Is it not amusing that a piece of red cloth, exhibited by a prostitute as a signal to spies, in the Old Testament is made to represent the blood of Jesus Christ shed in the New? If—according to this manner of interpreting allegorically all that is said, done, and practiced in the ancient law of the Jews—we should interpret in the same allegorical way all the discourses, the actions, and the adventures of the famous Don Quixote de la Mancha, we would find the same sort of mysteries and ridiculous figures.

It is nevertheless upon this absurd foundation that the whole Christian religion rests. Thus it is that there is scarcely anything in this ancient law that the Christ-worshiping doctors do not try to explain in a mystical way to build up their system. The most false and the most ridiculous prophecy ever made is that of Jesus, in Luke, where it is pretended that there will be signs in the sun and in the moon, and that the Son of Man will appear in a cloud to judge men; and this is predicted for the generation living at that time. Has it come to pass? Did the Son of Man appear in a cloud?

VII.

ERRORS OF DOCTRINE AND OF MORALITY.

The Christian Apostolical Roman Religion teaches, and compels belief, that there is but one God, and, at the same time, that there are three Divine persons, each one being God. This is absurd; for if there are three who are truly God, then there are three Gods. It is false, then, to say that there is but one God; or if this is true, it is false to say that there are really three who are God, for one and three can not be claimed to be one and the same number. It is also said that the first of these pretended Divine persons, called the Father, has brought forth the second person, which is called the Son, and that these first two persons together have produced the third, which is called the Holy Ghost, and, nevertheless, these three pretended Divine persons do not depend the one upon the other, and even that one is not older than the other. This, too, is manifestly absurd; because one thing can not receive its existence from another thing without some dependence on this other; and a thing must necessarily exist in order to give birth to another. If, then, the Second and the Third persons of Divinity have received their existence from the First person, they must necessarily depend for their existence on this First person, who gave them birth, or who begot them, and it is necessary also that the First person of the Divinity, who gave birth to the two other persons, should have existed before them; because that which does not exist can not beget anything. Nevertheless, it is repugnant as well as absurd to claim that anything could be begotten or born without having had a beginning. Now, according to our Christ-worshipers, the Second and Third persons of

Divinity were begotten and born; then they had a beginning, and the First person had none, not being begotten by another; it therefore follows necessarily that one existed before the other.

Our Christ-worshipers, who feel these absurdities and can not avoid them by any good reasoning, have no other resource than to say that we must ignore human reason and humbly adore these sublime mysteries without wishing to understand them; but that which they call faith is refuted when they tell us that we must submit; it is telling us that we must blindly believe that which we do not believe. Our Christ-worshipers condemn the blindness of the ancient Pagans, who worshiped several Gods; they deride the genealogy of those Gods, their birth, their marriages, and the generating of their children; yet they do not observe that they themselves say things which are much more ridiculous and absurd.

If the Pagans believed that there were Goddesses as well as Gods, that these Gods and Goddesses married and begat children, they thought of nothing, then, but what is natural; for they did not believe yet that the Gods were without body or feeling; they believed they were similar to men. Why should there not be females as well as males? It is not more reasonable to deny or to recognize the one than the other; and supposing there were Gods and Goddesses, why should they not beget children in the ordinary way? There would be certainly nothing ridiculous or absurd in this doctrine, if it were true that their Gods existed. But in the doctrine of our Christ-worshipers there is something absolutely ridiculous and absurd; for besides claiming that one God forms Three, and that these Three form but One, they pretend that this Triple and Unique God has neither body, form, nor face; that the First person of this Triple and Unique God, whom they call the Father, begot of Himself a

Second person, which they call the Son, and which is the same as His Father, being, like Him, without body, form, or face. If this is true, why is it that the First one is called Father rather than mother, or the Second called Son rather than daughter? For if the First one is really father instead of mother, and if the Second is son instead of daughter, there must be something in both of these two persons which causes the one to be father rather than mother, and the other to be son rather than daughter. Now who can assert that they are males and not females? But how should they be rather males than females, as they have neither body, form, nor face? That is not an imaginable thing, and destroys itself. No matter, they claim chat these two Persons, without body, form, or face, and, consequently, without difference of sex, are nevertheless Father and Son, and that they produced by their mutual love a third person, whom they called the Holy Ghost, who has, like the other two, no body, no form, and no face. What abominable nonsense!

As our Christ-worshipers limit the power of God the Father to begetting but one Son, why do they not desire that this Second person, and the Third, should have the same power to beget a Son like themselves? If this power to beget a son is perfection in the First person, it is, then, a perfection and a power which does not exist in the Second and in the Third person. Thus these two Persons, lacking a perfection and a power which is found in the First one, they are consequently not equal with Him. If, on the contrary, they say that this power to beget a son is no perfection, they should not attribute it, then, to the First person any more than to the other two; for we should attribute perfections only to an absolutely perfect being. Besides, they would not dare to say that the power to beget a Divine person is not a perfection; and if they claim that this First person could have begotten several sons and daughters, but that He desired but this only Son, and that the two other persons did not desire to beget any others, we could ask them, firstly, from whence they know this, for we do not see in their pretended Holy Scriptures that any One of these Divine personages reveals any such assertions; how, then, can our Christ-worshipers know anything about it? They speak but according to their ideas and to their hollow imaginations. Secondly, We could not avoid saying, that if these pretended Divine personages had the power of begetting several children, and did not wish to make use of it, the consequence would be that this Divine power was ineffectual. It would be entirely without effect in the Third person, who did not beget or produce any, and would be almost without effect in the two others, because they limited it. Then this power of begetting or producing an unlimited number of children would remain idle and useless; it would be inconsistent to suppose this of Divine Personages, One of whom had already produced a Son.

Our Christ-worshipers blame and condemn the Pagans because they attribute Divinity to mortal men, and worship them as Gods after their death; they are right in doing this. But these Pagans did only what our Christ-worshipers still do in attributing Divinity to their Christ; doing which, they condemn themselves also, because they are in the same error as these Pagans, in that they worship a man who was mortal, and so very mortal that He died shamefully upon a cross.

It would be of no use for our Christ-worshipers to say that there was a great difference between their Jesus Christ and the Pagan Gods, under the pretense that their Christ was, as they claim, really God and man at the same time, while the Divinity was incarnated in Him, by means of which, the Divine nature found itself united personally, as they say, with human nature; these two natures would have made of

Jesus Christ a true God and a true man; this is what never happened, they claim, in the Pagan Gods.

But it is easy to show the weakness of this reply; for, on the one hand, was it not as easy to the Pagans as to the Christians, to say that the Divinity was incarnated in the men whom they worshiped as Gods? On the other hand, if the Divinity wanted to incarnate and unite in the human nature of their Jesus Christ, how did they know that this Divinity would not wish to also incarnate and unite Himself personally to the human nature of those great men and those admirable women, who, by their virtue, by their good qualities, or by their noble actions, have excelled the generality of people, and made themselves worshiped as Gods and Goddesses? And if our Christ-worshipers do not wish to believe that Divinity ever incarnated in these great personages, why do they wish to persuade us that He was incarnated in their Jesus? Where is the proof? Their faith and their belief; but as the Pagans rely on the same proof, we conclude both to be equally in error.

But what is more ridiculous in Christianity than in Paganism, is that the Pagans have generally attributed Divinity but to great men, authors of arts and sciences, and who excelled in virtues useful to their country. But to whom do our God-Christ-worshipers attribute Divinity? To a nobody, to a vile and contemptible man, who had neither talent, science, nor ability; born of poor parents, and who, while He figured in the world, passed but for a monomaniac and a seditious fool, who was disdained, ridiculed, persecuted, whipped, and, finally, was hanged like most of those who desired to act the same part, when they had neither the courage nor skill. About that time there were several other impostors who claimed to be the true promised Messiah; amongst others a certain Judas, a Galilean, a Theodorus, a Barcon, and others who, under this vain pretext, abused the people, and tried to excite them, in order to win them, but they all perished.

Let us pass now to His discourses and to some of His actions, which are the most singular of this kind: "Repent," said He to the people, "for the kingdom of Heaven is at hand; believe these good tidings." And He went all over Galilee preaching this pretended approach of the kingdom of Heaven. As no one has seen the arrival of this kingdom of Heaven, it is evident that it was but imaginary. But let us see other predictions, the praise, and the description of this beautiful kingdom.

Behold what He said to the people:

The kingdom of Heaven is likened unto a man who sowed good seed in his field. But while he slept, his enemy came and sowed tares among the wheat, and went his way. Again, the kingdom of Heaven is like unto treasure hidden in a field, the which, when a man has found, he hideth again, and for joy thereof goes and sells all that he has, and buys that field. Again, the kingdom of Heaven is like unto a merchantman seeking goodly pearls, who, when he had found one pearl of great price, went and sold all he had, and bought it. Again, the kingdom of Heaven is like unto a net that was cast into the sea, and gathered of every kind; which, when it was full, they drew to shore, and sat down and gathered the good into vessels, but cast the bad away. It is like a grain of mustard-seed, which a man took and sowed in his field which, indeed, is the least of all seeds, but when it is grown it is the greatest among herbs, etc.

Is this a language worthy of a God? We will pass the same judgment upon Him if we examine. His actions more closely. Because, firstly, He is represented as running all over a country preaching the approach of a pretended kingdom; Secondly, As having been transported by the Devil upon a high mountain, from which He believed He saw all the kingdoms of the world; this could only happen to a visionist; for it is certain, there is no mountain upon the earth from which He could see even one entire kingdom, unless it was the little kingdom of Yvetot, which is in France; thus it was only in imagination that He saw all these kingdoms, and was transported upon this mountain, as well as upon the pinnacle of the temple. Thirdly, When He cured the deaf-mute, spoken of in St. Mark, it is said that He placed His fingers in the ears, spit, and touched his tongue, then casting His eyes up to Heaven, He sighed deeply, and said unto him: "Ephphatha!" Finally, let us read all that is related of Him, and we can judge whether there is anything in the world more ridiculous.

Having considered some of the silly things attributed to God by our Christ-worshipers, let us look a little further into their mysteries. They worship one God in three persons, or three persons in one God, and they attribute to themselves the power of forming Gods out of dough, and of making as many as they want. For, according to their principles, they have only to say four words over a certain quantity of wine or over these little images of paste, to make as many Gods of them as they desire. What folly! With all the pretended power of their Christ, they would not be able to make the smallest fly, and yet they claim the ability to produce millions of Gods. One must be struck by a strange blindness to maintain such pitiable things, and that upon such vain foundation as the equivocal words of a fanatic. Do not these blind theologians see that it means opening a wide door to all sorts of idolatries, to adore these paste images under the pretext that the priests have the power of consecrating them and changing them into Gods?

Can not the priests of the idols boast of having a similar ability?

Do they not see, also, that the same reasoning which demonstrates the vanity of the gods or idols of wood, of stone, etc., which the Pagans worshiped, shows exactly the same vanity of the Gods and idols of paste or of flour which our Christ-worshipers adore? By what right do they deride the falseness of the Pagan Gods? Is it not because they are but the work of human hands, mute and insensible images? And what kind of Gods are those which we preserve in boxes for fear of the mice?

What are these boasted resources of the Christ-worshipers? Their morality? It is the same as in all religions, but their cruel dogmas produced and taught persecution and trouble. Their miracles? But what people has not its own, and what wise men do not disdain these fables? Their prophecies? Have we not shown their falsity? Their morals? Are they not often infamous? The establishment of their religion? but did not fanaticism begin, and has not intrigue visibly sustained this edifice? The doctrine? but is it not the height of absurdity?

End Of The Abstract By Voltaire.

PUBLISHER'S PREFACE.

By translating into both the English and German languages Le Bon Sens, containing the Last Will and Testament of the French curate JEAN MESLIER, Miss Anna Knoop has performed a most useful and meritorious task, and in issuing a new edition of this work, it is but justice to her memory [Miss Knoop died Jan. 11, 1889.] to state that her translation has received the endorsement of our most competent critics.

In a letter dated Newburyport, Mass., Sep. 23, 1878, Mr. James Parton, the celebrated author, commends Miss Knoop for "translating Meslier's book so well," and says that:

"This work of the honest pastor is the most curious and the most powerful thing of the kind which the last century produced. . . . . Paine and Voltaire had reserves, but Jean Meslier had none. He keeps nothing back; and yet, after all, the wonder is not that there should have been one priest who left that testimony at his death, but that all priests do not. True, there is a great deal more to be said about religion, which I believe to be an eternal necessity of human nature, but no man has uttered the negative side of the matter with so much candor and completeness as Jean Meslier."

The value of the testimony of a catholic priest, who in his last moments recanted the errors of his faith and asked God's pardon for having taught the catholic religion, was fully appreciated by Voltaire, who highly commended this grand work of Meslier. He voluntarily made every effort to increase its circulation, and even complained to D' Alembert "that there were not as many copies in all Paris as he himself had dispersed throughout the mountains of Switzerland." [See Letter 504, Voltaire to D'Alembert] He earnestly entreats his associates to print and distribute in Paris an edition of at least four or five thousand copies, and at the suggestion of D'Alembert, made an abstract or abridgment of The Testament "so small as to cost no more than five pence, and thus to be fitted for the pocket and reading of every workman." [Letter 146, from D'Alembert.]

The Abbé Barruel claims in his Memoirs [See History of Jacobinism by the Abbé Barruel, 4 vols. 8 VO, translated by the Hon. Robert Clifford, F. R. S., and printed in London in 1798. The learned Abbé defines Jacobinism as "the error of every man who, judging of all things by the standard of his own reason, rejects in religious matters every authority that is not derived from the light of nature. It is the error of every man who denies the possibility of any mystery beyond the limits of his reason, of every one who, discarding revelation in defence of the pretended rights of Reason, Equality, and Liberty, seeks to subvert the whole fabric of the Christian religion." B. 4.] to detect in the writings of Voltaire and of the leading Encyclopedists, a conspiracy not only against the Altar but also against the Throne. He severely denounces the "Last Will of Jean Meslier,—that famous Curate of Etrepigni,—whose apostasy and blasphemies made so strong an impression on the minds of the populace," and he styles the plan of D'Alembert for circulating a few thousand copies of the Abstract of the Will, as a "base project against the doctrines of the Gospel." [Ibid, page 145] He even asserts his belief that:

"The Jacobins will one day declare that all men are free, that all men are equal; and as a consequence of this Equality and Liberty they will conclude that every man must be left to the light of reason. That every religion subjecting man's reason to mysteries, or to the authority of any revelation speaking in God's name, is a religion of constraint and slavery; that as such it should be annihilated in order to reestablish the indefeasible rights of Equality and Liberty as to the belief or disbelief of all that the reason of man approves or disapproves: and they will call this Equality and Liberty the reign of Reason and the empire of Philosophy." [History of Jacobinism, page 51.]

The results which the Abbé Barruel so clearly foresaw have at length been realized. The labors of the Jacobins have not been in vain, and the Revolution they incited has restored France to the government of the people!

"With ardent hope for the future," says President Carnot in his centennial address, May 5, 1889, "I greet in the palace of the monarchy the representatives of a nation that is now in complete possession of herself, that is mistress of her destinies, and that is in the full splendor and strength of liberty. The first thoughts on this solemn meeting turn to our fathers. The immortal generation of 1789, by dint of courage and many sacrifices, secured for us benefits which we must bequeath to our sons as a most precious inheritance. Never can our gratitude equal the grandeur of the services rendered by our fathers to France and to the human race. . . . The Revolution was based upon the rights of man. It created a new era in history and founded modern society."

This is literally true. The freethinkers of France have taught mankind the doctrines of Liberty, Equality, and Fraternity. They have taught the dignity of human reason, and the sacredness of human rights. They have broken the bondage of the altar, and severed the shackles of the throne; and it is to be regretted that at the centennial celebration held in this city on April 30th, 1889, the appointed orator [See the

Centennial Address of the Hon. Chauncey M. Depew.] did not realize the grandeur of the occasion, and did not, like Carnot, pay a just tribute to our allies, the reformers of Europe, as well as to the fathers of the republic. But the people of America will remember what the politician has forgotten. They will remember the names and deeds of their foreign benefactors as well as of the American patriots of '76. When they recall the illustrious Europeans who fought for our liberties they will remember the name of Lafayette; when they think of the Declaration of Independence they will not forget the name of Thomas Jefferson; and when they speak of "the times that tried men's souls" they will recall with gratitude the name of Thomas Paine.

Although the ecclesiastical conclave at Rome claims the power of working miracles in defiance of Nature's laws, yet with or without miracles, they have never answered the simple arguments advanced by Jean Meslier; although they claim to hold the keys of Paradise, and bind on earth the souls that are to be bound in heaven, yet year by year their waning power refutes their senseless boast; although they boldly assert the dogma of popish infallibility, yet the loss of the temporal power once wielded by Rome, and the death of each succeeding pontiff, attest both the Pope's fallibility and the Pope's mortality. Indeed, the successor of St. Peter is but human—the sacred college at Rome is but mortal; and faith and dogma cannot forever resist the influence of light and knowledge. The power of Catholicism is surely declining throughout Europe; and if it has become aggressive in our American cities, is it not because the friends of freedom have forgotten the well-known axiom that "eternal vigilance is the price of liberty"?

PETER ECKLER.

New York, May 21, 1889.

PREFATORY NOTE BY THE TRANSLATOR

Some years ago a copy of John Meslier fell into my hands. I was struck with the simple truthfulness of his arguments, and the thought never left me of the happy change that would be produced all over the world when the religious prejudices should be dispelled, and when all the different nations and sects would unite and lend each other a friendly hand.

Since I had the opportunity of hearing the speeches and lectures of liberal men, it has seemed to me that the time has come for this work of John Meslier to be appreciated, and I concluded to translate it into the language of my adopted country, presuming that many would be happy to study it.

In this faith I offer it now to the public, and I hope that the name of John Meslier will be honored as one of the greatest benefactors of humanity.

ANNA KNOOP.

PREFACE OF THE EDITOR OF THE FRENCH EDITION OF 1830.

It is said that truth is generally revealed by dying lips. When men full of health and enjoying all the pleasures of life, exert themselves without ceasing, to excite minds and to take advantage of their fanaticism by wearing the mask of religion, it will not be without interest or importance to know what other men, invested with the same ministry, have taught under the impulse of a conscience quickened by the approach of the final hour. Their confessions are more valuable because they carry with them the spirit of contrition. It is then that the truth, which is no longer obscured by narrow passions and sordid interests, presents itself in all its brilliancy, and imposes upon him who has kept it hidden during his life, the duty, and even the necessity, of unveiling it fully at his death. It is then that human speech, losing in a measure its terrestrial nature, becomes persuasive and convincing.

We know this fact of a celebrated preacher who in the beginning of the Revolution stood in the same pulpit which we are pleased to call the pulpit of truth, and with his hand upon his heart declared that till then he had taught only falsehood. He did more; he implored his parishioners to forgive him for the gross errors in which he had kept them, and congratulated them upon having at last arrived at a period when it was permitted to establish the empire of reason upon the ruins of prejudice. Times have changed very much, it is true; however, so long as the press shall be able to combat the fatal errors of religious fanaticism, and perhaps even to some extent prevent its violence, it will be the duty of every friend of humanity to reproduce continually the full retractions which opposed the sincerity and conscience of the dying to the bad faith and hypocritical avidity of the living. Guided by this intention, and ashamed to see the human race, in a land just freed from the yoke of prejudice, give birth to a disgraceful juggling which will terminate in dominating authority, and associate itself with the persecutions of which our incredulous or dissenting ancestors were the sad victims, we believe it useful to reprint the last lessons of a priest—an honest man—bequeathed to his fellow-citizens and to posterity. The service we render to Philosophy will be so much the greater when we can consider as immutable, perpetual, permanent, and ready to appear in the hour of need, the edition which we are preparing of "COMMON SENSE, BY THE PRIEST JEAN MESLIER, AND HIS DYING CONFESSION."

To do justice to these two works, to which we have added analytical notes, which will greatly facilitate our researches, we will limit ourselves by giving the imposing approbation of two philosophers of the eighteenth century—Voltaire and d'Alembert. They certainly understood much better the sublimity of evangelical morality, and spoke of it in a manner more worthy of its author, than did those who deified it to profit by its divinity, and who abused so cruelly the ignorance and barbarity of the first centuries, to establish, in the interest of their fortunes and power, so many base prejudices, so many puerile and superstitious practices.

Here is what Voltaire and d'Alembert thought of the curate Meslier and of his work. Their letters are presented here in order to excite curiosity and convince the judgment:

VOLTAIRE TO D'ALEMBERT.

FERNEY, February, 1762.

They have printed in Holland the Testament of Jean Meslier. I trembled with horror in reading it. The testimony of a priest, who, in dying, asks God's pardon for having taught Christianity, must be a great weight in the balance of Liberals. I will send you a copy of this Testament of the anti-Christ, because you desire to refute it. You have but to tell me by what manner it will reach you. It is written with great simplicity, which unfortunately resembles candor.

VOLTAIRE TO THE SAME.

FERNEY, February 25, 1762.

Meslier also has the wisdom of the serpent. He sets an example for you; the good grain was hidden in the chaff of his book. A good Swiss has made a faithful abstract and this abstract can do a great deal of good. What an answer to the insolent fanatics who treat philosophers like libertines. What an answer to you, wretches that you are, this testimony of a priest, who asks God's pardon for having been a Christian!

D'ALEMBERT'S ANSWER.

PARIS, March 31, 1762.

A misunderstanding has been the cause, my dear philosopher, that I received but a few days since the work of Jean Meslier, which you had sent almost a month ago. I waited till I received it to write to you. It seems to me that we could inscribe upon the tombstone of this curate: "Here lies a very honest priest, curate of a village in Champagne, who, in dying, asks God's pardon for having been a Christian, and who has proved by this, that ninety-nine sheep and one native of Champagne do not make a hundred beasts." I suspect that the abstract of his work is written by a Swiss, who understands French very well, though he affects to speak it badly. This is neat, earnest, and concise, and I bless the author of the abstract, whoever he may be. "It is of the Lord to cultivate the vine." After all, my dear philosopher, a little longer, and I do not know whether all these books will be necessary, and whether man will not have enough sense to comprehend by himself that three do not make one, and that bread is not God. The enemies of reason are playing a very foolish part at this moment, and I believe that we can say as in the song:

"To destroy all these people You should let them alone."

I do not know what will become of the religion of Christ, but its professors are in false garb. What Pascal, Nicole, and Arnaud could not do, there is an appearance that three or four absurd and ignorant fanatics will accomplish. The nation will give this vigorous blow within, while she is doing so little outside, and we will put in the abbreviated chronological pages of the year 1762: "This year France lost all its colonies and expelled the Jesuits." I know nothing but powder, which with so little apparent force, could produce such great results.

VOLTAIRE TO D'ALEMBERT.

DELICES, July 12, 1762.

It appears to me that the Testament of Jean Meslier has a great effect; all those who read it are convinced; this man discusses and proves. He speaks in the moment of death, at the moment when even liars tell the truth fully. This is the strongest of all arguments. Jean Meslier is to convert the world. Why is his gospel in so few hands? How lukewarm you are at Paris! You hide your tight under a bushel!

D'ALEMBERT'S ANSWER.

PARIS, July 31, 1762.

You reproach us with lukewarmness, but I believe I have told you already that the fear of the fagot is very cooling. You would like us to print the Testament of Jean Meslier and distribute four or five thousand copies. The infamous fanaticism, for infamous it is, would lose little or nothing, and we should be treated as fools by those whom we would have converted. Man is so little enlightened to-day only because we had the precaution or the good fortune to enlighten him little by little. If the sun should appear all of a sudden in a cave, the inhabitants would perceive only the harm it would do their eyes. The excess of light would result only in blinding them.

D'ALEMBERT TO VOLTAIRE.

PARIS, July 9, 1764.

Apropos, they have lent me that work attributed to St. Evremont, and which is said to be by Dumarsais, of which you spoke to me some time ago; it is good, but the Testament of Meslier is still better!

VOLTAIRE TO D'ALEMBERT.

FERNEY, July 16, 1764.

The Testament of Meslier ought to be in the pocket of all honest men; a good priest, full of candor, who asks God's pardon for deceiving himself, must enlighten those who deceive themselves.

VOLTAIRE TO THE COUNT D'ARGENTAL.

AUX DELICES, February 6, 1762.

But no little bird told me of the infernal book of that curate, Jean Meslier; a very important work to the angels of darkness. An excellent catechism for Beelzebub. Know that this book is very rare; it is a treasure!

VOLTAIRE TO THE SAME.

AUX DEUCES, May 31, 1762.

It is just that I should send you a copy of the second edition of Meslier. In the first edition they forgot the preface, which is very strange. You have wise friends who would not be sorry to have this book in their secret cabinet. It is excellent to form youthful minds. The book, which was sold in manuscript form for eight Louis-d'or, is illegible. This little abstract is very edifying. Let us thank the good souls who give it gratuitously, and let us pray God to extend His benedictions upon this useful reading.

VOLTAIRE TO D'AMILAVILLE.

AUX DEUCES, February 8, 1762.

My brother shall have a Meslier soon as I shall have received the order; it would seem that my brother has not the facts. Fifteen to twenty years ago the manuscript of this work sold for eight Louis-d'or; it was a very large quarto. There are more than a hundred copies in Paris. Brother Thiriot understands the facts. It is not known who made the abstract, but it is taken wholly, word for word, from the original. There are still many persons who have seen the curate Meslier. It would be very useful to make a new edition of this little work in Paris; it can be done easily in three or four days.

VOLTAIRE TO THE SAME.

FERNEY, December 6, 1762.

But I believe there will never be another impression of the little book of Meslier. Think of the weight of the testimony of one dying, of a priest, of a good man.

VOLTAIRE TO THE SAME.

FERNEY, July 6, 1764.

Three hundred Mesliers distributed in a province have caused many conversions. Ah, if I was assisted!

VOLTAIRE TO THE SAME.

FERNEY, September 29, 1764.

There are too few Mesliers and too many swindlers.

VOLTAIRE TO THE SAME.

AUX DELICES, October 8, 1764.

Names injure the cause; they awaken prejudice. Only the name of Jean Meslier can do good, because the repentance of a good priest in the hour of death must make a great impression. This Meslier should be in the hands of all the world.

VOLTAIRE TO MADAM DE FLORIAN.

AUX DELICES, May 20, 1762.

My dear niece, it is very sad to be so far from you. Read and read again Jean Meslier; he is a good curate.

VOLTAIRE TO THE MARQUIS D'ARGENCE.

March 2, 1763.

I have found a Testament of Jean Meslier, which I send you. The simplicity of this man, the purity of his manners, the pardon which he asks of God, and the authenticity of his book, must produce a great effect. I will send you as many copies as you want of the Testament of this good curate.

VOLTAIRE TO HELVETIUS.

AUX DEUCES, May 1, 1763.

They have sent me the two abstracts of Jean Meslier. It is true that it is written in the style of a carriage-horse, but it is well suited to the street. And what testimony! that of a priest who asks pardon in dying, for having taught absurd and horrible things! What an answer to the platitudes of fanatics who have the audacity to assert that philosophy is but the fruit of libertinage!

www.ingramcontent.com/pod-product-compliance
Lightning Source LLC
Chambersburg PA
CBHW050120170426
43197CB00011B/1650